The Accountant's Guide to XBRL

3rd Edition

Clinton White, Jr.

SkipWhite.com

www.skipwhite.com

The Accountant's Guide to XBRL (3rd edition)
By Clinton White, Jr.

Printed in the United State of America

Published by SkipWhite.com
www.skipwhite.com

Printing History:
May 2006: First Edition
December 2006: Second Edition
December 2008: Third Edition

ISBN: 0-9779525-4-1

To my friends, family, and colleagues – thanks for your encouragement and support.

The Accountant's Guide to XBRL

3rd Edition

Preface

The second edition of *The Accountant's Guide to XBRL* was published in December of 2006. Two years have passed, many important events have transpired, and the momentum of the XBRL movement has increased significantly. One major development is the support and funding of XBRL for financial reporting by the U.S. Securities and Exchange Commission. Since Christopher Cox, current Chairman of the SEC, coined the phrase "interactive data" in 2004 to describe financial data in a form that is easily accessible and processable with computerized applications, the SEC has been promoting the use of XBRL to improve the transparency of financial reporting and its usefulness to all interested parties. It began a pilot voluntary XBRL filing program in 2005. It issued contracts to upgrade the EDGAR database system to accommodate and support XBRL and to fund XBRL US to complete the development of the US GAAP taxonomy. XBRL US issued version 1.0 of the US GAAP taxonomy in December, 2007 and it reached approved status in August, 2008. Working closely with the SEC, XBRL US has released a new version of the US GAAP taxonomy for public comment and expects it to be released for use in February 2009. Also, the SEC has issued a proposed ruling to phase in over three years reporting in XBRL format for all publicly-traded companies. It is expected that the 500 largest US domestic publicly traded companies will be required to start furnishing supplemental financial statements in XBRL format with all of their SEC filings. Others will follow suit over a two year period. For details about these and other SEC activities see: http://www.sec.gov/spotlight/xbrl.shtml.

The US GAAP XBRL taxonomy v1.0 is significantly more robust than earlier XBRL taxonomies. It now contains over 12,000 standard element names representing accounting and financial reporting concepts to be used for tagging items in financial statements and footnote disclosures. It is composed of a number of industry "entry points" that include the commonly used statements and disclosures in major US GAAP industry categories; including, Commercial and Industrial, Banking and Savings Institutions, Brokers and Dealers, Insurance, and Real Estate.

XBRL is a vocabulary for financial and business operations reporting built on the XML foundation. As you will see in this text, my approach is that a person needs to understand the basics of the XML foundation in order to understand XBRL. A major new XML vocabulary for e-business documents is UBL (the Universal Business Language). I use it to introduce XML in this edition of the Accountant's Guide. I came to understand that XML is not simply another "language" with which to write code but instead a computing paradigm on which to build vocabularies for other purposes, such as business documents and financial and business operations reporting. I have researched, published articles, taught professional workshops and seminars, and built XBRL into a capstone course for accounting majors at the University of Delaware. The First Edition of *The Accountant's Guide to XBRL* (May, 2006) was the initial result of this experience. The Third Edition (December, 2008) is an improved, expanded, and up-to-date resource with which to learn the basics of XBRL. It is an emerging technology and my intent is to continue to publish it under my own name at **www.SkipWhite.com.**

The current XBRL Specification 2.1, as amended in April 2005, is considered to be stable but is evolving steadily based on the results of pilot programs and initiatives around the world. In the US, XBRL US, in conjunction with the SEC, plans to release an updated version of the US GAAP taxonomy on a yearly basis. XBRL GL 2007 – "the journal taxonomy," has reached recommended status and is beginning to be be used for internal accounting. This is emerging technology that is changing the face of financial and business operations reporting around the world. It will continue to evolve and you will need to keep posted on current events.

The Accountant's Guide to XBRL is the foundation. By publishing it and other materials under **SkipWhite.com**, I will be better able to provide current information, books, cases, and dynamic support. *The Accountant's Guide to XBRL* will be supported through the **www.SkipWhite.com** Web space. For academics, I will provide lesson plans, solutions, new exercises, and up-to-date information and techniques as they evolve. For accounting practitioners, I will provide exercise solutions and up-to-date information and new materials as they become available.

Who Should Read This Book

This book is for accounting and MIS academics and their students, practicing accountants, and anyone else involved with computerized financial and business operations reporting. If you fit into one of these categories, you will get the following from this book:

- A basic understanding of XML documents and the XML language foundation
- A basic understanding of UBL (the Universal Business Language)
- A basic understanding of XBRL and how to use XBRL taxonomies to build XBRL instance documents
- A basic understanding of the XSLT processing language to transform UBL and XBRL reports into Web pages
- A basic understanding of XBRL GL 2007

Organization of This Book

This book is organized according to the scheme that the author uses to teach XBRL to senior accounting majors at the University of Delaware and to accounting academics and practitioners in workshops and seminars. The chapters are designed to be read sequentially but several teaching schemes are discussed at the end of Chapter 1 in the section titled *Notes on Teaching.*

Chapter 1, *The Accountant's Guide to XBRL*

This chapter gives a non-technical introduction to XBRL, the role of markup in computerized information processing, and the business reasons for XBRL.

Chapter 2, *The XML Document Foundation*

UBL (the Universal Business Language) is a new XML vocabulary that defines a library of business documents to be used in e-business relationships. This chapter introduces the rules that all XML documents must follow and the basic XML foundation by way of UBL. Like UBL, XBRL is an XML vocabulary for a special purpose – financial and business operations reporting.

Chapter 3, *The XML Language Foundation*

Both the UBL and XBRL specifications were created using the tools provided in the XML family of languages. As such, this chapter introduces three members of the XML language foundation necessary for understanding XML vocabularies (e.g. XBRL): the XML Schema language, XML Namespaces, and XLink.

Chapter 4, *XBRL Instance Documents*

All XBRL documents are referred to as "instance documents." This chapter introduces the rules that XBRL documents must follow to be valid "instance documents."

Chapter 5, *Transforming Documents with XSLT*

XBRL instance documents are meant to be read by software applications. As such, they are likely to be "transformed" for many different purposes including Web pages for human consumption. This chapter introduces a simple scripting language to transform XML documents into human-readable form – Web pages.

Chapter 6, *The Current State of XBRL*

This chapter discusses the current state of XBRL including major adoption activities, tools available for XBRL instance document creation, and thoughts about its future.

Appendix, *XBRL GL 2007*

This appendix introduces XBRL GL 2007 – the "journal taxonomy." XBRL GL has now reached recommended status and is expected to have a major impact on XBRL and accounting in computerized information systems.

Conventions Used in This Book

Glossary: At the end of each chapter, you will find a Glossary of New Terms which were introduced in the chapter. In each chapter they are ***bold, italic, and underlined***. Refer to the glossary for further definitions and explanations.

Interactive exercises: In Chapters 2 through 6 and the Appendix, you will find "interactive exercises" that are designed to help you better understand the text materials. These often require you to use a computer with an Internet connection to access materials and challenge you to get actively engaged with the materials.

Exercises: At the end of Chapters 2 through 6 and the Appendix, you will find exercises which extend the chapter's material and challenge you to demonstrate and advance your understanding of the material.

Table of Contents

The Accountant's Guide to XBRL (3rd edition)

Chapter 1: Introduction

Overview

The Accountant's Guide to XBRL is designed to help those with a background in accounting and finance understand the basics of ***XBRL***: the Extensible Business Reporting Language. Although a basic knowledge of accounting is necessary to understand this book, it is not about debits and credits but about how to use XBRL in financial reporting. XBRL adds meaning and context to accounting, financial, and other business performance data, making it understandable, reusable, and precisely interpretable by computer applications. Although raw data are easily processed by computer applications, processing data with meaning and context represents a new and higher level because data can be more effectively exchanged and transmitted as information across networks and formerly manual processes can be automated.

Although XBRL is a technical computer language designed to standardize business and financial reporting, you do not need a degree in Computer Science to understand it. *The Accountant's Guide to XBRL* is written from a non-technical perspective. It reflects the way the author teaches XBRL to senior accounting majors at the University of Delaware and to accounting educators and practitioners in workshops and seminars.

This chapter introduces *The Accountant's Guide to XBRL*. It starts with an overview of XBRL and its role in computerized financial and business operations reporting and concludes with a preview of each chapter. New ***words*** and ***phrases*** are introduced and explained throughout. Each is also defined in the Glossary at the end of each chapter. If you don't understand a term in context, be sure to refer to its formal definition in the glossary; all entries are in alphabetical order. XBRL is an emerging technology that is impacting accounting, financial, and business reporting. Well educated accounting and finance professionals should have a familiarity with the basics of XBRL. *The Accountant's Guide to XBRL* is designed to provide you with those basics. With this knowledge, you will have the foundation on which to investigate further and build an expertise in the area or simply be comfortable with the technology.

XBRL

The Extensible Business Reporting Language is a "vocabulary," a special purpose language, of the Extensible Markup Language (***XML***). XML is a toolkit for adding meaning to data and storing and processing it as information. "Extensible" means that as long as you follow the rules, it can be extended or added to. "Markup" means surrounding pieces of data with tags that add meaning. "Language" means a method of communication. Using the XML toolkit, a piece of data, such as the amount of accounts payable at a specific point in time for a specific business, can be stored in an XML document as: **<AccountsPayable>** *1234567890*<**/AccountsPayable>**. In this form, the piece of data, *1234567890*, is surrounded by tags – a beginning tag **<AccountsPayable>** and an ending tag **</AccountsPayable>**, that give it meaning and differentiate it from other pieces of data. The piece of data is no longer raw data. It is information because it is contained within tags that give it "meaning," and it can be stored and communicated as such. XML provides the general tools, rules, and syntax with which to build vocabularies for specific purposes, such as XBRL for financial and business operations reporting. XBRL provides us with an additional set of tools, rules, and syntax with which to build business reporting applications, such as US GAAP financial statements.

XBRL is an emerging technology under the auspices of XBRL International. XBRL International is a world-wide consortium of over 400 companies, organizations, and government entities dedicated to creating an open international standard for computerized representation and reporting of financial and business operations information (see www.xbrl.org). XBRL is used to tag each piece of data in a standard way so that it becomes a piece of business information that can be validated, stored, and processed by computerized applications. It is an emerging technology in that there is now a core specification defining the XBRL vocabulary around which new XBRL extensions are being developed, one of which is the US GAAP taxonomy.

The core specification, ***XBRL Specification 2.1*** (November 7, 2005), defines the rules and syntax for XBRL documents and for ***XBRL taxonomies***. XBRL documents are referred to as "***instance documents***" because they are an instance of a class of documents defined by this specification. XBRL taxonomies define tag names to represent accounting and financial terms used to report data in XBRL instance documents. XBRL instance documents follow a standard format and contain pieces of data, each tagged with a name from an XBRL taxonomy. Therefore, each piece of data in an XBRL instance document is identifiable as information being reported by a specific entity, at a specific point in time, in a specific currency. The result is that the XBRL document and the data it contains can be validated, stored, and processed by software applications. Of equal importance, the data it contains can be efficiently analyzed, compared, and used for other purposes by software applications. The major benefit is the standardized representation of accounting and financial information so that it can be reported in such a way that it can be validated, analyzed, used for multiple purposes by multiple parties, and unambiguously understood. In addition, once tagged in XBRL format, the data does not need to be re-entered multiple times and it can be communicated in its original form between software applications on computer networks.

Markup is very important in computerized systems. Every piece of data that is processed by a software application is marked up in some way to distinguish it from any other piece of data. Consider the Excel™ spreadsheet in Figure 1-1.

Figure 1-1: An Excel™ spreadsheet – 3M Company, Inc.'s current assets and liabilities

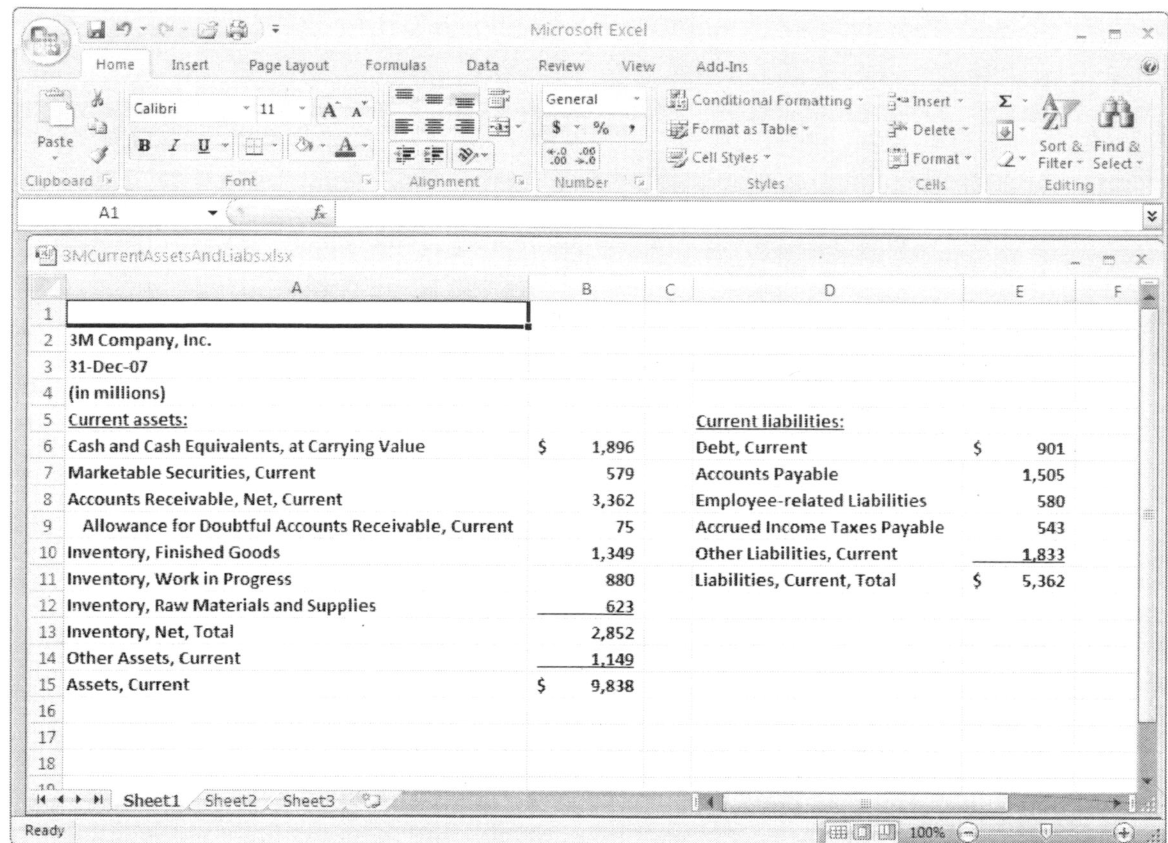

	A	B	D	E
1				
2	3M Company, Inc.			
3	31-Dec-07			
4	(in millions)			
5	Current assets:		Current liabilities:	
6	Cash and Cash Equivalents, at Carrying Value	$ 1,896	Debt, Current	$ 901
7	Marketable Securities, Current	579	Accounts Payable	1,505
8	Accounts Receivable, Net, Current	3,362	Employee-related Liabilities	580
9	Allowance for Doubtful Accounts Receivable, Current	75	Accrued Income Taxes Payable	543
10	Inventory, Finished Goods	1,349	Other Liabilities, Current	1,833
11	Inventory, Work in Progress	880	Liabilities, Current, Total	$ 5,362
12	Inventory, Raw Materials and Supplies	623		
13	Inventory, Net, Total	2,852		
14	Other Assets, Current	1,149		
15	Assets, Current	$ 9,838		

Anyone familiar with accounting or finance recognizes this as a spreadsheet reporting 3M Company, Inc.'s current assets and liabilities, in millions of dollars, as of December 31, 2007. In a spreadsheet software application, each piece of data is separated from every other piece of data and marked up by its physical location in Excel™ format. Cell A6 contains the text string "Cash and Cash Equivalents, at Carrying Value" and cell B6 contains the number "1896" formatted for currency, and so on. With this data in this spreadsheet, we could jump to another cell and write a formula to calculate 3M Company's current ratio or we could email the entire spreadsheet to someone else connected to our network or the Internet. Those we send it to could, if they also had the same version of Excel™, open it and see the same spreadsheet. We could not, however, query the Excel™ spreadsheet to find a value for "Cash and Cash Equivalents, at Carrying Value." Likewise, we could not have a separate software application read a value in a cell and understand what it represents.

A basic problem with proprietary software like an Excel™ spreadsheet is that data are marked up by their physical location or by a proprietary method that makes sense for the software application itself. XML and its special purpose languages enable the marking up of data in a universal, non-proprietary fashion so they can be unambiguously interpreted and processed by any XML-enabled software application. Markup that adds meaning to data is referred to as ***meta-data***. XBRL is an XML vocabulary for adding standardized meaning to data for accounting and financial reporting so they can be unambiguously reported, stored, and communicated over computer networks. We could query an XBRL instance document with the information found in the spreadsheet in Figure 1-1 and find a value for "Cash and cash equivalents" because the value is surrounded by standardized meta-data.

Why is it important to markup accounting, financial, and business operations data with meta-data so they are specified precisely in a standard format? For better computer processing!

In today's interconnected world of computerized applications, processing, analyzing, reporting, and understanding data are critical for business success. Accounting is "an information system that measures, processes, and communicates financial information about an identifiable economic entity" (Needles and Powers, *Financial Accounting*, 2004, pg. 4). Most accounting employs computerized applications. XBRL is a tool box to make computerized accounting and financial and business reporting in general more effective and efficient.

Accounting adds value to decision making through reporting financial and business operations information. XBRL instance documents contain "facts" reported by a specific entity, at a specific point in time, in a specific currency, and under identifiable accounting guidelines, such as U.S. GAAP or IFRS. Each fact reported in an XBRL instance document can be identified, addressed individually, analyzed in relation to other facts, and reused for other purposes. These are distinct business advantages because of the large amount and variety of accounting, financial, and operations reporting that business entities must do and because of the interpretability of the items and facts reported.

Consider, for example, a publicly-traded company's annual reporting of operations, including the annual 10-K report to the ***SEC*** (U.S. Securities and Exchange Commission) in HTML (Hypertext Markup Language) and PDF (Portable Document Format), the glossy printed annual report for shareholders, and its Web page for Internet consumption. Typically, each of these reports is created individually, even though each is based on the same basic items of information in one form or another, including the company's financial statements with and without detailed footnotes, its management discussion and analysis, its auditor's report, and its discussion of operations. The detailed items of information that make up these reports can be tagged with XBRL and stored in instance documents. They can then be processed by software applications for filings with the SEC, the printed annual report, and the Web page without time-consuming, error-prone human intervention.

In addition, when the SEC receives a company's 10-K in HTML and PDF (the current required filing formats), it is a block of text marked up for presentation purposes (i.e., both HTML and PDF are presentation format standards), making automated analysis difficult at best. The same is true for users of the company's Web page. Try searching for "Net income" for a specific time period in either an SEC filing in the ***EDGAR*** (Electronic Data Gathering and Retrieval) database or a company's Web page. You will find the words "Net income" and, with additional visual searching, the value you are looking for. If you then want to use that value in a spreadsheet, or any other software application, you have to read the value and type it in and go from there.

With an XBRL instance document as your source document, on the other hand, you could write a few lines of code to perform the same search and find and copy all of the values reporting "Net income," each tagged with its specific time period and currency. You could reuse each individually or in total along with relevant footnotes in any other application without human intervention. You could even compare them to similar values found in other XBRL instance documents of other companies. If all companies reported 10-K information in XBRL instance document format, the efficiency and effectiveness of the analyses that the SEC, as well as all users of the EDGAR database, could do would be improved exponentially. XBRL instance documents are a tool to support transparency of accounting and financial information.

The SEC began a pilot program in 2005, referred to as their "interactive data initiative," to encourage companies to voluntarily file XBRL financial statements as supplemental documents. After analyzing the participant company filings for 2005 and 2006, they issued contracts worth many millions of dollars to upgrade their 20-year old databases to handle XBRL instance documents. As of this writing, the SEC has issued a proposal to phase in XBRL reporting over the next three years. The U.S. Federal Deposit Insurance Corporation (***FDIC***) has required since October 2005 that member banks submit quarterly "Call Reports" in XBRL format directly to a Central Data Repository established by the U.S. Federal Financial Institutions Examination Council (***FFIEC***). The FDIC reports dramatic improvements in the accuracy of the data that its 8,300 member banks submit and the ability to analyze the information in the reports in days rather than months.

A Preview of *The Accountant's Guide to XBRL*

Since XBRL is a vocabulary of XML, you must understand some of the basics of the XML foundation before jumping into XBRL. XML is not like other computer languages with which you may be familiar. XML is a set of rules and syntax, a meta-language used to create other languages. **Chapter 2** describes the rules for XML documents and the Universal Business Language (UBL) – a new XML vocabulary for creating business documents. XML documents and their behavior when processed are the foundation of the formal XML specification. XML documents contain data surrounded by tags that add meaning to them. Data are tagged with XML "elements" and "attributes." Properly formatted XML documents can be processed by any XML-enabled software application. In the examples and exercises in this book, we will use the MS Internet Explorer™ as our

XML processor. The XML documents that you create in the end-of-chapter exercises will be used in other exercises in later chapters.

Continuing with the XML foundation, **Chapter 3** discusses the XML Schema language and two companion languages, Namespaces and XLink. XML documents contain data, while XML languages are used to validate and process XML documents. The XML Schema language is a very technical computer language used to define XML elements and attributes and the structure of XML documents. The formal UBL and XBRL specifications are written in the XML Schema language, as are all UBL and XBRL taxonomies. A basic knowledge of the principles, not the technical details, of the XML Schema language is helpful for understanding XML vocabularies such as UBL and XBRL. Two additional supporting languages, XML Namespaces and XLink, are also covered from a non-technical perspective.

Building on the XML foundation, **Chapter 4** describes XBRL instance documents and taxonomies. You can think of XML as the foundation toolkit and UBL and XBRL as the business document and reporting toolkits. The XBRL Specification 2.1 (November 7, 2005) defines the rules and structure that XBRL documents must follow and a language for building XBRL taxonomies, which are dictionaries of elements and relationships for specific reporting purposes, such as the XBRL US GAAP v1.0 taxonomy (April 28, 2008). Like all XML documents, XBRL documents contain data surrounded by tags that add meaning. XBRL tags have very specific accounting and financial reporting meanings (i.e., each tag represents a well-defined accounting/financial reporting concept) as defined in XBRL taxonomies (e.g., the XBRL US GAAP v1.0 taxonomy). And each XBRL document is linked to at least one XBRL taxonomy that supports the document's specific reporting purpose.

XBRL documents contain data representing business facts reported for a particular purpose, such as sending a financial statement to your bank or filing a 10-K with the SEC. Although XBRL documents are human-readable, they are meant to be processed by software applications. **Chapter 5** explains how to transform XBRL documents into human-readable output using the Extensible Stylesheet Language for Transformations (XSLT). XSLT is a relatively simple language for transforming XML documents for other purposes, such as presentation as a Web page. Chapter 5 presents the basics of the XSLT language and uses it to build the code to transform UBL and XBRL instance documents into Web pages for human consumption.

Chapter 6 discusses the current state of XBRL in financial and business operations reporting, some of the tools available for instance document creation and validation, and the potential impact of XBRL and several related technologies on accounting, auditing, and financial reporting. The chapter introduces the new SEC filing program and other significant XBRL adoption programs around the world. It also introduces a few of the tools available for XBRL document and taxonomy creation and validation. It finishes with several predictions about the future of XBRL.

The **Appendix** introduces a relatively new member of the XBRL family of technologies, XBRL GL (April 17, 2007), known as the "journal taxonomy." XBRL GL, "Global Ledger," was first introduced in November, 2005 and version 2.1 is currently an XBRL International "recommended" taxonomy (i.e., it has been tested and is ready for use). It is an evolving specification that is independent of any chart of accounts or reporting standard to support drill-up and drill-down for financial and performance measurement reporting, mandatory audit trails, and tax reporting. It is expected to have a major impact in the future.

The Accountant's Guide to XBRL is designed as a textbook on XBRL for those with an accounting or finance background. It is based on the way the author teaches XBRL in five weeks in his Accounting Information Systems class at the University of Delaware. **Week one** includes coverage of Chapters 1 and 2 and requires students to create two basic XML documents using the UBL vocabulary. The author uses a lab setting in which students create a simple XML document as presented in Chapter two. Students then complete as a homework assignment one of the end-of-chapter exercises. **Week two** includes coverage of Chapter 3 along with a simple in-class exercise as presented in the chapter. Students then complete as a homework assignment one of the end-of-chapter exercises; building a UBL document schema. **Week three** includes coverage of Chapter 4 and requires the creation of two XBRL documents – a simple one in class followed by a more complex one as homework using one of the end-of-chapter exercises. **Week four** includes coverage of Chapter 5 and requires the creation of at least two XSLT documents – one to transform a simple UBL document to a Web page in class and another as homework to transform an XBRL instance document into a financial statement using one of the end-of-chapter exercises. **Week five** includes coverage of Chapter 6 and the Appendix and requires the creation of a basic XBRL GL instance document using one of the end-of-chapter exercises. Instructors can register for detailed lesson plans, PowerPoint™ slides, instructor's notes, and exercise solutions.

For those with less than five weeks to devote to XBRL, there are several recommended alternatives. A four week introduction to XBRL would simply not include week number five. A three week introduction to XBRL would include weeks one, two, and three but not weeks four and five. A two week introduction to XBRL would include coverage of Chapters 1, 2, and 4 as follows: Week one – cover Chapters 1 and 2 and assign the creation of at least one XML document; Week two – cover Chapter 4 and assign the creation of at least one XBRL instance document. Material skipped in Chapter 3, such as XML schemas and Namespaces, would need to be covered briefly in order to make sense of some of the material in Chapter 4.

For software, you can use MS Notepad™, or any other "text editor" (i.e., not a Word processor), to create XML, UBL, and XBRL documents and the Internet Explorer™, or any other current browser, to process them. The basics of using Notepad™, which can be found under *Accessories* on a Windows™ computer, are explained at the end of Chapter 2. A more sophisticated text editor for the Windows environment is the free *Programmer's File Editor*, available from various archive sites, including http://www.lancs.ac.uk/staff/ steveb/cpaap/pfe/default.htm. A more sophisticated text editor for the Macintosh OSX environment is TextMate, a commercial package with a 30-day free trial version available from http://macromates.com/.

I hope you enjoy the Third edition of *The Accountant's Guide to XBRL* and find it to be a useful tool for learning about this emerging technology that is changing the face of accounting, financial, and business operations reporting. It will be important in your future as a professional!

Glossary of new terms introduced in Chapter 1

EDGAR (The Electronic Data Gathering and Retrieval database): The public database in which all submissions to the SEC are stored.

FDIC (The U.S. Federal Deposit Insurance Corporation): The regulatory authority to which all federally insured banks in the U.S. must report.

FFIEC (The U.S. Federal Financial Institutions Examination Council): A U.S. regulatory authority consisting of the FDIC, the Federal Reserve Board, and the Controller of the Currency.

Instance documents: An XBRL document. It is referred to as an "instance" document because it is an instance of the class of documents described in the XBRL Specification 2.1.

Meta-data: Data about data. It means data describing data by adding meaning to it.

SEC (The U.S. Securities and Exchange Commission): The regulatory authority to which all publicly-traded companies must report financial performance. The annual 10K report is a complete, audited report of financial and performance information required from all publicly-traded companies.

XBRL (Extensible Business Reporting Language): A toolbox for creating accounting, finance, and business reports.

XBRL Specification 2.1: The most recent XBRL specification. It was issued on December 31, 2003 and reissued with errata corrections on November 7, 2005. It is a formal specification of the rules and syntax that XBRL instance documents and taxonomies must follow to be valid.

XBRL taxonomies: Lists of elements and relationships for specific reporting purposes, such as reporting financial information under U.S. GAAP. Each tag used in an XBRL instance document must be defined as an element in an XBRL taxonomy.

XML (Extensible Markup Language): A toolbox, including a meta-language, a language for creating other languages, that forms the foundation for all XML vocabularies, such as XBRL. Following the rules of the XML language, data are surrounded with tags that add meaning and allow them to be processed as information.

Downloadable files:

Available at: http://www.skipwhite.com/Guide2008/Chapter1/3MAssetsAndLiabs.xlsx

- 3MAssetsAndLiabs.xlsx (Figure 1-1)

References:

Needles, Belverd E. and Marian Powers, *Financial Accounting*, Houghton Mifflin Company (NY) 2004

Programmer's File Editor, http://www.lancs.ac.uk/staff/steveb/cpaap/pfe/default.htm.

SEC (U.S. Securities & Exchange Commission), http://www.sec.gov/.

TextMate, http://macromates.com/.

XBRL International, www.xbrl.org.

XBRL US, http://xbrl.us/Pages/default.aspx.

The Accountant's Guide to XBRL

Chapter 2: The XML Document Foundation

Overview

XML (the Extensible Markup Language) is a meta-language – a language used to create other languages. XML is not like other languages with which you may be familiar as it describes basic rules and syntax that XML documents must follow instead of a specific programming vocabulary. XML is used as the foundation on which to build vocabularies for specific purposes. We will cover two XML vocabularies in this book: Universal Business Language (UBL) (UBL OASIS, 2006) and XBRL. This chapter focuses on business documents as defined in the ***UBL vocabulary***.

XML was developed to meet a number of design goals: to be usable over the Internet, to support a variety of applications, and to be human-readable. To meet these design goals, the XML Specification 1.0 (XML, W3C) describes a class of data objects known as XML documents and their behavior when processed by software. A data object is simply a computer processable item containing data and instructions. As you might expect, the XML specification is quite technical. It describes the rules and syntax that XML documents must follow to be ***well-formed*** and ***valid***. Well-formed XML documents are those that follow the basic rules for all XML documents and can be processed by XML-enabled software. Valid XML documents must follow additional rules for specific classes of XML documents as described in XML schemas and DTDs (Data Type Definitions). (Schemas are covered in Chapter 3: The XML Language Foundation.) This chapter is devoted to introducing, in a non-technical manner, well-formed XML documents and their role in business. As you will see, XML documents are a very important part of the XML family of technologies. They contain tagged items of data and conform to specific rules and syntax that make them processable by all XML-enabled software applications. As such, they have become the preferred way to move data between software applications on a computer network and are being built into business processes.

The Rules for Well-formed XML Documents

XML documents are designed to be human-readable as well as processable by computer applications. Figure 2-1 is a basic well-formed XML document processed by the MS Internet Explorer ™ (then "collapsed" for illustration purposes).

Figure 2-1: *A well-formed XML document (a "collapsed" UBL Catalogue document)*

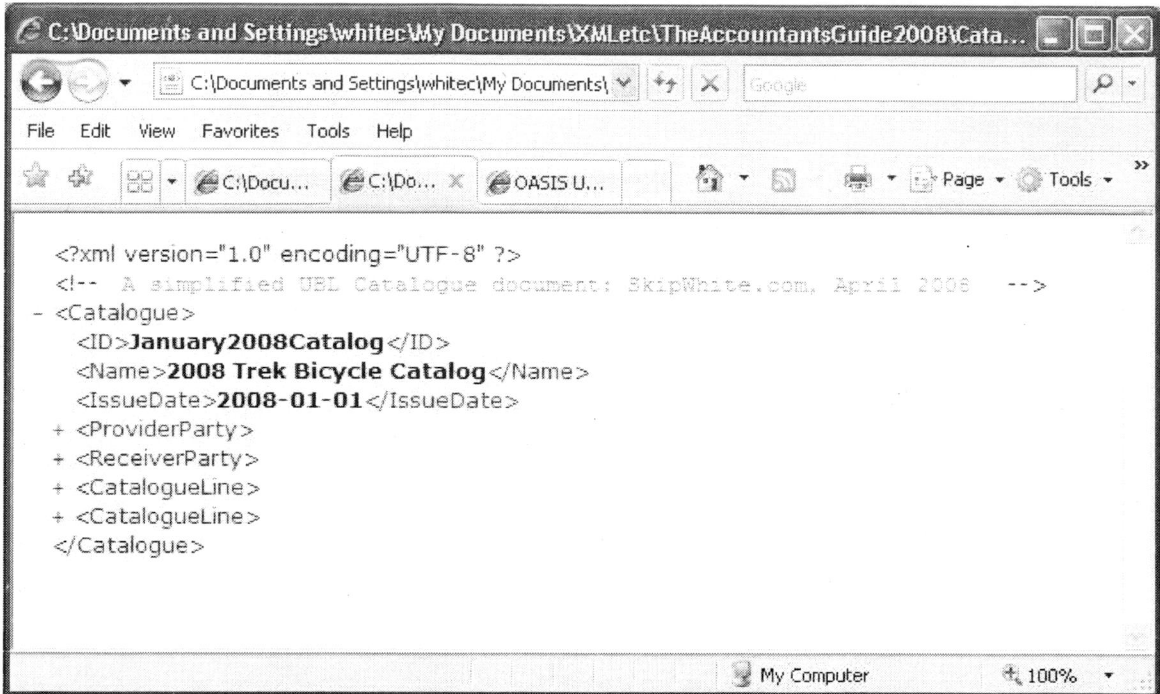

(File: *http://www.skipwhite.com/Guide2008/Chapter2/CatalogueItemExampleSimple .xml*)

In addition to being a well-formed XML document, Figure 2-1 is a document (collapsed for viewing) representing the major components of a catalog as defined in the UBL vocabulary. UBL 2.0 is an XML vocabulary that defines the structure and contents of common business documents. A UBL Catalogue (English spelling) is defined as a business document that describes items, prices, and other details about products or services available for sale. Like Catalogue, the UBL language defines the structure and contents of a family of common business documents, such as Order, Invoice, and Remittance advice, and the reusable data components that appear in them, such as ID, Name, IssueDate, and Item. If you have Internet access, point your browser to *http://www.skipwhite.com/Guide2008/Chapter2/CatalogueItemExampleSimple.xml*. Here you will find the complete "expanded" version of the UBL Catalogue document (as shown in Figure 2-2). To "collapse" Figure 2.2 to the document shown in Figure 2.1, click the "–" beside the ProviderParty, ReceiverParty, and CatalogueLine tag names; notice that each "–" is replaced by a "+" indicating nested contents within.

Figure 2-2: A well-formed, "expanded" UBL Catalogue document

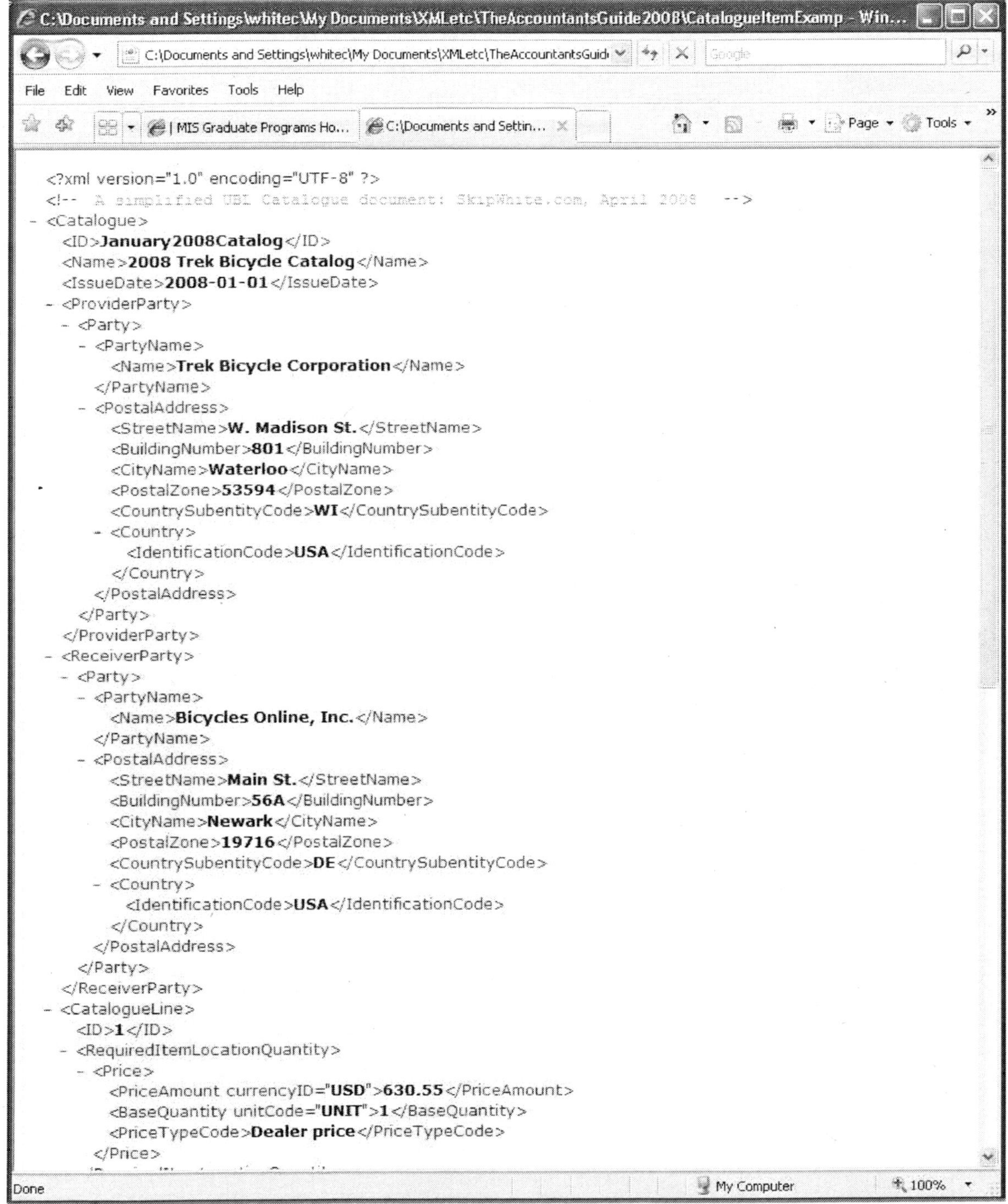

(File: *http://www.skipwhite.com/Guide2008/Chapter2/CatalogueItemExampleSimple.xml*)

Well-formed XML documents contain tags and data items in a nested hierarchy. A tag set and its contents is called an ***element***. An element consists of a matching beginning and ending tag name along with its content. Thus, **<ID>** *January2008Catalog***</ID>** in Figure 2-1 (or Figure 2-2) is an XML element with the name **ID** and the content "*January2008Catalog*" (all element names will be **bolded** in the remainder of this book). Notice that element names are surrounded with "< >" brackets and an ending element name is preceded by a "/" slash. In Figure 2-1, the elements **ID, Name,** and **IssueDate** contain data, while the elements **Catalogue, ProviderParty, ReceiverParty,** and **CatalogueLine** contain other elements nested within them. Notice also that element names are descriptive, and when two words are used, as in **IssueDate, ProviderParty, ReceiverParty,** and **CatalogueLine**, the first letter of each word is capitalized (no spaces allowed). These are referred to as "camel" characters.

All elements in a well-formed XML document are arranged in a hierarchy known as a parent-child relationship. Thus **Catalogue** is the parent of the entire XML document. It is referred to as the ***root element***. Likewise, the **ProviderParty, ReceiverParty,** and **CatalogueLine** elements are parents of other elements nested within them. Before getting into the details of XML and the UBL Catalogue document, you need to understand the general rules that all XML documents must follow.

To be well-formed, XML documents must follow a basic set of rules:

1. An XML document can have one and only one root element. The root element is the parent element of an XML document (often referred to as the "document element"). All other elements are its children and its children's children. **Catalogue** is the root element name for a UBL Catalogue document as defined in the UBL 2.0 vocabulary.
2. All elements must have matching beginning and ending names, and XML is case sensitive. XML documents can also have "empty" elements that do not contain data or other elements. (Empty elements are introduced in Chapter 3: The XML Language Foundation.)

3. Elements can contain ***attributes*** that add information about a specific element and appear following the beginning element name (see the **PriceAmount** and **BaseQuantity** elements within the **Price** elements in Figure 2-2). Attributes always consist of an attribute name and a value in the format: ***attributeName=*** *"attributeValue"* and always appear within the < > brackets of the beginning element name (see: **currencyID="**USD**"** in the **PriceAmount** elements and **unitCode="**Unit**"** in the **BaseQuantity** elements in Figure 2-2).
4. All elements must be properly nested.

XML documents that follow these basic rules can be processed by any software that is XML-enabled. XML is so popular for storing and transferring data on computer networks because XML documents are easy to create, easy for humans to understand, and efficient for computers to process. The basic rules for XML documents are simple yet powerful from two perspectives. First, they provide the foundation for the creation of humanly-understandable tags (element names) to "markup" data items with descriptive metadata (data about data). Second, they provide a structure that enforces a strict hierarchy that results in very efficient computer processing. The result is documents that are both easily understandable by humans and efficiently processable by computer applications.

The UBL Catalogue

The Universal Business Language was created by an international consortium devoted to the creation of ***open-source software standards*** for e-business and Web services known as ***OASIS*** (the Organization for the Advancement of Standard Information Standards). UBL provides a complete XML-based library of business documents to be used in e-business transactions. Since XML is "extensible," it has been adopted for a wide variety of business purposes, including the creation of industry-specific versions of basic business documents. Industry-specific versions of business documents creates problems for exchanging documents in trading relationships and integrating business processes in supply chain or other business relationships. UBL provides a generic XML interchange format for business documents that can be used between disparate software applications and across industries. Remember that XML is a set of rules and syntax for creating XML vocabularies for specific purposes. UBL is one such vocabulary for business documents to be used in e-business relationships.

Since the majority of businesses have a number of products and services to sell, the UBL Catalogue is a good example e-business document with which to start. A UBL Catalogue is a standard way for a business to encode in computer-readable form the information necessary to describe the products and services it has available. A UBL Catalogue could be rendered as a printed document or a Web page or simply transmitted from a seller to a potential buyer by way of the Internet. The catalog as shown in Figure 2-2 is simply a well-formed XML document written using the UBL 2.0 vocabulary. It would be used to transmit information from a seller to a potential buyer. An XML document does not include formatting instructions for how to display its contents. (We will cover this in Chapter 5: Transforming Documents with XSLT). Since the UBL Catalogue shown in Figure 2-2 is written in a standard, open-source language and can be processed by any XML-enabled software application, it is ideal to be used to transfer this information from one business to another. In this book we will use the MS Internet Explorer™ as our XML processor. If you have not done so, point your browser to *http://www.skipwhite.com/Guide2008/Chapter2/CatalogueItemExampleSimple.xml*. Then, if you are using IE, *click* View/Source and the XML source code will be loaded into MS Notepad™. The example e-business entity we will use in this book is Bicycles Online, Inc., a fictitious company that sells bicycles by way of the Web. As you will understand, the UBL Catalogue in Figure 2-2 is an example of a catalog that might be provided by Trek Bicycle Corporation to Bicycles Online, Inc. This catalog is meant to symbolize the beginning of the procurement process for Bicycles Online, Inc.

Like all XML vocabularies, UBL has its own rules and guiding principles. One rule is that each UBL document has its own unique root element name. As mentioned previously, an XML document can have one and only one root element. According to the rules of UBL, **Catalogue** is the root element name for this type of business document. One guiding principle is that each UBL document will be made up of ***reusable data components*** each with its own unique name, such as **ID**, **Name**, **IssueDate**,

ProviderParty, etc. Each reusable data component has its own meaning within UBL and can be used over and over again in any UBL document. A goal of UBL is to become an international standard for e-commerce.

If you think about it, every catalog that a business provides should have an **ID** with which it can be uniquely identified, a **Name** with which it can be referred to by humans, and an **IssueDate** to fix it in time and differentiate it from any other version of the same catalog. In addition, according to the rules of UBL, a catalog must also have a **ProviderParty** to identify the business entity providing the catalog, a **ReceiverParty** to identify an association between buyer and seller, and at least one **CalatogueLine** to describe the details of each product or service available. Think of the catalog shown in Figure 2-2 as an XML document written in the UBL vocabulary.

Looking at the top of Figure 2-2, you see that all XML documents start with a ***prolog***. A prolog contains processing instructions to be used by an XML processor and additional information such as documentation and structure information. All XML document prologs start with an XML declaration and version information: **<?xml version="**1.0" **encoding="**UTF-8"**?>**. This tells the XML processor which version of XML is being used and that all characters in the document are encoded in 8-bit Unicode - the preferred encoding scheme for e-mail and Web pages. Prologs often contain documentation statements. For example, <!-- A simplified UBL Catalogue document: SkipWhite.com, April 2008 --> identifies the file and its origin and date created. Documentation statements can appear anywhere in an XML document and are always in the form <!-- *documentation statement* -->.

Following the prolog is the beginning root element name: **<Catalogue>**. The beginning root element name is always the first tag in an XML document after the prolog; the root element is also referred to as the "document element" because it contains all of the document's other elements nested within it. Notice that the ending root element name is the last tag in the document: **</Catalogue** >. An XML document always starts and ends with its root element name. The root element name is always carefully chosen to be descriptive about the contents and purpose of the XML document; for instance, **xrbl** is the root element name for all XBRL documents. As with the root element name **Catalogue**, all other element names in the UBL vocabulary are defined in computer-readable XML taxonomies (essentially dictionaries of element names to be used for specific purposes).

UBL Element Names – Metadata

Remember that an XML element consists of a beginning and ending name and its contents, and all elements in an XML document are arranged in a strict hierarchical parent-child relationship. In XML documents, an element can have one and only one parent. In Figure 2-2, **Catalogue** is the root element; by definition it has no parent. It is, however, the parent of each element one step below it in the hierarchy. Thus, the **Catalogue** element is the parent of the **ID, Name, IssueDate, ProviderParty, ReceiverParty,** and two **CatalogueLine** elements (as illustrated in the collapsed XML document in Figure 2-1). Likewise, the **ProviderParty** and **ReceiverParty** elements are the parent of a single **Party** element. Each **Party** element is the parent of a **PartyName** element and a **PostalAddress** element. And, each of the **CatalogueLine** elements is the parent of an **ID, RequiredItemLocationQuantity,** and **Item** elements.

Question 2-1: What are the child elements of the **PostalAddress** element(s)?

Answer:

____

____

____

____

____

____

(Try to answer it first! See Question 2-1 in the Answer section.)

Notice that each of the two **PostalAddress** elements has exactly the same elements nested within it; each with its own data values. This element is a great example of a “reusable” UBL component. In other words, the **PostalAddress** element can be reused in all UBL documents that require it (e.g. an Order document or an Invoice document). Notice also that the **ProviderParty** and the **ReceiverParty** elements have exactly the same **Party** element nested within them. This is because each of these elements identifies a “party” to a business relationship with the only difference being that one is a “provider” and the other is a “receiver.” These elements are all reusable UBL components. As you will see, UBL is a very flexible XML vocabulary that takes maximum advantage of this idea of reusable components. (We will cover this in more detail in Chapter 3: The XML Language Foundation.)

Remember that XML is a set of rules and syntax for creating XML documents and other XML specifications. UBL and XBRL are both XML specifications/vocabularies for specific purposes--UBL for common business documents to be exchanged electronically by business partners and XBRL for computerized financial and business operations reporting. The general concepts in this discussion apply to both.

Notice that each element name in our UBL Catalogue makes sense and adds meaning to the data items it contains. Both the individual element names and their hierarchical nesting are important from the perspective of adding meaning. For example, the authors of the UBL specification decided that the root element name for a UBL catalog must be **Catalogue** and that its first <u>required</u> child element must be **ID**, followed by an <u>optional</u> **Name** element, and a second <u>required</u> element, **IssueDate**. All UBL documents have both required and optional elements. Notice that with only a minimal understanding of XML documents, it is obvious to a reader that the data contained in this UBL document pertains to a catalog named “*2008 Trek Bicycle Catalog*” issued on “*2008-01-01*” (the international date format for January 1, 2008). The point is that both the element names and their position in the document hierarchy add meaning and context to the data values within the elements in the document. In this sense, they are metadata – data about data. Processing data in context with standardized metadata is a significant improvement over processing data on its own. In addition, the metadata and context help a human better understand the data in the document.

The UBL specification requires that a UBL Catalogue include the **ProviderParty**, **ReceiverParty,** and one or more **CatalogueLine** elements. As the author of this UBL Catalogue document (Figure 2-2), I chose to use the elements that you see within the **ProviderParty** and **ReceiverParty** elements. Also, as the author of this Catalogue document, I chose to use the **Party** element and for it to contain the **PartyName** and **PostalAddress** elements and their contents. Within the **CatalogLine** element, the **ID** and **Item** elements are required, but the rest of the elements I chose to use to describe the catalog item. UBL is very flexible, and as long as a UBL document author follows the rules of UBL, he/she can create a business document to meet the purpose at hand. The great advantage to using UBL instead of creating your own XML business documents is that UBL is a standardized XML vocabulary that can be used for any e-business document. If you created your own vocabulary and your business partners created their own, each would use different element names and structure and each would have to be translated before being processed. As you will see in Chapter 3, using a standard XML vocabulary has significant advantages over creating your own.

XML Attributes – Additional Meaning for Elements

All XML elements can have one or more attributes. All attributes are contained within the beginning element name brackets (< >) and serve to further explain the meaning of an individual element. All attributes have their own name and a value in the following format: ***attributeName***=“*attributeValue*” – referred to as a “name-value pair.” UBL uses attributes sparingly. Consider the **PriceAmount** element in each of the **Price** elements in Figure 2-2. The **PriceAmount** element is required to have a **currencyID** attribute so that its data value can be properly interpreted. Thus, within the **Price** element in the first **CatalogueLine** element, the element **<PriceAmount currencyID=**"*USD*"**>***630.55* **</PriceAmount>** can be properly interpreted as “630.55 in U.S. dollars;” USD is the international abbreviation for U.S. dollars. The element name, **PriceAmount**, did not change (i.e., its matching ending element name is still **</PriceAmount>**), but the attribute **currencyID**="*USD*" appears within the brackets of the beginning element name. So even though a beginning element name looks different when an attribute is added, the element name has not changed. XML attributes are used when necessary to add meaning to specific elements so that a human or a software application can precisely interpret the element's contents.

Question 2-2: In your own words, how would you interpret all of the data values in the **Price** element within the second **CatalogueLine** element?

____

____

____

____

____

____

____

In the UBL vocabulary, attributes are required on elements that contain monetary amounts and object measurements. As you will see, attributes are used very heavily in the XBRL vocabulary.

A UBL Purchase Order Document

Remember that XML documents are used in business to store and transmit data along with its meaning. Each item of data is contained within an element whose name and attributes add meaning to it. Each element is contained within a hierarchy that adds context to it. Thus, a software application processing an XML document is processing data objects with meaning and in context. When data can be processed with meaning and context, instead of as a string of raw numbers or characters, the data are easily understandable and can be more readily reused for other purposes. This is especially true when the element and attribute names and the document structure are standardized, as in UBL. Data in this form is considered to be "information."

A business could develop its own elements, attributes, and document structures in XML or choose from one of several XML vocabularies developed for specific business purposes. As you will see, there are significant advantages to using an established XML vocabulary such as UBL. The purchase order presented and discussed in detail in this section is a complete UBL Order; simplified by removing XML-specific schema references and namespaces (which are covered in Chapter 3: The XML Language Foundation).

In this Chapter and several that follow, we will work with examples of important steps and documents used in the business procurement cycle (also referred to as the purchasing and cash disbursement cycle) involving two business partners. The business scenario is that Trek Bicycle Corporation has provided its 2008 bicycle catalog in UBL Catalogue format (as shown in Figure 2-2) to Bicycles Online, Inc., one of its dealers. Bicycles Online, Inc. has used the information in the catalog to create a purchase order in UBL Order format and is ready to send it to Trek Bicycle Corporation.

At the top of the UBL Purchase Order document shown in Figure 2-3 (available for viewing and download at: *http://www.skipwhite.com/Guide2008/Chapter2/OrderExampleSimple.xml*) the required root element is **Order**. In UBL, a purchase order is a type of Order, as is a sales order. As you will see, they differ by their required structure. A UBL Order is required to have an **ID** element and an **IssueDate** element. Since this **ID** element's data value, *12345*, was assigned by the buyer/customer, it will be used as an order reference number. A UBL Order is also required to have a **BuyerCustomer Party** element, a **SellerSupplierParty** element, and at least one **OrderLine** element.

Figure 2-3: A simplified UBL Purchase Order document

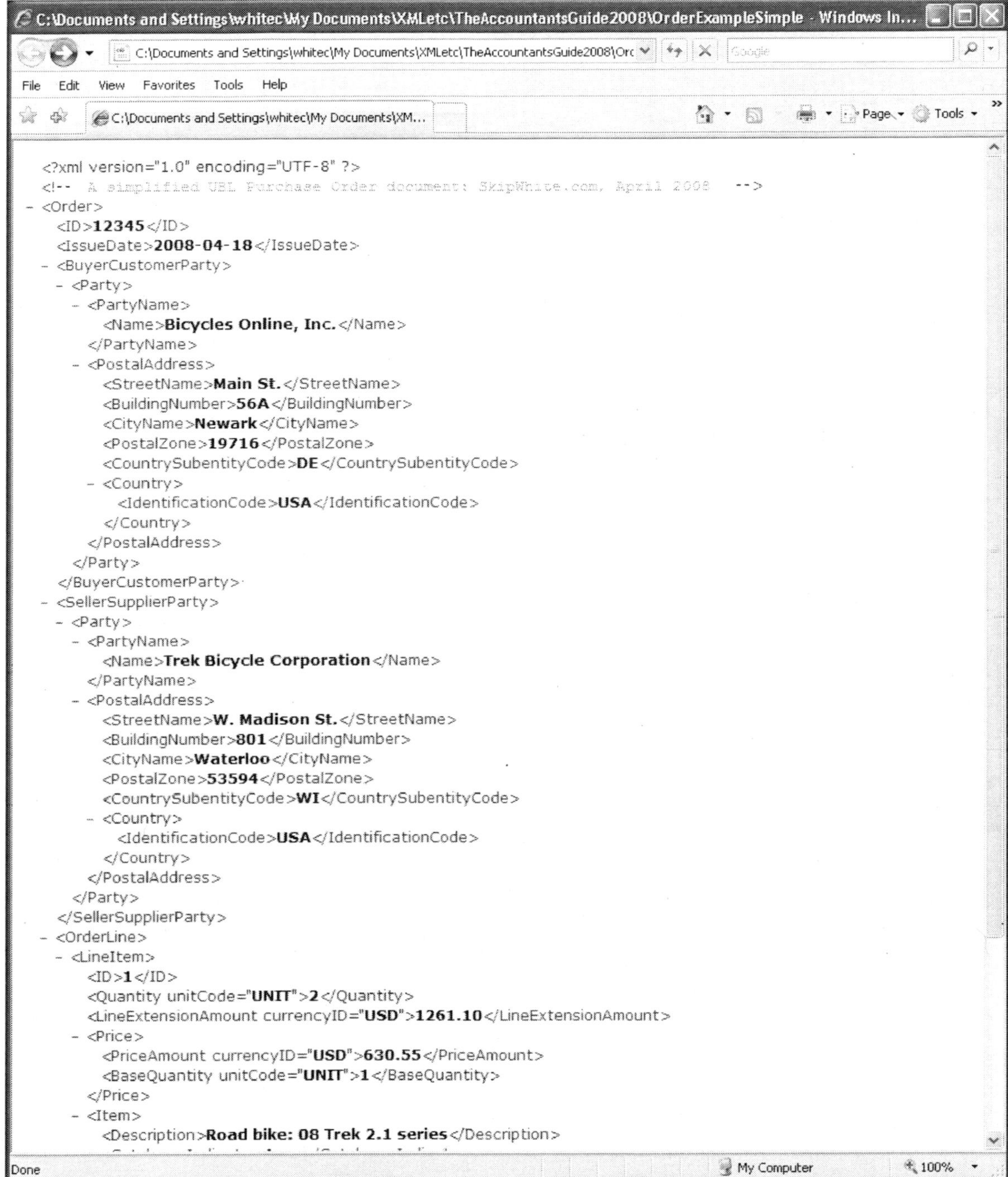

```
<?xml version="1.0" encoding="UTF-8" ?>
<!-- A simplified UBL Purchase Order document: SkipWhite.com, April 2008 -->
- <Order>
    <ID>12345</ID>
    <IssueDate>2008-04-18</IssueDate>
  - <BuyerCustomerParty>
    - <Party>
      - <PartyName>
          <Name>Bicycles Online, Inc.</Name>
        </PartyName>
      - <PostalAddress>
          <StreetName>Main St.</StreetName>
          <BuildingNumber>56A</BuildingNumber>
          <CityName>Newark</CityName>
          <PostalZone>19716</PostalZone>
          <CountrySubentityCode>DE</CountrySubentityCode>
        - <Country>
            <IdentificationCode>USA</IdentificationCode>
          </Country>
        </PostalAddress>
      </Party>
    </BuyerCustomerParty>
  - <SellerSupplierParty>
    - <Party>
      - <PartyName>
          <Name>Trek Bicycle Corporation</Name>
        </PartyName>
      - <PostalAddress>
          <StreetName>W. Madison St.</StreetName>
          <BuildingNumber>801</BuildingNumber>
          <CityName>Waterloo</CityName>
          <PostalZone>53594</PostalZone>
          <CountrySubentityCode>WI</CountrySubentityCode>
        - <Country>
            <IdentificationCode>USA</IdentificationCode>
          </Country>
        </PostalAddress>
      </Party>
    </SellerSupplierParty>
  - <OrderLine>
    - <LineItem>
        <ID>1</ID>
        <Quantity unitCode="UNIT">2</Quantity>
        <LineExtensionAmount currencyID="USD">1261.10</LineExtensionAmount>
      - <Price>
          <PriceAmount currencyID="USD">630.55</PriceAmount>
          <BaseQuantity unitCode="UNIT">1</BaseQuantity>
        </Price>
      - <Item>
          <Description>Road bike: 08 Trek 2.1 series</Description>
```

(File: *http://www.skipwhite.com/Guide2008/Chapter2/OrderExampleSimple.xml*)

Since we will compare the elements in the UBL Catalogue to those in the UBL Purchase Order, it may be helpful to place the UBL Catalogue side by side with the UBL Purchase Order; as in Figure 2-4.

Figure 2-4: The UBL Catalogue and the UBL Purchase Order

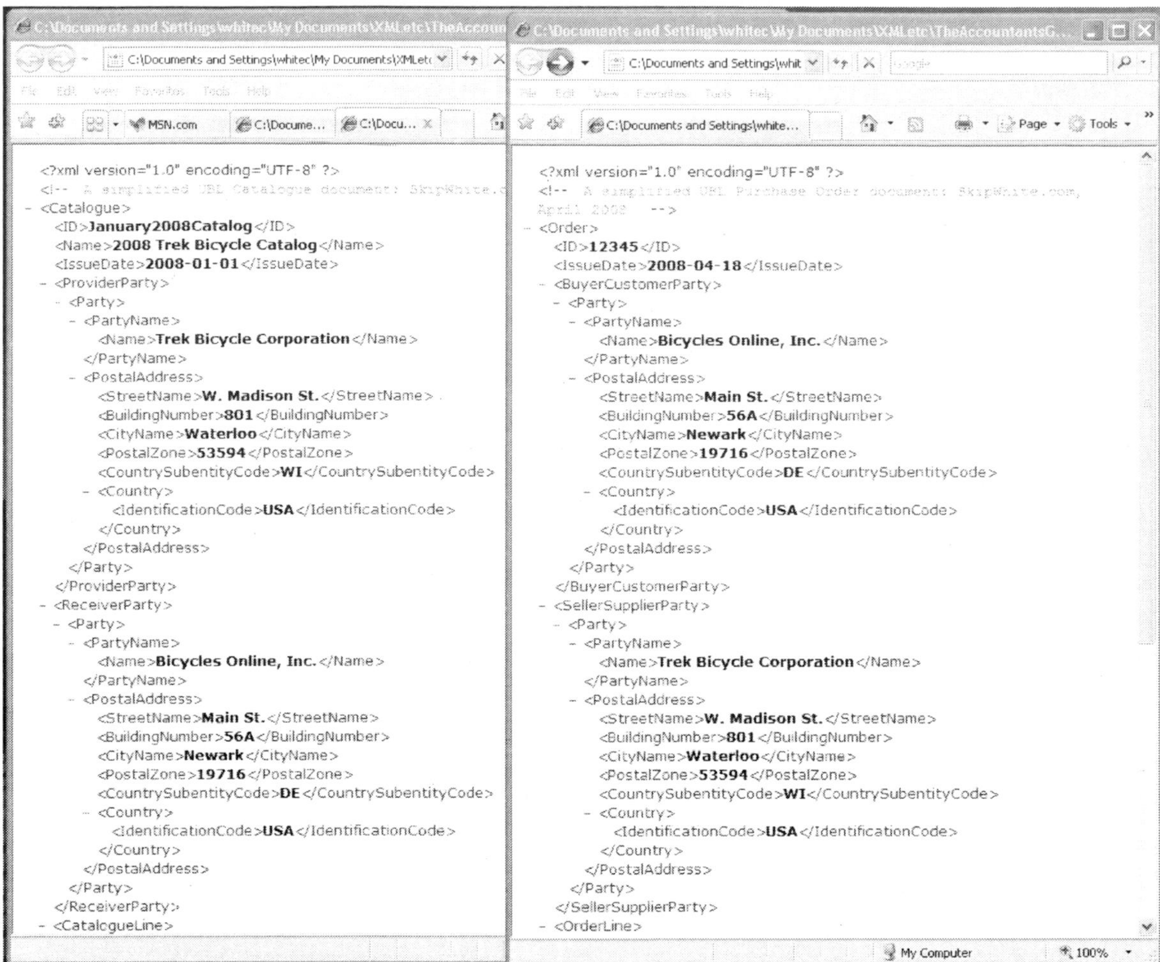

```
<?xml version="1.0" encoding="UTF-8" ?>
<!-- A simplified UBL Catalogue document: SkipWhite.c
- <Catalogue>
    <ID>January2008Catalog</ID>
    <Name>2008 Trek Bicycle Catalog</Name>
    <IssueDate>2008-01-01</IssueDate>
  - <ProviderParty>
    - <Party>
      - <PartyName>
          <Name>Trek Bicycle Corporation</Name>
        </PartyName>
      - <PostalAddress>
          <StreetName>W. Madison St.</StreetName>
          <BuildingNumber>801</BuildingNumber>
          <CityName>Waterloo</CityName>
          <PostalZone>53594</PostalZone>
          <CountrySubentityCode>WI</CountrySubentityCode>
        - <Country>
            <IdentificationCode>USA</IdentificationCode>
          </Country>
        </PostalAddress>
      </Party>
    </ProviderParty>
  - <ReceiverParty>
    - <Party>
      - <PartyName>
          <Name>Bicycles Online, Inc.</Name>
        </PartyName>
      - <PostalAddress>
          <StreetName>Main St.</StreetName>
          <BuildingNumber>56A</BuildingNumber>
          <CityName>Newark</CityName>
          <PostalZone>19716</PostalZone>
          <CountrySubentityCode>DE</CountrySubentityCode>
        - <Country>
            <IdentificationCode>USA</IdentificationCode>
          </Country>
        </PostalAddress>
      </Party>
    </ReceiverParty>
  - <CatalogueLine>
```

```
<?xml version="1.0" encoding="UTF-8" ?>
<!-- A simplified UBL Purchase Order document: SkipWhite.com,
April 2008 -->
- <Order>
    <ID>12345</ID>
    <IssueDate>2008-04-18</IssueDate>
  - <BuyerCustomerParty>
    - <Party>
      - <PartyName>
          <Name>Bicycles Online, Inc.</Name>
        </PartyName>
      - <PostalAddress>
          <StreetName>Main St.</StreetName>
          <BuildingNumber>56A</BuildingNumber>
          <CityName>Newark</CityName>
          <PostalZone>19716</PostalZone>
          <CountrySubentityCode>DE</CountrySubentityCode>
        - <Country>
            <IdentificationCode>USA</IdentificationCode>
          </Country>
        </PostalAddress>
      </Party>
    </BuyerCustomerParty>
  - <SellerSupplierParty>
    - <Party>
      - <PartyName>
          <Name>Trek Bicycle Corporation</Name>
        </PartyName>
      - <PostalAddress>
          <StreetName>W. Madison St.</StreetName>
          <BuildingNumber>801</BuildingNumber>
          <CityName>Waterloo</CityName>
          <PostalZone>53594</PostalZone>
          <CountrySubentityCode>WI</CountrySubentityCode>
        - <Country>
            <IdentificationCode>USA</IdentificationCode>
          </Country>
        </PostalAddress>
      </Party>
    </SellerSupplierParty>
  - <OrderLine>
```

(File: *http://www.skipwhite.com/Guide2008/Chapter2/CatalogueItemExampleSimple.xml* and *http://www.skipwhite.com/Guide2008/Chapter2/OrderExampleSimple.xml*)

Compare the **BuyerCustomerParty** element in the Purchase Order document to the **ReceiverParty** element in the Catalogue document. Also compare the **SellerSupplier Party** element in the Purchase Order document to the **ProviderParty** element in the Catalogue document. All of these elements contain a **Party** element with exactly the same structure. And the corresponding receiver/buyer and provider/seller **Party** elements contain exactly the same information. Since both of these documents are in computer-readable form in a standardized vocabulary, a few lines of computer code can be used to move the complete **Party** element within the **ReceiverParty** element in the Catalogue document to the **BuyerCustomerParty** element in the Purchase Order document. This illustrates one of the significant business benefits of using the UBL vocabulary for business documents both internally and externally in business relationships: data are reusable and easily moved from one business application to another without expensive, error-prone human intervention.

A UBL Purchase Order is required to have at least one **OrderLine** element and a **LineItem** element. The **LineItem** element is required to have an **ID** element and an **Item** element. Within the **LineItem** element, the **ID** element is the identifier for the line item being ordered, and the **<Quantity unitCode=**"UNIT"**>**_2_**</Quantity>** and **<LineExtensionAmount currencyID=**"USD"**>**_1261.10_**</LineExtensionAmount>** elements and their attributes identify the quantity ordered and the total amount for the two items. Notice the similarity between the **Price** elements in the Catalogue document and the Purchase Order document (i.e., the **<PriceAmount currencyID=**"USD"**>** _630.55_**</PriceAmount>** and **<BaseQuantity unitCode=**"UNIT"**>**_1_**</BaseQuantity>** elements are exactly the same). Also notice the similarity between the **Item** elements in the Catalogue document and the Purchase Order document (i.e., the **<Description>**_Road bike: 08 Trek 2.1 series_**</Description>**, **<Name>**_Mens 2008 Trek 2.1_**</Name>,** and the **<ID>**_08T2.1M_ **</ID>** element within the **SellersItemIdentification** elements are exactly the same).

It is important to remember that XML documents contain elements which contain data values and that all of the elements are in a hierarchy that adds context to everything in the document. Data in this form is actually information because it has meaning – it is surrounded by metadata. In addition, it can be easily processed by computer applications and the information can be easily reused for other purposes. The first two steps in the procurement process are to uncover information about the items to be purchased, often done by way of a catalog, and then to create a purchase order. In this section, we compared a UBL Purchase Order to a UBL Catalogue. Since both are XML documents written in the UBL vocabulary, they are very similar in structure and reuse many basic components. Both start with a root element name that describes the purpose of the document and both have an **ID** for unique identification and an **IssueDate** for fixing the document in time. Both documents use the same **Party** structure and the same **Price** and

Item structures, modified appropriately for their separate purposes. In addition, the Purchase Order has two new elements to indicate the quantity and price of the items ordered and two new elements to identify the catalog in which they are described by the seller. The **<Quantity unitCode=**"UNIT"**>***2* **</Quantity>** element within the **LineItem** element indicates the quantity being ordered, and the **<LineExtensionAmount currencyID=**"USD"**>***1261.10* **</LineExtensionAmount>** element indicates the total amount for the items. Similarly, the **<CatalogueIndicator>***true***</CatalogueIndicator>** element within the **Item** element is used to indicate that this item in this Purchase Order is from a Catalogue, and the **CatalogueItemIdentification** element with its required **<ID>***January2008Catalog***</ID>** element is used to identify which Catalogue. Notice that this **ID** element in the Purchase Order document is exactly the same as the **ID** element used to uniquely identify the entire Catalogue document; the **ID** element is the required first child element of the Catalogue root element.

The following rules apply to all UBL documents:

1. Each has a unique root element chosen to correspond to the document's purpose.
2. Each has a required **ID** element to uniquely identify the document and an **IssueDate** element to fix it in time (an optional **IssueTime** element can also be used).
3. Each has two party elements appropriately named for the purpose of the document to identify the provider/supplier and the customer/buyer parties to the document (e.g., **ProviderParty** and **ReceiverParty** in the Catalogue document; and **BuyerCustomerParty** and **SellerSupplierParty** in the Purchase Order document).
4. Each has at least one line element appropriately named for the purpose of the document (e.g., **CatalogueLine** in the Catalogue document; and **OrderLine** in the Purchase Order document). And, each line element is required to have an **ID** element and appropriate item information.

The objective of discussing in detail the UBL Catalogue and UBL Purchase Order is to help you understand the basics of XML documents (i.e., how data is tagged with elements and attributes and how XML documents are structured) and to introduce you to UBL documents and the concept of reusable components. In addition, the UBL Catalogue and Purchase Order represent documents used in the initial steps of a business procurement process. As discussed in the next section, exchanging information in XML documents between business partners can significantly reduce data re-entry and manual processing steps in business relationships. This is especially true with a standardized XML language like UBL.

XML and UBL in Business

Standardization of documents and the data they contain is a very old issue. The ideas behind ***Electronic Data Interchange*** (EDI) are traceable to the 1948 Berlin Airlift and the earliest days of computer processing. At the end of World War II, the Soviet Union occupied East Germany, including the eastern half of Berlin. In June 1948, the Soviets began blockading access to West Berlin. The United States, United Kingdom, France, and West Germany created what became known as the Berlin Airlift to fly in all manner of supplies to keep the citizens alive and thwart the Soviet attempt to make all of Berlin part of the Soviet empire. The task of coordinating the delivery of massive amounts of supplies from different countries using different documents containing different terms, data, and in different languages, was solved through a standardized manifest containing standard data in a standard format. (Historical note: the Soviets lifted their blockage about a year later and provided access points to West Berlin. In 1961, they built the Berlin Wall to stop people fleeing from East to West Berlin. The Wall stood until 1989.)

From this early beginning, there have been many attempts at standardizing the structure and contents of business documents. While EDI formatted document exchanges by way of proprietary, third-party value-added networks (VAN) are still common, two major problems persist: there are four separate major sets of EDI standards, and before software applications can send or receive EDI documents the data must be translated to/from EDI format. The new emerging technology for the exchange of business information is ***XML web services***. XML web services are standardized software systems designed to support direct computer-to-computer interaction over a network, including the Internet. Since most current software applications are XML-enabled and XML vocabularies for business documents (UBL) and operations reporting (XBRL) are maturing, businesses are finding ways to exchange information directly between software applications using XML web services over the Internet.

Consider a buyer and a seller exchanging business documents in a relatively simple trading relationship as depicted in Figure 2-5 (i.e., a procurement process from the buyer's standpoint). Using the UBL language, the supplier creates a UBL Catalogue document using an XML-enabled software application such as MS Notepad™ or a special XML editor such as XMLSpy (Altova Software, *http://www.altova.com/simpledownload2.html?gclid=CIjz-Mv2gJMCFR11lgod8iAyGQ*). The supplier would likely send a catalog directly to his trading partners and render a version, without specific buyer information, as a Web page on its e-commerce Web site (we will cover rendering XML documents as Web pages in Chapter 5). The buyer would likely render the UBL Catalogue document using a browser and also save the complete document as an XML file.

Figure 2-5: Document exchange in a simple procurement process

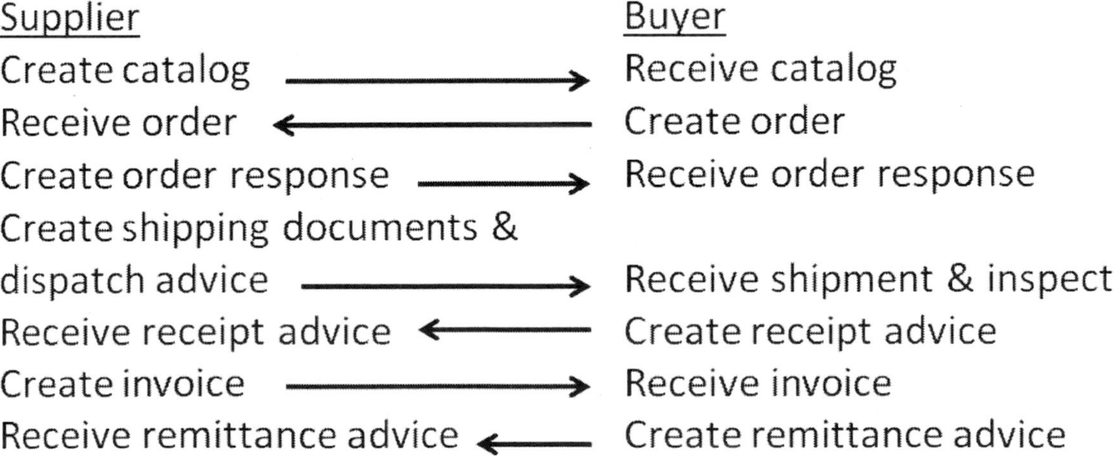

The buyer would load the UBL Catalogue document into an XML-enabled software package or an XML editor, or any text editor, and reuse the catalog information to create her UBL Purchase Order document. The supplier would receive the UBL Purchase Order

and reuse the order information to create a UBL Order Response document to inform the buyer that the Purchase Order has been received; the buyer would receive it and store it. The supplier would then fulfill the order and create a UBL Packing List to include with the order shipment and create and send to the buyer a UBL Despatch Advice (English spelling for "dispatch") describing the dispatch and delivery of the ordered items; and if necessary a UBL Waybill (shipping document) containing carrier and delivery information to be sent to the carrier. The buyer would receive the UBL Despatch Advise and store it and later receive and inspect the ordered items and create a UBL Receipt Advice describing the receipt and condition of the items and send it to the supplier. The supplier would create a UBL Invoice and send it to the buyer who would receive it and create a UBL Remittance Advice and send it along with payment for the ordered items. Notice that UBL supports the entire trading relationship with a set of business documents, all of which have a similar structure and reuse common information such as buyer and seller demographic and specific item information.

As with the standardized manifest to support the Berlin Airlift, standardization of documents and their contents translates into efficient and effective information processing. Since XML documents are independent of any specific computing platform and most current generation software applications are XML-enabled, they have become the standard way to encode data for the exchange of information between heterogeneous information systems. Since all business today involves trading partners communicating by way of computer networks and UBL supports the complete end-to-end exchange of computer-readable business documents in a standard format using reusable data components, it has taken off in Europe and is gaining traction in the United States. In the example UBL Catalogue and UBL Purchase Order developed in this Chapter, it is easy to see that standard information elements in standardized documents create business process benefits. Some of these benefits include being able to exchange information in documents directly between disparate software applications without having to transform or translate it (as in an EDI system); reusing information components in new documents without having to manually re-enter the data; and streamlining business processes to receive documents by way of the Internet, analyze their contents with software tools, generate new documents and send them back by way of the Internet. In addition, the contents of XML documents, or complete documents, can be efficiently stored in databases with very little human intervention.

Summary

XML is a meta-language that is defined in the XML specification 1.0 (http://www.w3.org/TR/REC-xml/). Well-formed XML documents are a class of data objects that can be processed by XML-enabled software applications. XML documents are a key part of the XML foundation. XML documents contain data "tagged" with meaningful XML elements (metadata) in a strict hierarchy. The basic unit of information in an XML document is an "element." An element consists of a beginning and ending element name, attributes, and data values or other elements nested within it. All well-formed XML documents follow a basic set of rules: one and only one root element; matching beginning and ending element names; all elements can contain attributes; all elements must be properly nested. These simple yet powerful rules help standardize XML documents so they can be efficiently processed by software applications.

XML documents are used in business to store and transmit data. One advantage is that XML documents allow businesses to process data in context. An XML document's context is provided by the element names, attributes, and element hierarchy, all of which add meaning to the actual data values contained within individual elements. Businesses can develop their own elements, attributes, and document structures to represent their business information or choose one of a number of already developed XML document vocabularies. One such vocabulary is UBL (Universal Business Language), which defines an XML library of common business documents and their reusable components (http://www.oasis-open.org/committees/tc_home.php?wg_abbrev=ubl). Another is XBRL. A final advantage is that all well-formed XML documents can be processed by all XML-enabled software – which is to say essentially all current generation software applications. This allows businesses to avoid the extra costs of purchasing and maintaining proprietary software for individual applications.

The XML specification and its rules for well-formed XML documents are one part of the foundation of the XML paradigm. The XML paradigm is a large and growing family of technologies that follow the XML specification. In this Chapter, we have discussed XML documents by introducing the UBL vocabulary for business documents. In Chapter 3 we will discuss several technical components of the XML language necessary for processing XML documents: XML Namespaces; the XML Schema language; and the XLinking language. As you will understand, these form the foundation for all XML vocabularies, including UBL and XBRL, and other parts of the XML paradigm.

Glossary of new terms introduced in Chapter 2

Attributes: Add meaning to a specific XML element. XML attributes always have a name-value pair in the format: ***attributeName=****"attributeValue"*. They can appear in any XML element and are always found in the beginning element name tag.

Electronic Data Interchange (EDI): A standard format for communicating data in standard business transactions between and within businesses, organizations, and government entities. EDI usually involves third-party value-added networks to translate and transmit the data between software applications.

Element: A matching beginning and ending tag set and its contents, or an empty element. An XML element can contain a data item or other elements nested within it. It is the basic unit of content in an XML document.

OASIS (The Organization for the Advancement of Standard Information Standards): An international not-for-profit consortium that administers the development and adoption of open standards for the global information society (http://www.oasis-open.org/who/).

Open-source software standards: Standards for the development of non-proprietary computer software that is available in the public domain free of charge.

Prolog: The first part of an XML document that contains processing instructions to be used by an XML processor and often contains comments. The prolog always appears before the root element.

Reusable data component: XML elements developed for specific purposes, such as UBL or XBRL.

Root element: The first element in an XML document. It is the parent element for the entire XML document – often referred to as the "document" element. All other elements in the XML document are nested within it.

UBL vocabulary: An XML language that defines a generic format for common business documents (such as "Order," "Invoice," and "Remittance advice") and their contents (such as "Address," "Name," and "Item."). See: http://www.oasis-open.org/committees/tc_home.php?wg_abbrev=ubl.

Valid XML documents: XML documents that are well-formed and also follow rules specified in a DTD (data type definition) or XML schema (covered in Chapter 3).

Well-formed XML documents: Documents that follow the basic rules for all XML documents and can therefore be processed by an XML processor.

XML web services: The exchange of XML documents directly between software applications on a network. It also refers to the use of XML messages to send data to a remote software application on the Web, which then performs a service and returns a result.

Using Notepad™

XML documents are text, and you should use a text editor such as Notepad™ to create them. Warning: do not use a word processor such as Word™ because all word processors add proprietary codes that will cause errors when the document is processed by an XML processor!

With Notepad™, you have to take two special steps when you save your XML file. First, when you are ready to "Save" your XML document, be sure to change **"Save as type:"** to **"All Files"** – this bypasses the default save as a ".txt" file. Second, add a **".xml"** extension on your file name (as in ***myfilename*.xml**), **before** hitting the Save button (see below – notice the File name: and Save as type: dialog boxes).

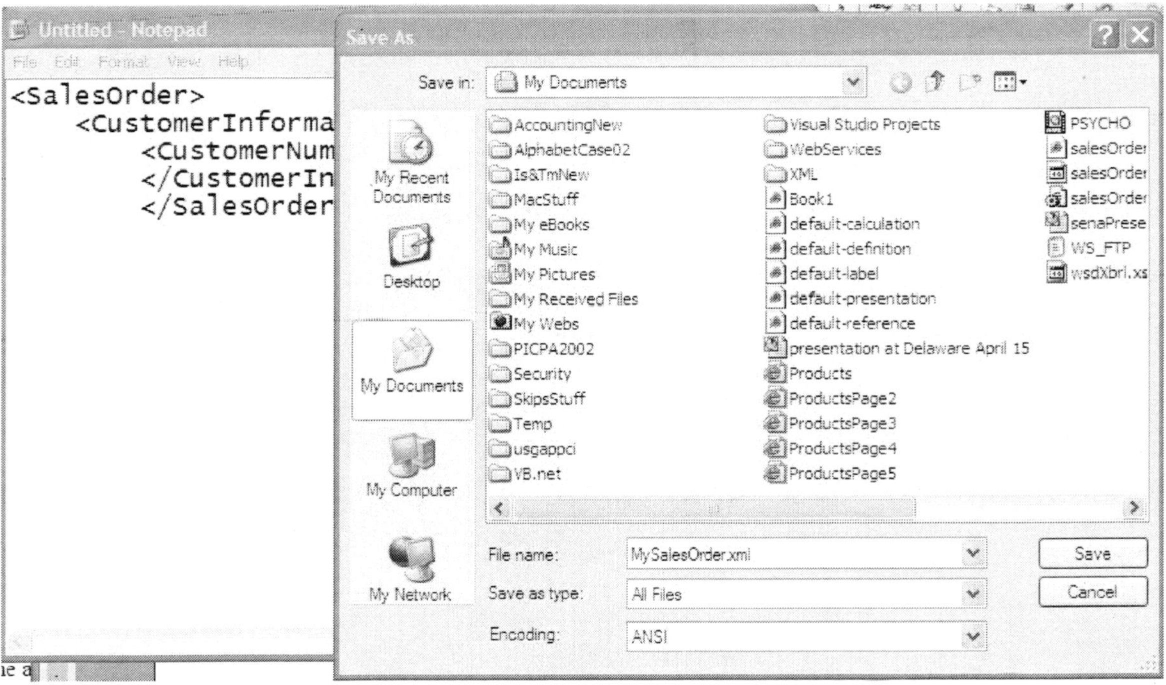

These procedures are necessary because Notepad™ by default saves files as Text and adds a ".txt" extension, which would cause it not to be recognized as an xml file. The Programmer's File Editor is an excellent and more sophisticated text editor. It can be found at various locations including: http://www.lancs.ac.uk/staff/steveb/cpaap/pfe/default.htm. One for the Macintosh OSX environment is TextMate, a commercial package with a 30-day free trial version available from http://macromates.com/.

Processing XML Documents with a Web Browser

Well-formed XML documents can be processed by any XML-enabled software application. Since we are all familiar with Web browsers and the Internet Explorer™ is heavily used in universities, we use it as our XML processor in the examples in this book. However, any current generation Web browser should work. When an XML document is processed by an XML-enabled software application, the processor reads the document and any associated instructions. Since the XML documents we will create in the following exercises do not contain any additional instructions, an XML processor will simply read each individual document and check to see if it is well-formed. Figures 2-2 and 2-3 illustrate what a well-formed XML document should look like when processed by an XML-enabled Web browser like IE. Remember that you can collapse a well-formed XML document processed by a Web browser by clicking the "–" to the left of any element that has other elements nested within it (see Figure 2-1). If your XML document is not well-formed, you will get an error message.

Exercises

Exercise 2-1: Creating an Order Response document

Figure 2-5 illustrates the document exchange between a buyer and a supplier in a relatively standard ordering process. We have already considered a UBL Catalogue document (*http://www.skipwhite.com/Guide2008/Chapter2/CatalogueItem ExampleSimple.xml*) and a UBL Purchase Order document (*http://www.skipwhite.com/ Guide2008/Chapter2/OrderExampleSimple.xml*). Your challenge in this exercise is to create your own XML document representing an Order Response document. Since you are now familiar with the rules that all XML documents must follow and you understand some of the basics of UBL documents, you are to create an Order Response document that conforms to the following rules. It must have:

- A root element name that makes sense (Hint: What root element name do you think might be used for a UBL Order Response document?)
- An ID element, a Sales Order ID element, and an Issue Date element
- An Order Reference element with data referencing the buyer's purchase order number
- Elements containing supplier and buyer information
- An Item element with ordered item information.

Additional instructions:

Structure your Order Response document similar to the UBL Catalogue and Purchase Order documents and reuse as much information as you can. Include a Note element containing text about whether or not the items are in stock and how soon they can be shipped. As with the Note element, make up your own data values for your elements when necessary. When you are finished, save your file with a .xml extension (as in *MyOrderResponse.xml*) and open it in the IE (or your favorite browser) to make sure it is well-formed.

Exercise 2-2: Creating a Dispatch Advice document

Figure 2-5 illustrates the document exchange between a buyer and a supplier in a relatively standard ordering process. We have already considered a UBL Catalogue document (*http://www.skipwhite.com/Guide2008/Chapter2/CatalogueItem ExampleSimple.xml*) and a UBL Purchase Order document (*http://www.skipwhite.com/ Guide2008/Chapter2/OrderExampleSimple.xml*). Your challenge in this exercise is to create your own XML document representing a Dispatch Advice document. Since you are now familiar with the rules that all XML documents must follow and you understand some of the basics of UBL documents, you are to create a Dispatch Advice document that conforms to the following rules. It must have:

- A root element name that makes sense (Hint: What root element name do you think might be used for a UBL Despatch Advice document?)
- An ID element and an Issue Date element
- An Order Reference element with an ID element, a Sales Order ID element (assigned by the supplier), and its Issue Date
- Elements containing supplier and buyer information
- A Dispatch Line element containing an ID element, a Delivery Quantity element, an Order Line Reference element containing an Order Reference element, and an Item element with ordered item information.

Additional instructions:

Structure your Dispatch Advice document similar to the UBL Catalogue and Purchase Order documents and reuse as much information as you can. Include a Note element containing text about shipment and delivery of the ordered items. As with the Note element, make up your own data values for your elements when necessary. When you are finished, save your file with a .xml extension (as in *MyDispatchAdvice.xml*) and open it in the IE (or your favorite browser) to make sure it is well-formed.

Downloadable files:

Available from: www.SkipWhite.com/Guide2008/Chapter2/ *file name*:

- File name: CatalogueItemExampleSimple.xml (Figure 2-21 and 2-2) http://www.skipwhite.com/Guide2008/Chapter2/CatalogueItemExampleSimple.xml
- File name: OrderExampleSimple.xml (Figure 2-3) http://www.skipwhite.com/Guide2008/Chapter2/OrderExampleSimple.xml

References & more information:

XML, W3C: Extensible Markup Language (XML) 1.0 (Third Edition), W3C, 2004-02-04 (http://www.w3.org/TR/REC-xml/#sec-physical-struct)

UBL: Universal Business Language 2.0, Oasis, 2006-12-12 (http://www.oasis-open.org/committees/tc_home.php?wg_abbrev=ubl)

XMLSpy, Altova Software (http://www.altova.com/simpledownload2.html?gclid=CIjz-Mv2gJMCFR11lgod8iAyGQ)

Answers:

Question 2-1: What are the child elements of the **<PostalAddress>** element(s)?

Refer to Figure 2-2.The following elements are the children of the **<PostalAddress>** element(s):
<StreetName>
<BuildingNumber>
<CityName>
<PostalZone>
<CountrySubentityCode>
and
<Country>
Remember that an element's children are found one step below it in the document hierarchy, and a child element has one and only one parent element.

Question 2-2: In your own words, how would you interpret the data in the **<Price>** element within the second **<CatalogueLine>** element?

```
<Price>
   <PriceAmount currencyID="USD">575.55</PriceAmount>
   <BaseQuantity unitCode="UNIT">1</BaseQuantity>
   <PriceTypeCode>Dealer price</PriceTypeCode>
</Price>
```

This element can be interpreted as: the "per unit" price of this item is "575.55 in U.S. dollars," and this is a "Dealer price."

The Accountant's Guide to XBRL

Chapter 3: The XML Language Foundation

Overview

As you learned in Chapter 2, well-formed XML documents contain data values surrounded by XML elements and attributes in a nested hierarchy. The rules and syntax for creating well-formed XML documents are one portion of the XML foundation as described in the XML Specification 1.0 (XML, W3C). This chapter focuses on XML languages that form another portion of the XML foundation.

The XML language foundation is a family of languages for processing and validating XML documents and for creating other specifications/vocabularies, such as UBL and XBRL, which extend the XML family of technologies for specific purposes. The XML Schema language is a key part of the foundation because it is used to specify the structure and contents of XML documents. All specifications that extend the XML family, including UBL and XBRL, are formally expressed using the XML Schema language. As you might expect, the XML Schema language is quite complex. In this Chapter we introduce the XML Schema language in a non-technical manner along with two other XML languages necessary for understanding UBL and XBRL – XML Namespaces and XLink.

The XML Schema Language

The ***XML Schema language*** is an XML language used to create XML schema documents. Note that by convention, Schema (with a capital S) refers to the XML Schema language (http://www.w3.org/TR/xmlschema-0/) and schema (with a small s) refers to a ***schema document*** created using the XML Schema language. The purpose of an individual XML schema document, which itself is a well-formed XML document, is to define the rules that a class of XML documents must follow. An individual schema document defines each element and attribute that can appear in a class of XML documents, such as UBL Purchase Orders, as well as their overall structure. As you will see, the UBL vocabulary consists of a number of XML schemas defining elements and attributes (such as **ID**, **IssueDate**, **Party**, **PostalAddress**, and **Item**) to be used in UBL documents (such as **Catalogue**, **Order**, **Receipt Advice**, **Despatch Advice**, and **Invoice**). Likewise, the XBRL vocabulary is made up of a number of XML schemas defining elements and attributes used for financial reporting, the structure of XBRL documents, and a host of financial reporting taxonomies, such as U.S. GAAP for Commercial and Industrial companies, U.S. GAAP for Banking and Savings institutions, Management Discussion and Analysis reports, and Accountants reports. The objective of covering the basics of XML schema documents is not to make you an expert in the XML Schema language but to introduce you to how XML vocabularies work.

Each XML vocabulary is created for a specific purpose, and each has its own ***XML namespace*** with which it can be identified. An XML namespace is a unique identifier, referred to as a URI (Universal Resource Identifier), indicating where information about an XML resource can be found. A URI can be a local name or a URL (Universal Resource Locator). Since XML documents are often made up of elements and attributes created for different purposes, XML namespaces unambiguously identify their source. Namespaces are meant to be human readable and computer processable. Since there are numerous XML vocabularies being developed for a variety of purposes and each has a number of XML schemas defining elements and attributes used for that purpose, XML namespaces are used to uniquely identify each one to avoid naming collisions (i.e., two or more elements with the same name but different meanings). As you will see, by identifying each schema's location with an XML namespace we can differentiate the elements and attributes defined in one schema from those defined in any other schema. In this Chapter, we will cover the basics of two simplified UBL schemas and use them to build several UBL document schemas.

Two basic types of elements can appear in XML documents: ***simple elements*** and ***complex elements***. A simple element contains a data value and no attributes, while a complex element contains other elements nested within it and/or attributes. In the UBL Catalogue (Figure 2-2) and Purchase Order (Figure 2-3) documents, elements such as **ID**,

IssueDate, **Name**, and **StreetName** are all simple elements (i.e., each one has a data value and no attributes). In the same documents, elements such as **ProviderParty**, **ReceiverParty**, **BuyerCustomerParty**, **SellerSupplierParty**, **Party**, **PartyName**, and **PostalAddress** are all complex elements (i.e., each one has other elements nested within it). And elements such as **PriceAmount** and **BaseQuantity** have a data value, referred to as "simple content," but are considered to be complex because each has an attribute.

Question 3-1: Referring to Figure 2-3 (OrderExampleSimple.xml): What type of element (simple or complex) is each of the following?

Country - simple or complex

Price - simple or complex

Item - simple or complex

LineExtensionAmount - simple or complex

The UBL language is made up of many schemas. We will work with simplified versions of two UBL schemas – the "Common Aggregate Components" schema and the "Common Basic Components" schema. Each of these schemas define the UBL ***reusable data components*** – XML elements that are defined once and then reused over and over again in various UBL documents. As its name suggests, the UBL Common Aggregate Components schema defines the structure of complex elements, such as the **ProviderParty**, **ReceiverParty**, and **CatalogueLineItem** elements (Figure 2-3), that are used in UBL documents. Similarly, the UBL Common Basic Components schema defines all elements that are simple (such as the **ID**, **IssueDate**, and **Name** elements) and all elements that have simple content and an attribute (such as **Quantity**, **LineExtension-Amount**, **PriceAmount**, and **BaseQuantity**; seeFigure 2-3). Since elements and attributes from each of these schemas appear in XML documents, it is important to identify the namespace from which each element comes. It is common practice to append a prefix to each element name identifying its namespace and thereby its schema. Thus, since the **ProviderParty** element is defined in the Common Aggregate Components schema, we would append a prefix as follows: **cac:ProviderParty**. Each namespace has its own "preferred prefix" with which it is identified – **cac** for UBL Common Aggregate

Components and **cbc** for UBL Common Basic Components. As you will see, a namespace prefix is actually a short-hand way to identify the URI of a namespace. Consider Figure 3-1.

Figure 3-1: UBL Catalogue with namespaces

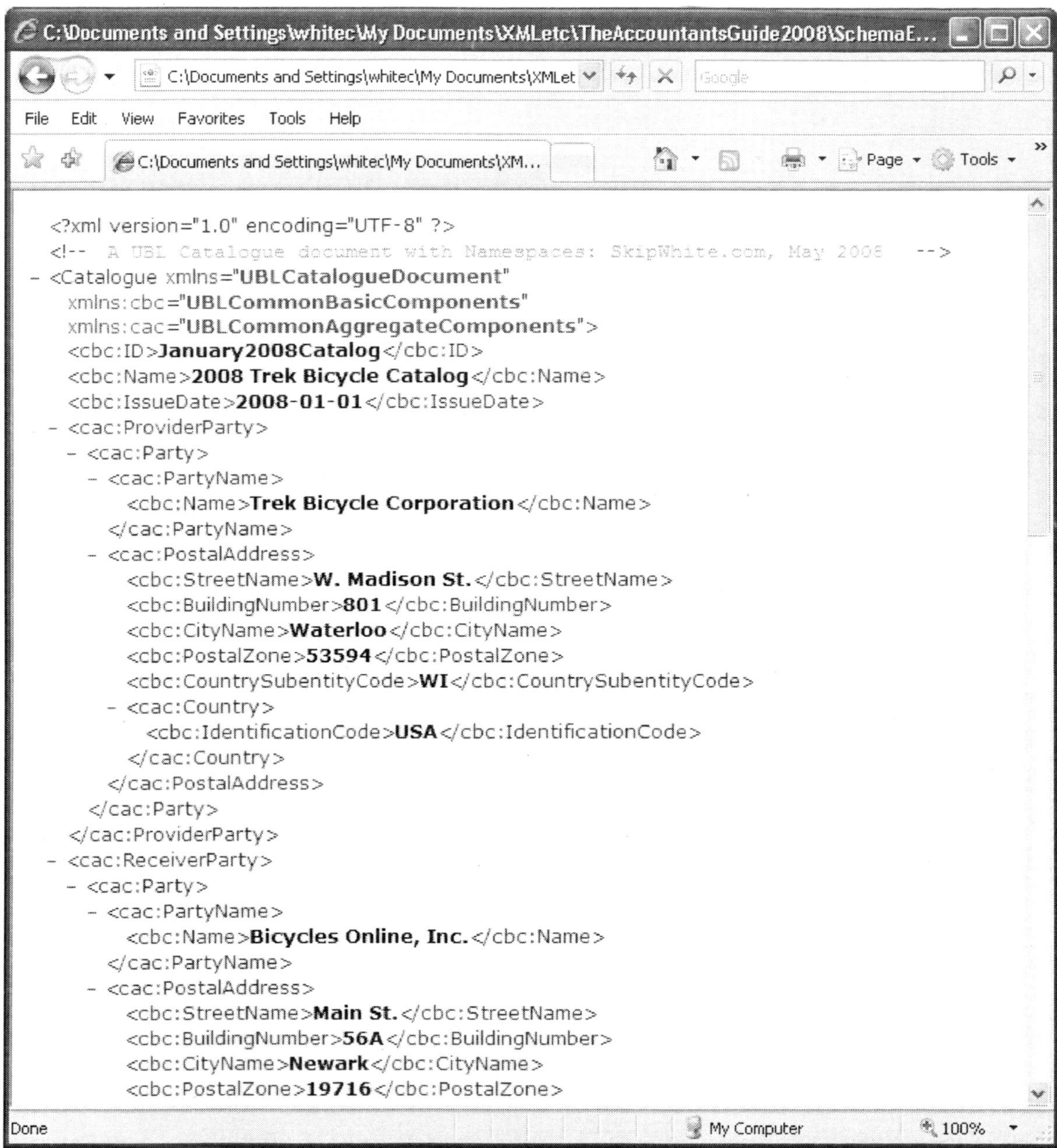

```
<?xml version="1.0" encoding="UTF-8" ?>
<!-- A UBL Catalogue document with Namespaces: SkipWhite.com, May 2008 -->
- <Catalogue xmlns="UBLCatalogueDocument"
    xmlns:cbc="UBLCommonBasicComponents"
    xmlns:cac="UBLCommonAggregateComponents">
    <cbc:ID>January2008Catalog</cbc:ID>
    <cbc:Name>2008 Trek Bicycle Catalog</cbc:Name>
    <cbc:IssueDate>2008-01-01</cbc:IssueDate>
  - <cac:ProviderParty>
    - <cac:Party>
      - <cac:PartyName>
          <cbc:Name>Trek Bicycle Corporation</cbc:Name>
        </cac:PartyName>
      - <cac:PostalAddress>
          <cbc:StreetName>W. Madison St.</cbc:StreetName>
          <cbc:BuildingNumber>801</cbc:BuildingNumber>
          <cbc:CityName>Waterloo</cbc:CityName>
          <cbc:PostalZone>53594</cbc:PostalZone>
          <cbc:CountrySubentityCode>WI</cbc:CountrySubentityCode>
        - <cac:Country>
            <cbc:IdentificationCode>USA</cbc:IdentificationCode>
          </cac:Country>
        </cac:PostalAddress>
      </cac:Party>
    </cac:ProviderParty>
  - <cac:ReceiverParty>
    - <cac:Party>
      - <cac:PartyName>
          <cbc:Name>Bicycles Online, Inc.</cbc:Name>
        </cac:PartyName>
      - <cac:PostalAddress>
          <cbc:StreetName>Main St.</cbc:StreetName>
          <cbc:BuildingNumber>56A</cbc:BuildingNumber>
          <cbc:CityName>Newark</cbc:CityName>
          <cbc:PostalZone>19716</cbc:PostalZone>
```

(File: *http://www.skipwhite.com/Guide2008/Chapter3/CatalogueItemExampleWNS.xml*)

Starting at the top, notice that the root element, **Catalogue**, has three attributes all starting with **xmlns**. These are known as ***namespace declarations***. Namespace declarations are necessary in an XML document to identify the namespaces that "support" the document. In other words, since elements from different namespaces are used in this document, each must be identified with a namespace declaration. Namespaces can be confusing, but as should become clear as we work through this Chapter, they are necessary to specifically identify the namespace and schema in which an element is defined to avoid naming collisions in XML documents. **xmlns** is the reserved key word in the XML language with which to declare a namespace, and the root element is where this is done. Namespaces are always declared as attributes of the root element. The namespace declarations in Figure 3-1 are interpreted as follows:

- **xmlns**="UBLCatalogueDocument" – identifies the namespace for the UBL Catalogue Document schema. The document in Figure 3-1 is a simplified version of an actual UBL Catalogue document, and, as you will see, its structure is defined with a schema in this namespace
- **xmlns:cbc**="UBLCommonBasicComponents" – identifies the namespace in which the UBL Common Basic Components schema is located
- **xmlns:cac**="UBLCommonAggreagateComponents" – identifies the namespace in which the UBL Common Aggregate Components schema is located

Remember that XML schemas define the structure and content of XML documents. Each element appearing in an XML document is defined in an XML schema, and each schema has its own unique namespace identifier. When elements from different schemas are used in the same XML document, XML namespaces provide a method with which to identify where each individual element is defined. The **xmlns**="UBLCatalogueDocument" namespace declaration is referred to as the "default" namespace for this document. A default namespace does not have a namespace prefix (like **cbc** or **cac**). The absence of a prefix signifies that any element in this document without a prefix (i.e., the **Catalogue** element) by default belongs to the default namespace. The **xmlns:cbc**="UBLCommon-BasicComponents" namespace declaration means that any element in this document with a **cbc** prefix is defined in ("belongs to") this namespace. Likewise, the **xmlns:cac**="UBL-CommonAggreagateComponents" namespace declaration means that any element in this document with a **cac** prefix is defined in/belongs to this namespace. As you will see, namespaces are used heavily in UBL and XBRL documents.

The UBL Catalogue Schema Document

A UBL Catalogue document (Figure 3-1) is created by reusing data components defined in schemas in the Common Basic Components and the Common Aggregate Components namespaces. The UBL Catalogue schema (Figure 3-2) defines the structure and contents of the class of XML documents known as UBL Catalogue documents. Each document that corresponds to this schema is referred to as an "instance" of the schema. As you will see, an instance of a UBL Catalogue document can be "validated" against the UBL Catalogue schema to make sure it adheres to its schema's definition.

Figure 3-2: The UBL Catalogue schema document

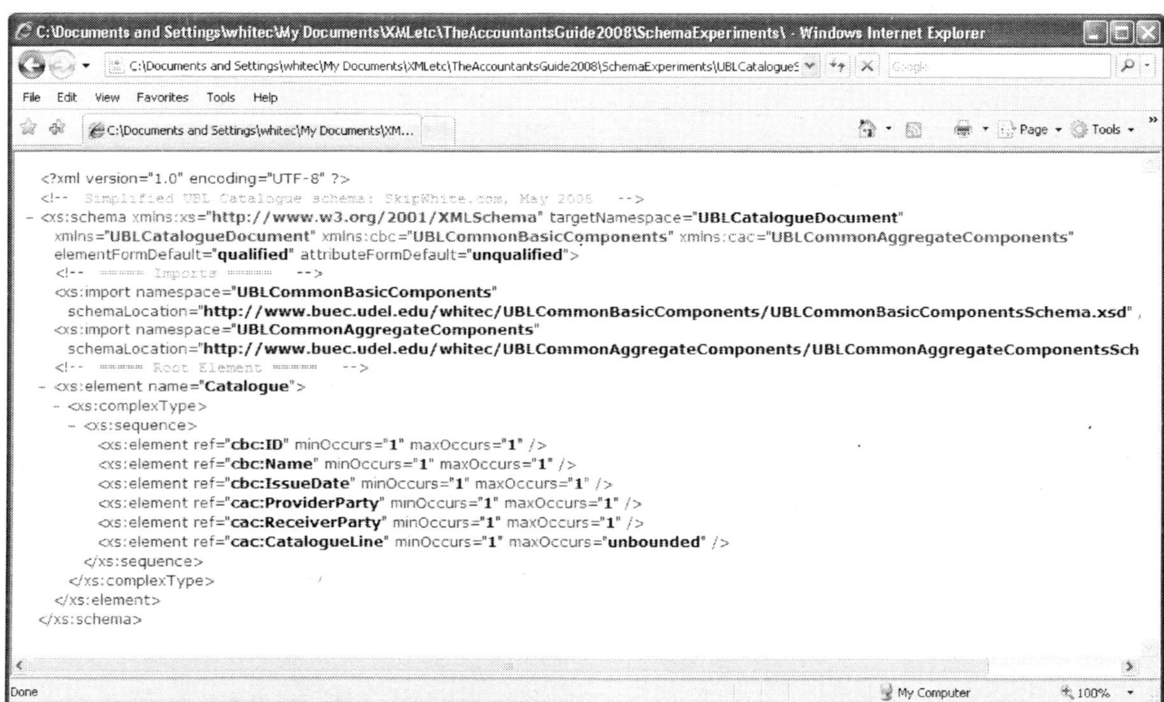

```
<?xml version="1.0" encoding="UTF-8" ?>
<!-- Simplified UBL Catalogue schema: SkipWhite.com, May 2006 -->
- <xs:schema xmlns:xs="http://www.w3.org/2001/XMLSchema" targetNamespace="UBLCatalogueDocument"
    xmlns="UBLCatalogueDocument" xmlns:cbc="UBLCommonBasicComponents" xmlns:cac="UBLCommonAggregateComponents"
    elementFormDefault="qualified" attributeFormDefault="unqualified">
    <!-- ====== Imports ====== -->
    <xs:import namespace="UBLCommonBasicComponents"
      schemaLocation="http://www.buec.udel.edu/whitec/UBLCommonBasicComponents/UBLCommonBasicComponentsSchema.xsd" ,
    <xs:import namespace="UBLCommonAggregateComponents"
      schemaLocation="http://www.buec.udel.edu/whitec/UBLCommonAggregateComponents/UBLCommonAggregateComponentsSch
    <!-- ====== Root Element ====== -->
  - <xs:element name="Catalogue">
    - <xs:complexType>
      - <xs:sequence>
          <xs:element ref="cbc:ID" minOccurs="1" maxOccurs="1" />
          <xs:element ref="cbc:Name" minOccurs="1" maxOccurs="1" />
          <xs:element ref="cbc:IssueDate" minOccurs="1" maxOccurs="1" />
          <xs:element ref="cac:ProviderParty" minOccurs="1" maxOccurs="1" />
          <xs:element ref="cac:ReceiverParty" minOccurs="1" maxOccurs="1" />
          <xs:element ref="cac:CatalogueLine" minOccurs="1" maxOccurs="unbounded" />
        </xs:sequence>
      </xs:complexType>
    </xs:element>
  </xs:schema>
```

(File: *http://www.skipwhite.com/Guide2008/Chapter3/UBLCatalogueSchema.xml*)

Although it looks complex, the UBL Catalogue schema is easy to understand. If you download the *UBLCatalogueSchema.xml* file and open it in your browser, you will notice that it is a well-formed XML document written in the XML Schema language. An XML schema document normally has a **.xsd** extension, but I chose to use a **.xml** extension because some browsers, including IE, do not open **.xsd** files directly. To understand an XML schema and an instance, it is helpful to open them in side-by-side browser windows. Figure 3-3 shows the UBL Catalogue instance (*http://www.skipwhite.com/ Guide2008/Chapter3/CatalogueItemExampleWNS.xml*), collapsed to its major child elements (those that are direct children of the root element), and its corresponding schema (*http://www.skipwhite.com/Guide2008/Chapter3/UBLCatalogueSchema.xml*) in side-by-side browser windows.

<u>Figure 3-3</u>: The UBL Catalogue instance and schema documents

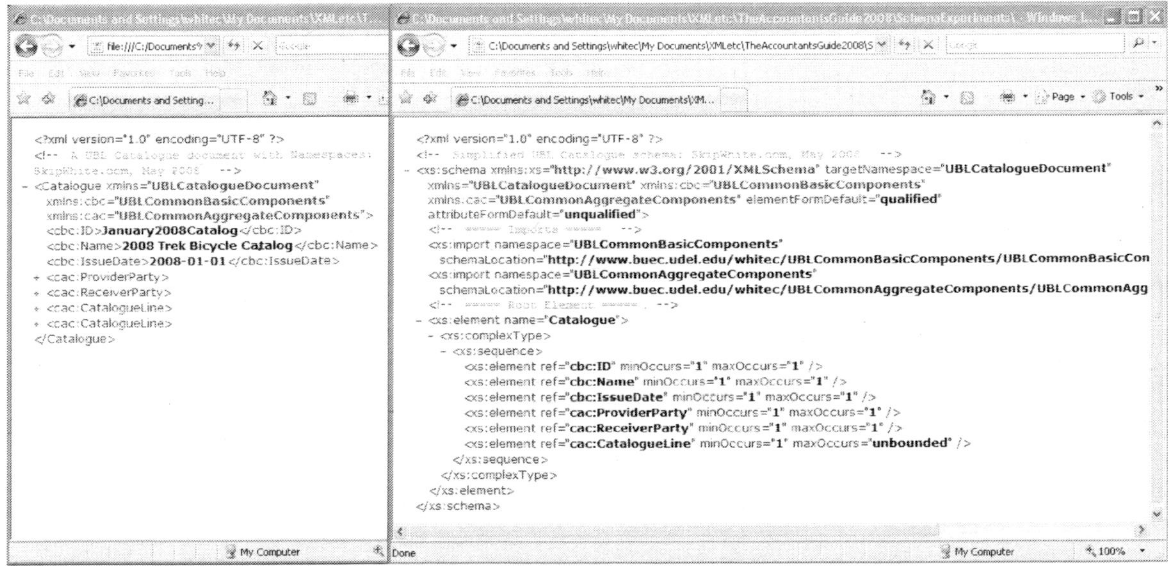

(<u>Files</u>: *http://www.skipwhite.com/ Guide2008/Chapter3/CatalogueItemExampleWNS.xml* <u>and</u> *http://www.skipwhite.com/Guide2008/Chapter3/UBLCatalogueSchema.xml*)

Starting at the top of the UBL Catalogue schema, you see that all XML schemas start with the root element name **schema,** usually “qualified” with an **xs** namespace prefix (some authors use the prefix **xsd**). The root element **xs:schema** will always be followed by the namespace declaration **xmlns:xs=**"http://www.w3.org/2001/XMLSchema" that identifies the namespace of the XML Schema language. Note that this namespace is the URL for the XML Schema language. If you go there with your browser, you will see a humanly readable page with links to various XML Schema resources. Every element from this namespace that appears in the remainder of this XML schema document will have the **xs** prefix appended to it; which is the short-hand way of saying that the element is defined in this namespace. The next attribute, **targetNamespace=** "UBLCatalogueDocument," tells the XML processor that this schema applies to (is "targeted at") the UBL Catalogue namespace. The next three attributes (**xmlns=**"UBLCatalogueDocument", **xmlns:cbc=**"UBLCommonBasicComponents", and **xmlns:cac=**"UBLCommon-AggregateComponents") are the same namespace declarations that appear in the UBL Catalogue document; they must be exactly the same in both documents and they are interpreted exactly the same by an XML processor. Notice that a namespace URI can be either a local name or an actual URL. The last two attributes, **elementFormDefault=** "qualified" and **attributeFormDefault=**"unqualified," tell an XML processor that all elements in this XML schema will be "qualified" by namespace prefixes and that all attributes will not be qualified (i.e., attributes will be "unqualified" – they will not have a namespace prefix). As you will see, these qualifiers often appear in XML schema documents.

The next line, <!-- ===== Imports ===== -->, is a comment line meant to identify where other schemas are "imported" into this schema so that the XML processor can find them. The element, **<xs:import namespace=**"UBLCommonBasicComponents" **schema-Location=**"http://www.buec.udel.edu/whitec/UBLCommonBasicComponents/UBL CommonBasicComponentsSchema.xsd"/> is a special element that associates the "UBLCommonBasicComponents" namespace with a specific **schemaLocation**. In other words, the **import** element identifies a local namespace, *UBLCommonBasicComponents*, and ties it to a URL so that the XML processor can find it. This makes the elements found in the schema at the specified URL available for use in this schema document. The element **<xs:import namespace=**"UBLCommonAggregate-Components" **schemaLocation=**"http://www.buec.udel.edu/whitec/UBLCommonAggregate-Components/UBLCommonAggregateComponentsSchema.xsd"/> does the same for the elements in the *UBLCommonAggregateComponents* namespace. Both of these **import** elements end with a /> bracket that designates them as ***empty elements*** (i.e., they have attributes but do not have a data value or other elements nested within them). This is shorthand for indicating that no closing element is necessary.

The **xs:schema** and **xs:import** elements and their attributes are necessary to set up this XML schema document so a processor can find and validate the contents of an associated instance document. The next line, <!-- ===== Root Element ===== -->, is a comment line that identifies the beginning of the schema to define the contents and structure of the class of documents known as UBL Catalogue documents. The purpose of this schema is to define each element and attribute and the overall structure of all UBL Catalogue documents. **xs:element** is the keyword in the XML Schema language for defining an element. Starting with the root element, every element must have a **name** and a **type**. Since by definition the root element of an XML document contains all of the other elements nested within it, it must be a complex element. The following block of code names the root element, identifies it as a **complexType**, and begins to define the document's overall structure with the **sequence** element that indicates the elements nested within this element must appear in sequence in a Catalogue instance document:

```
<xs:element name="Catalogue">
  <xs:complexType>
    <xs:sequence>
```

The format for defining an element name in the XML Schema language is **xs:element name="***elementName***"** (where *elementName* is replaced by an actual name; no spaces allowed). The basic unit in an XML document is the element and all XML elements are either complex or simple.

The next block of code defines the elements that must appear in sequence as children of the **Catalogue** root element. Each of these elements is defined in either the **cbc** or the **cac** namespace (i.e., the UBL Catalogue document is constructed from the reusable data components defined in the schemas in the *UBLCommonBasicComponents* and *UBLCommonAggregateComponents* namespaces):

```
<xs:element ref="cbc:ID"  minOccurs="1" maxOccurs="1"/>
<xs:element ref="cbc:Name"  minOccurs="1"  maxOccurs="1"/>
<xs:element ref="cbc:IssueDate"  minOccurs="1" maxOccurs="1"/>
<xs:element ref="cac:ProviderParty"  minOccurs="1" maxOccurs="1"/>
<xs:element ref="cac:ReceiverParty" minOccurs="1" maxOccurs="1"/>
<xs:element ref="cac:CatalogueLine" minOccurs="1" maxOccurs="unbounded"/>
```

Since each of these elements is defined (i.e., assigned a name and a data type) in a separate schema imported to this schema, we simply reference each one here using a **ref=***"element name"* attribute and define its ***cardinality*** (i.e., how many times it can occur in this document). For example, the first element in this block of code **<xs:element ref="cbc:ID" minOccurs=**"1" **maxOccurs=**"1"/> is interpreted as "an element named **ID** in the imported **cbc** schema must occur one and only one time, in this document." Likewise, the **cbc:Name**, **cbc:IssueDate**, **cac:ProviderParty**, and **cac:ReceiverParty** elements must appear one and only one time in sequence, while the **cac:CatalogueLine** element must appear once but can appear an unbounded number of times in sequence. Notice that each of these elements is an empty element, as indicated by />. The remaining tags, </**xs:sequence**>, </**xs:complexType**> and </**xs:element**>, are the properly nested closing element name tags and the </**xs:schema**> tag closes the schema document. Since UBL documents are constructed from reusable data components, creating a UBL document schema is relatively simple because it adheres to the following pattern:

- Declare the appropriate namespaces and qualifiers in the **schema** root element.
- Import the necessary schemas with **import** elements.
- Define the root element with a **name**, a **complexType**, and a **sequence** indicator if appropriate and reference (**ref**) the appropriate reusable data component elements from other UBL schemas.

If you compare the collapsed UBL Catalogue instance document to the UBL Catalogue schema (Figure 3-3), you see that the instance adheres to the rules specified in this schema. The instance document has the root element **Catalogue**, with the appropriate namespace declarations, followed in sequence by the elements defined in the UBL Catalogue schema. Notice that the first three child elements(**cbc:ID**, **cbc:Name**, and **cbc:IssueDate)** are all simple elements (i.e., each contains a data value and no attributes), and are all defined in the **cbc** namespace..The next elements (**cac:ProviderParty**, **cac:ReceiverParty)** and the two **cac:CatalogueLine** elements are complex elements (i.e., each contains other elements nested within it) and are defined in the **cac** namespace.

As you will see, all simple UBL elements are defined in the **cbc** schema, and all complex UBL elements are defined in the **cac** schema.

The UBL Common Basic Components Schema

If you expand the UBL Catalogue instance document (as in Figure 3-1), you see that each complex element defined in the **cac** schema contains elements from both the **cac** and **cbc** schemas. Figure 3-4, Parts 1 and 2, shows the **cbc** schema.

Figure 3-4 (Part 1): The UBL Common Basic Components schema

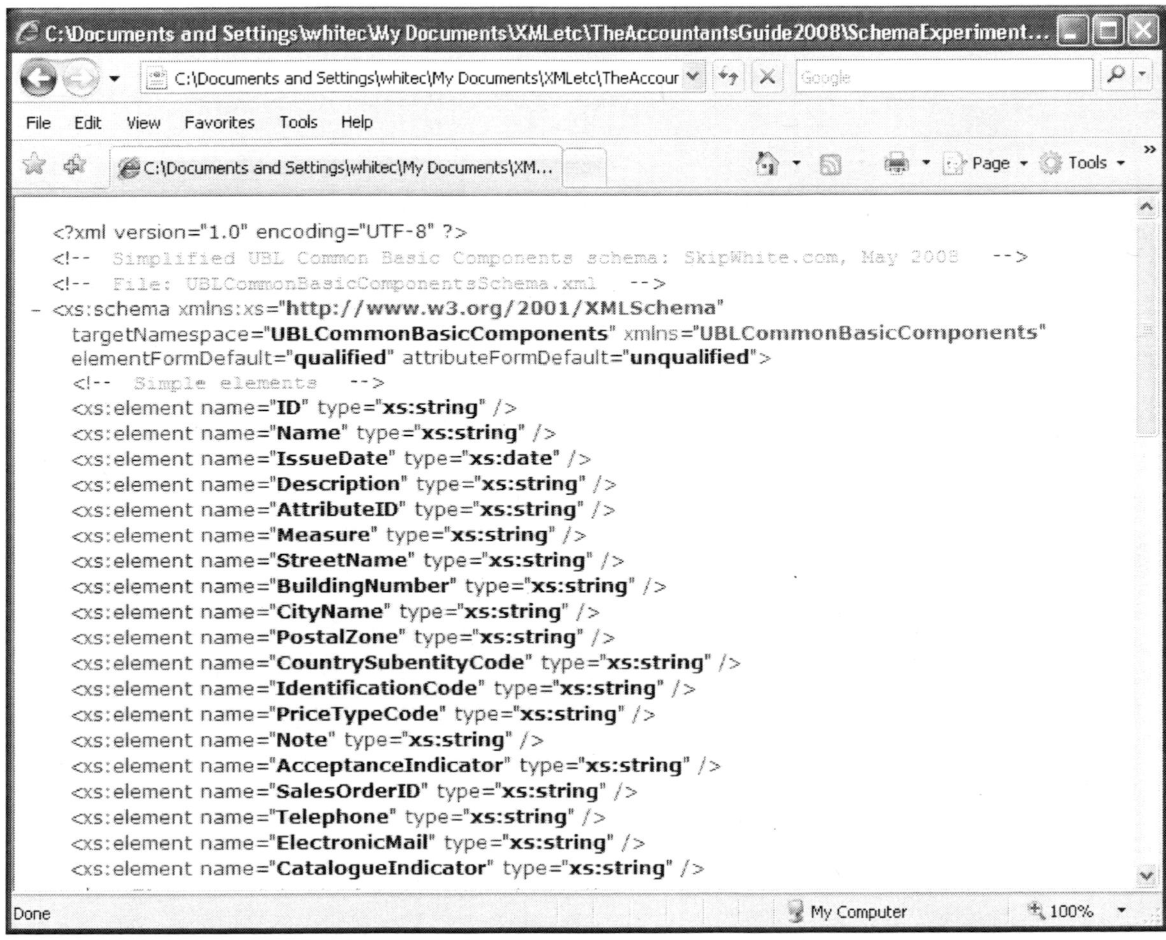

```
<?xml version="1.0" encoding="UTF-8" ?>
<!--  Simplified UBL Common Basic Components schema: SkipWhite.com, May 2008   -->
<!--  File: UBLCommonBasicComponentsSchema.xml   -->
- <xs:schema xmlns:xs="http://www.w3.org/2001/XMLSchema"
   targetNamespace="UBLCommonBasicComponents" xmlns="UBLCommonBasicComponents"
   elementFormDefault="qualified" attributeFormDefault="unqualified">
   <!--  Simple elements   -->
   <xs:element name="ID" type="xs:string" />
   <xs:element name="Name" type="xs:string" />
   <xs:element name="IssueDate" type="xs:date" />
   <xs:element name="Description" type="xs:string" />
   <xs:element name="AttributeID" type="xs:string" />
   <xs:element name="Measure" type="xs:string" />
   <xs:element name="StreetName" type="xs:string" />
   <xs:element name="BuildingNumber" type="xs:string" />
   <xs:element name="CityName" type="xs:string" />
   <xs:element name="PostalZone" type="xs:string" />
   <xs:element name="CountrySubentityCode" type="xs:string" />
   <xs:element name="IdentificationCode" type="xs:string" />
   <xs:element name="PriceTypeCode" type="xs:string" />
   <xs:element name="Note" type="xs:string" />
   <xs:element name="AcceptanceIndicator" type="xs:string" />
   <xs:element name="SalesOrderID" type="xs:string" />
   <xs:element name="Telephone" type="xs:string" />
   <xs:element name="ElectronicMail" type="xs:string" />
   <xs:element name="CatalogueIndicator" type="xs:string" />
```

Figure 3-4 (Part 2): The UBL Common Basic Components schema

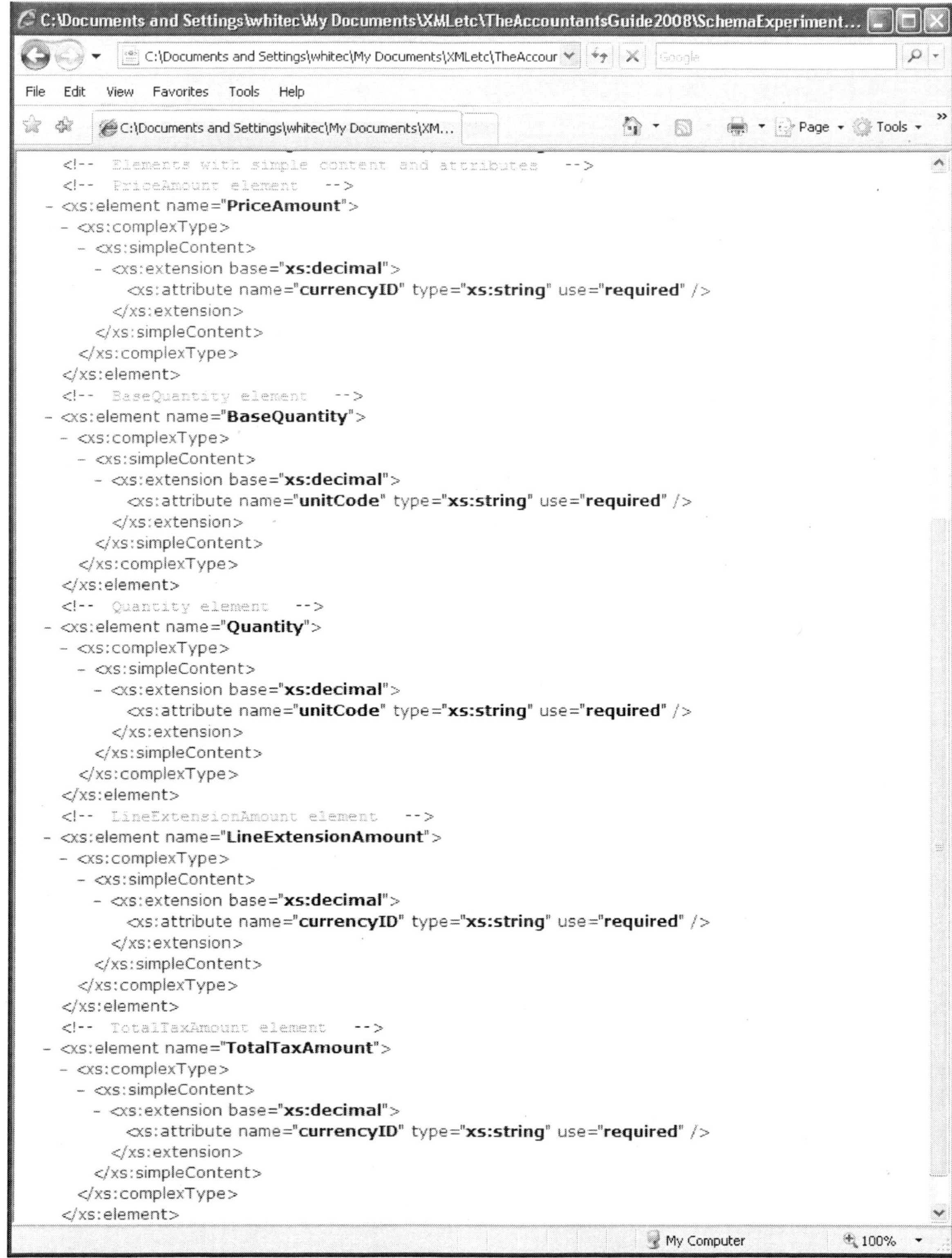

```
<!-- Elements with simple content and attributes -->
<!-- PriceAmount element -->
- <xs:element name="PriceAmount">
  - <xs:complexType>
    - <xs:simpleContent>
      - <xs:extension base="xs:decimal">
          <xs:attribute name="currencyID" type="xs:string" use="required" />
        </xs:extension>
      </xs:simpleContent>
    </xs:complexType>
  </xs:element>
  <!-- BaseQuantity element -->
- <xs:element name="BaseQuantity">
  - <xs:complexType>
    - <xs:simpleContent>
      - <xs:extension base="xs:decimal">
          <xs:attribute name="unitCode" type="xs:string" use="required" />
        </xs:extension>
      </xs:simpleContent>
    </xs:complexType>
  </xs:element>
  <!-- Quantity element -->
- <xs:element name="Quantity">
  - <xs:complexType>
    - <xs:simpleContent>
      - <xs:extension base="xs:decimal">
          <xs:attribute name="unitCode" type="xs:string" use="required" />
        </xs:extension>
      </xs:simpleContent>
    </xs:complexType>
  </xs:element>
  <!-- LineExtensionAmount element -->
- <xs:element name="LineExtensionAmount">
  - <xs:complexType>
    - <xs:simpleContent>
      - <xs:extension base="xs:decimal">
          <xs:attribute name="currencyID" type="xs:string" use="required" />
        </xs:extension>
      </xs:simpleContent>
    </xs:complexType>
  </xs:element>
  <!-- TotalTaxAmount element -->
- <xs:element name="TotalTaxAmount">
  - <xs:complexType>
    - <xs:simpleContent>
      - <xs:extension base="xs:decimal">
          <xs:attribute name="currencyID" type="xs:string" use="required" />
        </xs:extension>
      </xs:simpleContent>
    </xs:complexType>
  </xs:element>
```

(File: *http://www.skipwhite.com/Guide2008/Chapter3/UBLCommonBasicComponents Schema.xml*)

Starting with Part 1, you see that all XML schemas start with the **xs:schema** root element and the XML schema namespace declaration. The **targetNamespace**="UBLCommon-BasicComponents" declaration ties this schema to the **cbc** namespace, the **xmlns**="UBL CommonBasicComponents" namespace declaration makes this the default namespace (i.e., all elements with no namespace prefix belong to this namespace), and the element and attribute form qualifiers are the same as in the UBL Catalogue schema. The first element defined in this schema is the **ID** element. Since it is a simple element it is defined by giving it a name and a data type as follows: **<xs:element name**="ID" **type**="xs:string"/>. Remember that a simple element contains data, as opposed to other elements nested within it, so its type, **type**="xs:string" (i.e., a string of text), is referred to as a "primitive" type. There are many primitive data types defined in the XML schema language, but we will use only string, date, integer, and decimal. The **Name**, **IssueDate**, **Description**, **AttributeID**, and other simple elements in Figure 3-4 (Part 1) are defined exactly the same way: each is given a name and an appropriate primitive data type.

Although the remaining elements in the UBL Common Basic Components schema (Figure 3-4 -Part 2) are considered to be complex, they do not contain other elements nested within them. They are a special type of element because each contains a data value like a simple element but also an attribute that provides additional information about it. As such, they are defined as **complexType** with **simpleContent,** as in the following block of code defining the **PriceAmount** element:

```
<xs:element name="PriceAmount">
  <xs:complexType>
  <xs:simpleContent>
       <xs:extension base="xs:decimal">
          <xs:attribute name="currencyID" type="xs:string" use="required"/>
        </xs:extension>
  </xs:simpleContent>
  </xs:complexType>
  </xs:element>
```

The element is named as usual and defined as a **complexType** with **simpleContent**. Then the **<xs:extension base=**"xs:decimal"> element is used to assign a primitive type to the base **PriceAmount** element. Following that, the **<xs:attribute name=**"currencyID"

type="xs:string" **use=**"required"/> element defines its attribute by giving it a name, a type, and a usage attribute. Like elements, all attributes must also be defined with a name and a type, and most attributes are "required" to be used. As shown in Figure 3-4 (Part 2), the **BaseQuantity, Quantity**, **LineExtensionAmount**, and **TotalTaxAmount** elements are also **complexType** elements with **simpleContent** and are defined in the same way. This type of element is best understood by looking at it in an instance document.

<u>**Figure 3-5**</u>: A **CatalogueLine** element in a UBL Catalogue document

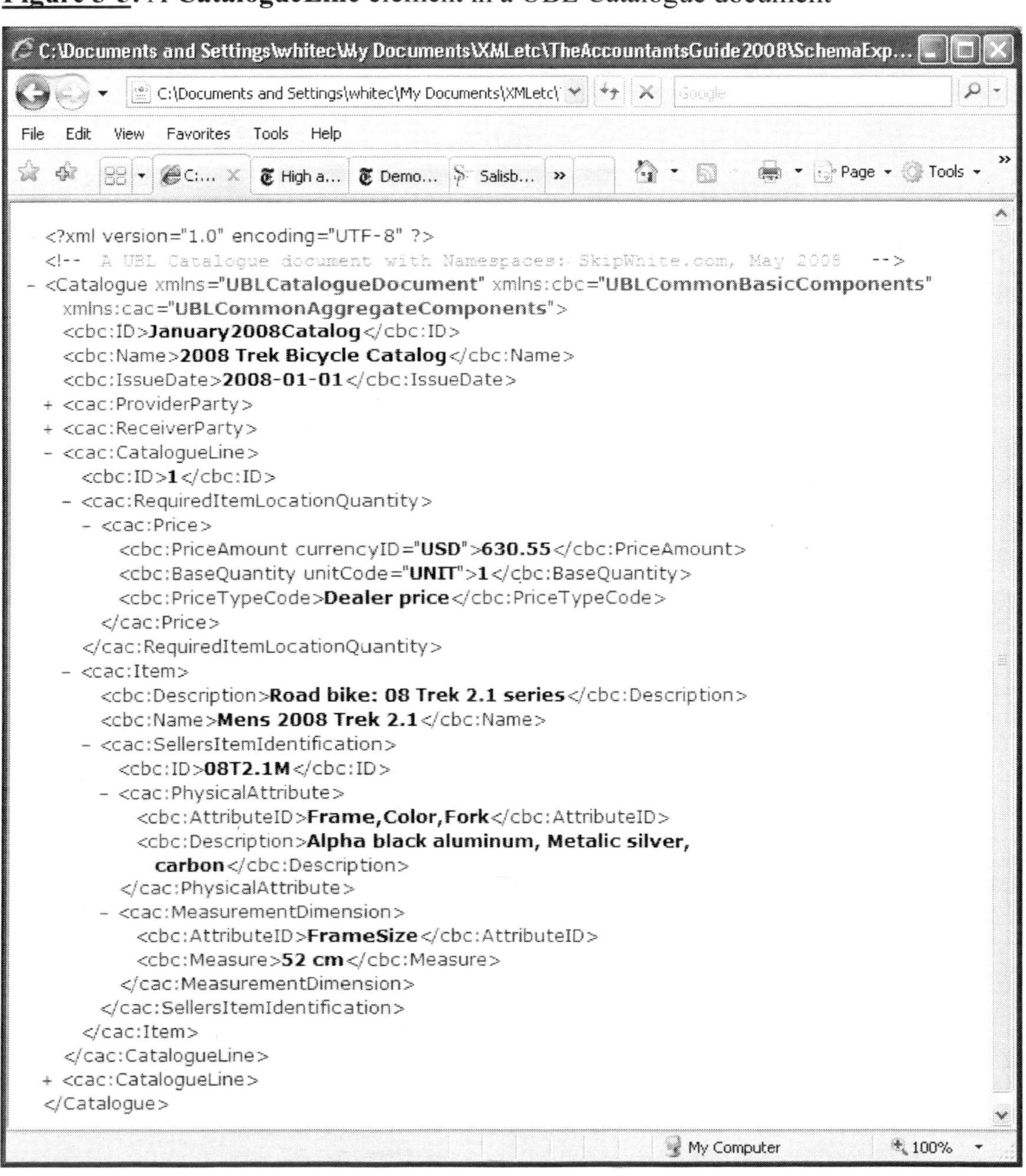

```
<?xml version="1.0" encoding="UTF-8" ?>
<!-- A UBL Catalogue document with Namespaces: SkipWhite.com, May 2008 -->
- <Catalogue xmlns="UBLCatalogueDocument" xmlns:cbc="UBLCommonBasicComponents"
    xmlns:cac="UBLCommonAggregateComponents">
    <cbc:ID>January2008Catalog</cbc:ID>
    <cbc:Name>2008 Trek Bicycle Catalog</cbc:Name>
    <cbc:IssueDate>2008-01-01</cbc:IssueDate>
  + <cac:ProviderParty>
  + <cac:ReceiverParty>
  - <cac:CatalogueLine>
      <cbc:ID>1</cbc:ID>
    - <cac:RequiredItemLocationQuantity>
      - <cac:Price>
          <cbc:PriceAmount currencyID="USD">630.55</cbc:PriceAmount>
          <cbc:BaseQuantity unitCode="UNIT">1</cbc:BaseQuantity>
          <cbc:PriceTypeCode>Dealer price</cbc:PriceTypeCode>
        </cac:Price>
      </cac:RequiredItemLocationQuantity>
    - <cac:Item>
        <cbc:Description>Road bike: 08 Trek 2.1 series</cbc:Description>
        <cbc:Name>Mens 2008 Trek 2.1</cbc:Name>
      - <cac:SellersItemIdentification>
          <cbc:ID>08T2.1M</cbc:ID>
        - <cac:PhysicalAttribute>
            <cbc:AttributeID>Frame,Color,Fork</cbc:AttributeID>
            <cbc:Description>Alpha black aluminum, Metalic silver,
              carbon</cbc:Description>
          </cac:PhysicalAttribute>
        - <cac:MeasurementDimension>
            <cbc:AttributeID>FrameSize</cbc:AttributeID>
            <cbc:Measure>52 cm</cbc:Measure>
          </cac:MeasurementDimension>
        </cac:SellersItemIdentification>
      </cac:Item>
    </cac:CatalogueLine>
  + <cac:CatalogueLine>
  </Catalogue>
```

As shown in Figure 3-5, the data value in the **<cbc:PriceAmount currencyID=**"USD">630.55**</cbc:PriceAmount>** element, within the **cac:Price** element, can be precisely interpreted by a human or software as "the price of this catalogue line item is $630.55 in U.S. dollars." Likewise, the data value in the **<cbc:BaseQuantity unitCode=**"UNIT">1**</cbc:BaseQuantity>** element, within the **cac:Price** element, can be precisely interpreted as "a unit of 1." In other words, elements in an instance document that have both a data value and an attribute are defined as **complexType** with **simpleContent** in a schema so that both the element's data value and its attribute can be precisely interpreted together.

Each of the elements defined in the UBL Common Basic Components schema will be reused in UBL instance documents and in the UBL Common Aggregate Components schema.

<u>Interactive exercise 3-2</u>: Using the XML Schema language, how would you define each of the following two elements appearing in an instance document?

1. **<AccountantName>**Skip White**</AccountantName>**

   ____

2. **<AccountantFee units=**"USD">10000**</AccountantFee>**

   ____

   ____

   ____

   ____

   ____

   ____

The UBL Common Aggregate Components Schema

The UBL Common Aggregate Components schema (see Figure 3-6) defines the UBL elements that, as the name suggests, contain other UBL elements nested within.

Figure 3-6: The UBL Common Aggregate Components schema

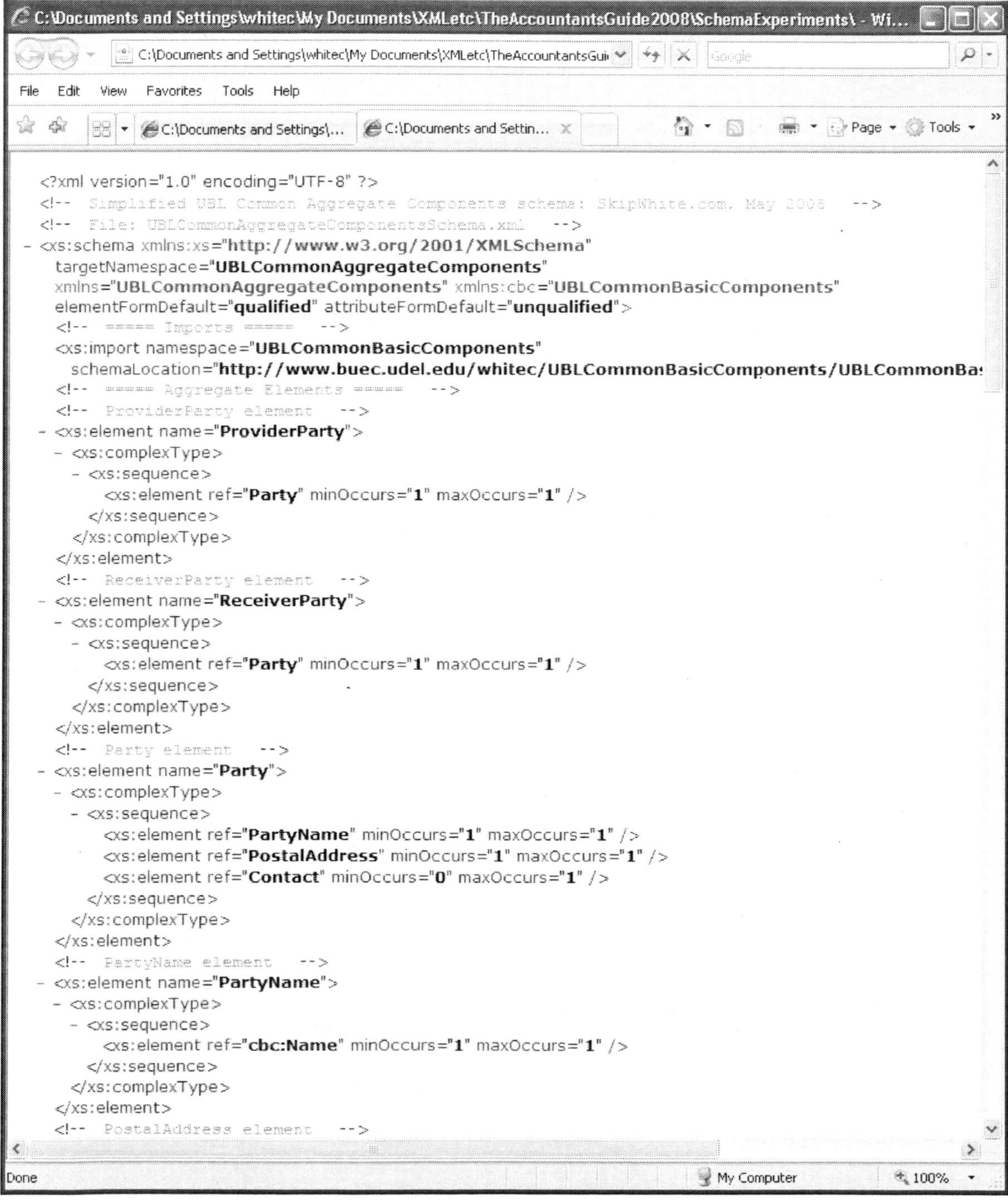

```
<?xml version="1.0" encoding="UTF-8" ?>
<!-- Simplified UBL Common Aggregate Components schema: SkipWhite.com, May 2008 -->
<!-- File: UBLCommonAggregateComponentsSchema.xml -->
- <xs:schema xmlns:xs="http://www.w3.org/2001/XMLSchema"
    targetNamespace="UBLCommonAggregateComponents"
    xmlns="UBLCommonAggregateComponents" xmlns:cbc="UBLCommonBasicComponents"
    elementFormDefault="qualified" attributeFormDefault="unqualified">
    <!-- ===== Imports ===== -->
    <xs:import namespace="UBLCommonBasicComponents"
      schemaLocation="http://www.buec.udel.edu/whitec/UBLCommonBasicComponents/UBLCommonBa
    <!-- ===== Aggregate Elements ===== -->
    <!-- ProviderParty element -->
  - <xs:element name="ProviderParty">
    - <xs:complexType>
      - <xs:sequence>
          <xs:element ref="Party" minOccurs="1" maxOccurs="1" />
        </xs:sequence>
      </xs:complexType>
    </xs:element>
    <!-- ReceiverParty element -->
  - <xs:element name="ReceiverParty">
    - <xs:complexType>
      - <xs:sequence>
          <xs:element ref="Party" minOccurs="1" maxOccurs="1" />
        </xs:sequence>
      </xs:complexType>
    </xs:element>
    <!-- Party element -->
  - <xs:element name="Party">
    - <xs:complexType>
      - <xs:sequence>
          <xs:element ref="PartyName" minOccurs="1" maxOccurs="1" />
          <xs:element ref="PostalAddress" minOccurs="1" maxOccurs="1" />
          <xs:element ref="Contact" minOccurs="0" maxOccurs="1" />
        </xs:sequence>
      </xs:complexType>
    </xs:element>
    <!-- PartyName element -->
  - <xs:element name="PartyName">
    - <xs:complexType>
      - <xs:sequence>
          <xs:element ref="cbc:Name" minOccurs="1" maxOccurs="1" />
        </xs:sequence>
      </xs:complexType>
    </xs:element>
    <!-- PostalAddress element -->
```

(File: *http://www.skipwhite.com/Guide2008/Chapter3/UBLCommonAggregate ComponentsSchema.xml*)

Starting at the top, you see that all XML schemas start with the **xs:schema** root element and the XML schema namespace declaration. The **targetNamespace**="UBLCommon-AggregateComponents" declaration ties this schema to the **cac** namespace, and the **xmlns**="UBLCommonAggregateComponents" namespace declaration makes this the default namespace (i.e., all elements with no namespace prefix belong to this namespace). The **xmlns:cbc**="UBLCommonBasicComponents" namespace declaration is necessary because its elements are reused in this schema, and the element and attribute form qualifiers are the same as in the UBL Basic Components and UBL Catalogue schemas. The **xs:import** element identifies the *UBLCommonBasicComponents* namespace and ties it to a URL so that the XML processor can find it and its elements can be reused in this schema document. As you will see, every element defined in the UBL Common Aggregate Components schema is complex and is made up of one or more elements defined in the UBL Common Basic Components schema and/or other elements from the UBL Common Aggregate Components schema.

The first aggregate element defined is the **ProviderParty** element. Consider the following block of code:

```
<xs:element name="ProviderParty">
  <xs:complexType>
  <xs:sequence>
      <xs:element ref="Party" minOccurs="1" maxOccurs="1"/>
  </xs:sequence>
  </xs:complexType>
  </xs:element>
```

The **ProviderParty** element is a **complexType** element with one and only one child element, **Party**. Since the **Party** element does not have a prefix, it is also an aggregate element. It is also a complex element and is defined with the following block of code:

```
<xs:element name="Party">
  <xs:complexType>
  <xs:sequence>
      <xs:element ref="PartyName" minOccurs="1" maxOccurs="1"/>
      <xs:element ref="PostalAddress" minOccurs="1" maxOccurs="1"/>
      <xs:element ref="Contact" minOccurs="0" maxOccurs="1"/>
  </xs:sequence>
```

```
</xs:complexType>
</xs:element>
```

The **Party** element contains three child elements in sequence – one and only one **PartyName** and **PostalAddress** elements and an optional **Contact** element (i.e., **minOccurs="0"** and **maxOccurs="1"**); all are also aggregate elements and do not have a prefix. The **PartyName** element is defined as a complex element containing one and only one **cbc:Name** element. Though this seems complex, it is easy to understand if you open both the UBL Catalogue and the Common Aggregate Components schema in side-by-side browser windows.

Figure 3-7: UBL Catalogue and Common Aggregate Components schema document

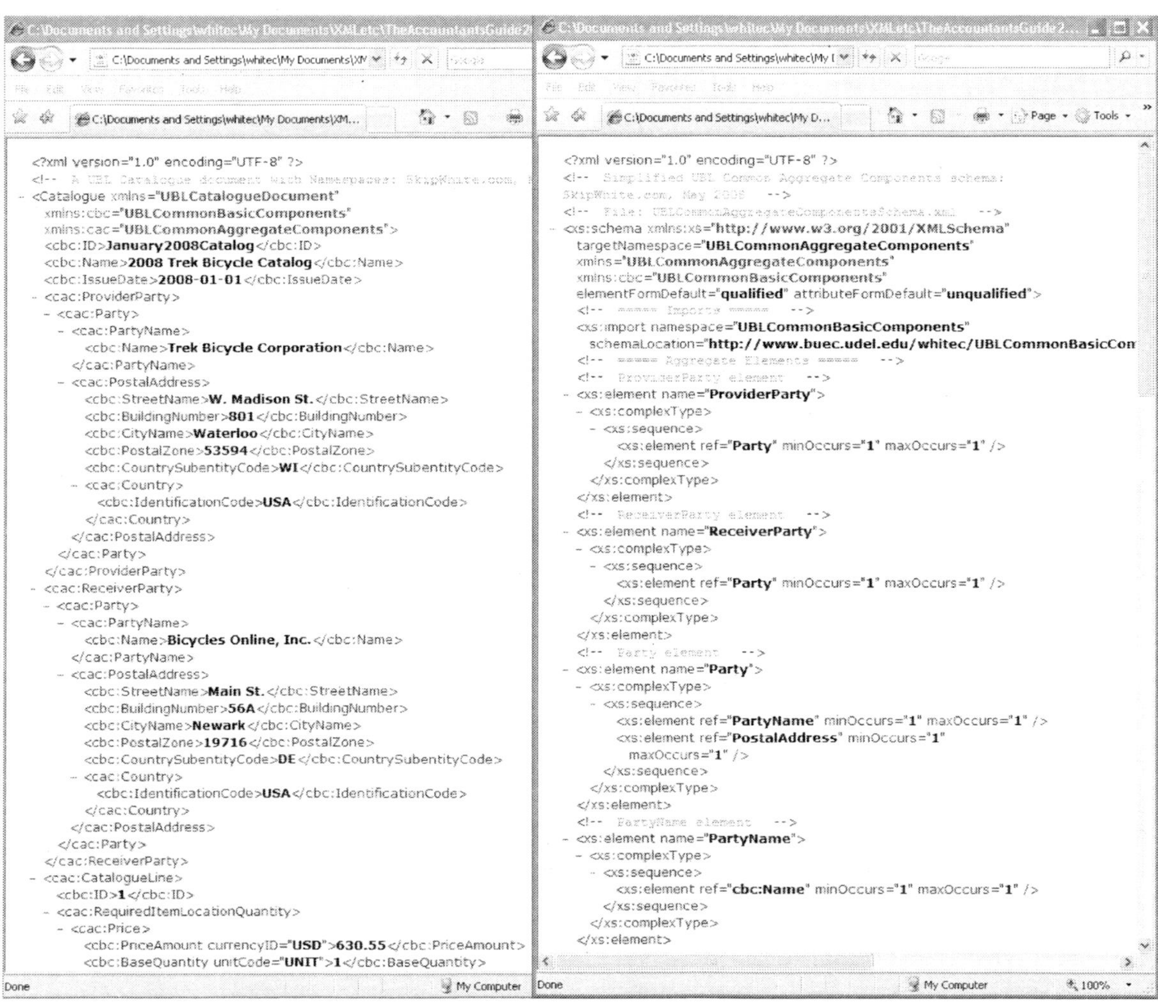

(Files: *http://www.skipwhite.com/Guide2008/Chapter3/CatalogueItemExampleWNS.xml* and *http://www.skipwhite.com/Guide2008/Chapter3/UBLCommonAggregate ComponentsSchema.xml*)

In the UBL Catalogue document, **cac:ProviderParty** has one child **cac:Party**, which has two children, **cac:PartyName** and **cac:PostalAddress**. Then the **cac:ProviderParty** element has one child element **cbc:Name** that contains a data value, *Trek Bicycle Corporation*. If you open the UBLCommonAggregateComponentsSchema in your browser and scroll down, you will see that the **cac:PostalAddress** element has five child elements from the UBL Common Basic Components schema, each of which contains a data value, and one child element from the UBL Common Aggregate Components schema (see Figure 3-8).

Figure 3-8: UBL Catalogue and Common Aggregate Components schema document

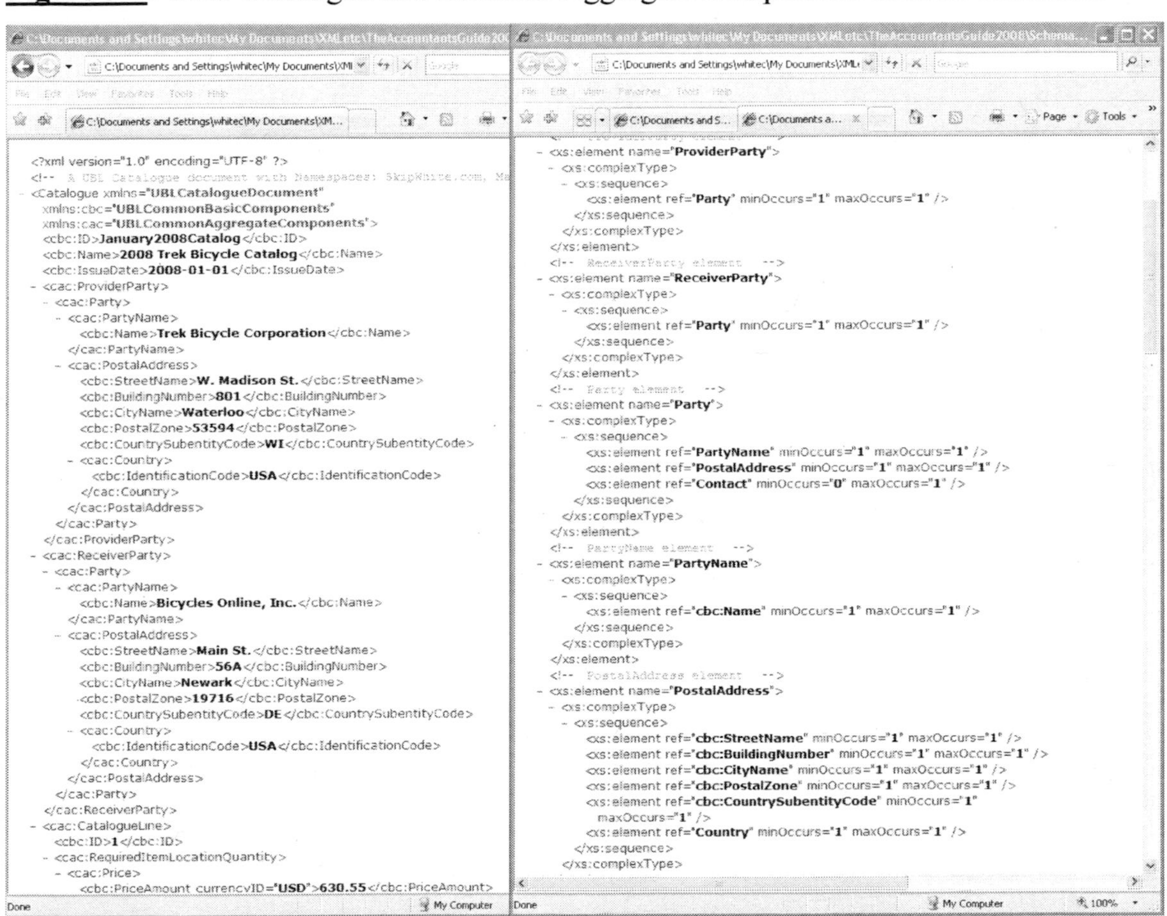

```
<?xml version="1.0" encoding="UTF-8" ?>
<!-- A UBL Catalogue document with Namespaces: SkipWhite.com, M
- <Catalogue xmlns="UBLCatalogueDocument"
    xmlns:cbc="UBLCommonBasicComponents"
    xmlns:cac="UBLCommonAggregateComponents">
    <cbc:ID>January2008Catalog</cbc:ID>
    <cbc:Name>2008 Trek Bicycle Catalog</cbc:Name>
    <cbc:IssueDate>2008-01-01</cbc:IssueDate>
  - <cac:ProviderParty>
    - <cac:Party>
      - <cac:PartyName>
          <cbc:Name>Trek Bicycle Corporation</cbc:Name>
        </cac:PartyName>
      - <cac:PostalAddress>
          <cbc:StreetName>W. Madison St.</cbc:StreetName>
          <cbc:BuildingNumber>801</cbc:BuildingNumber>
          <cbc:CityName>Waterloo</cbc:CityName>
          <cbc:PostalZone>53594</cbc:PostalZone>
          <cbc:CountrySubentityCode>WI</cbc:CountrySubentityCode>
        - <cac:Country>
            <cbc:IdentificationCode>USA</cbc:IdentificationCode>
          </cac:Country>
        </cac:PostalAddress>
      </cac:Party>
    </cac:ProviderParty>
  - <cac:ReceiverParty>
    - <cac:Party>
      - <cac:PartyName>
          <cbc:Name>Bicycles Online, Inc.</cbc:Name>
        </cac:PartyName>
      - <cac:PostalAddress>
          <cbc:StreetName>Main St.</cbc:StreetName>
          <cbc:BuildingNumber>56A</cbc:BuildingNumber>
          <cbc:CityName>Newark</cbc:CityName>
          <cbc:PostalZone>19716</cbc:PostalZone>
          <cbc:CountrySubentityCode>DE</cbc:CountrySubentityCode>
        - <cac:Country>
            <cbc:IdentificationCode>USA</cbc:IdentificationCode>
          </cac:Country>
        </cac:PostalAddress>
      </cac:Party>
    </cac:ReceiverParty>
  - <cac:CatalogueLine>
      <cbc:ID>1</cbc:ID>
    - <cac:RequiredItemLocationQuantity>
      - <cac:Price>
          <cbc:PriceAmount currencyID="USD">630.55</cbc:PriceAmount>
```

```
- <xs:element name="ProviderParty">
  - <xs:complexType>
    - <xs:sequence>
        <xs:element ref="Party" minOccurs="1" maxOccurs="1" />
      </xs:sequence>
    </xs:complexType>
  </xs:element>
  <!-- ReceiverParty element -->
- <xs:element name="ReceiverParty">
  - <xs:complexType>
    - <xs:sequence>
        <xs:element ref="Party" minOccurs="1" maxOccurs="1" />
      </xs:sequence>
    </xs:complexType>
  </xs:element>
  <!-- Party element -->
- <xs:element name="Party">
  - <xs:complexType>
    - <xs:sequence>
        <xs:element ref="PartyName" minOccurs="1" maxOccurs="1" />
        <xs:element ref="PostalAddress" minOccurs="1" maxOccurs="1" />
        <xs:element ref="Contact" minOccurs="0" maxOccurs="1" />
      </xs:sequence>
    </xs:complexType>
  </xs:element>
  <!-- PartyName element -->
- <xs:element name="PartyName">
  - <xs:complexType>
    - <xs:sequence>
        <xs:element ref="cbc:Name" minOccurs="1" maxOccurs="1" />
      </xs:sequence>
    </xs:complexType>
  </xs:element>
  <!-- PostalAddress element -->
- <xs:element name="PostalAddress">
  - <xs:complexType>
    - <xs:sequence>
        <xs:element ref="cbc:StreetName" minOccurs="1" maxOccurs="1" />
        <xs:element ref="cbc:BuildingNumber" minOccurs="1" maxOccurs="1" />
        <xs:element ref="cbc:CityName" minOccurs="1" maxOccurs="1" />
        <xs:element ref="cbc:PostalZone" minOccurs="1" maxOccurs="1" />
        <xs:element ref="cbc:CountrySubentityCode" minOccurs="1"
          maxOccurs="1" />
        <xs:element ref="Country" minOccurs="1" maxOccurs="1" />
      </xs:sequence>
    </xs:complexType>
```

(Files: *http://www.skipwhite.com/ Guide2008/Chapter3/CatalogueItemExampleWNS.xml* and *http://www.skipwhite.com/Guide2008/Chapter3/UBLCommonAggregateComponentsSchema.xml*)

Notice the relationship between the UBL Catalogue document and the Common Aggregate Components schema. Each element in the Catalogue that contains other elements nested within it is defined in the Common Aggregate Components schema as a **complexType** element made up of other **complexType** elements also defined in the Common Aggregate Components schema and simple elements defined in the Common Basic Components schema. Each contains a data value. This explains how UBL works - each complex element in the UBL vocabulary is defined in the Common Aggregate Components schema and is made up of reusable data components from the Common Aggregate Components schema and the Common Basic Components schema. And each UBL document is defined in its own schema and is made up of the same reusable data components.

As an example, notice that the **cac:ReceiverParty** element in the UBL Catalogue document contains exactly the same child elements as the **cac:ProviderParty** element and that each of these elements and their children are defined once in either the Common Aggregate Components schema or the Common Basic Components schema (see Figure 3-8).

Interactive exercise 3-3: To answer these questions, you should open the UBL Catalogue document (*http://www.skipwhite.com/Guide2008/Chapter3/CatalogueItem-ExampleWNS.xml*) and the UBL Common Aggregate Components schema (*http://www.skipwhite.com/Guide2008/Chapter3/UBLCommonAggregateComponents-Schema.xml*) in side by side browser windows.

1. What are the child elements of the **cac:CatalogueLine** element? (Hint: A child element has one and only one parent element.)

   ____

   ____

   ____

2. What are the child elements of the **cac:Item** element?

   ____

The objective of exposing you to UBL and its XML schemas is to introduce the concept and purpose of XML schema documents, the potential of standardized reusable data components, and their role in e-business documents. As you might expect, the real UBL schemas are significantly more complex than what is presented here.

Validating XML Documents

As we have seen, all well-formed XML documents can be read and processed by XML-enabled software applications. Schemas support the processing of XML documents by describing in computer-readable form their structure and contents. When a "schema aware" computer application reads a schema for a class of XML documents, it knows "what to expect" when it receives an instance of that class of documents and can validate the instance against the schema. In business applications, it is common practice to validate an XML document before processing it. In a typical business process, such as processing a sales order, validating it first enables the sales order to be checked for obvious errors, such as missing or inappropriate data, and to make sure it follows the business rules specified in its schema – such as an acceptable customer and billing address. When a customer completes a sales order on a Web site, it can be validated by an XML-enabled software application that compares it to its schema document before it is processed further. This step results in obvious processing efficiencies and can also prevent inappropriate, incorrect data from being transmitted to a database or other application, such as an accounting ledger. Figure 3-9 illustrates the schemas involved in the validation process for a UBL instance document.

Figure 3-9: The UBL validation process

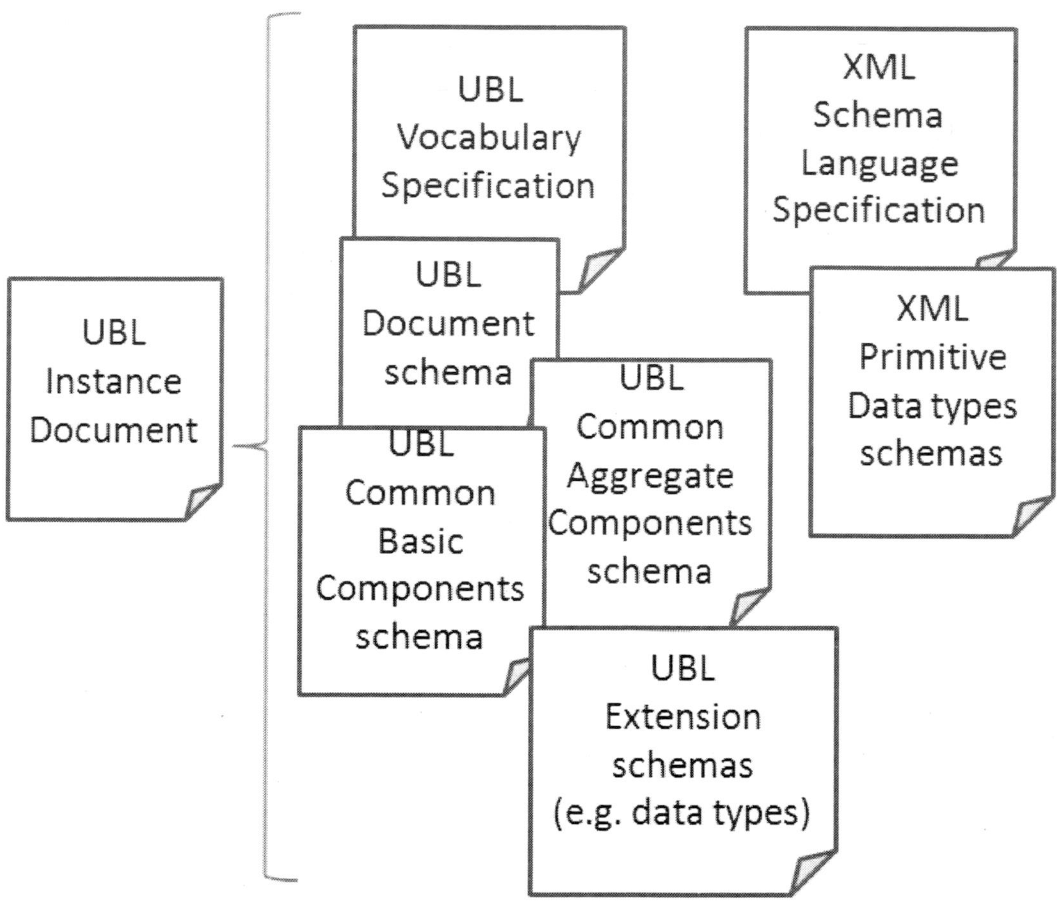

The validation process is somewhat complex because most XML vocabularies, including UBL and XBRL, are "supported" by a number of schemas. A validating XML application would read a UBL instance document and its supporting UBL document schema, which must conform to the UBL Vocabulary Specification and must be made up of reusable data components from the UBL Aggregate and Basic schemas or an extension schema. Since all schema documents are written in the XML Schema language, they must follow the rules formalized in the XML Schema Language Specification. As you saw in the schema documents in this chapter, a UBL document schema imports the UBL Common Aggregate Components schema and the Common Basic Components schema. Each of these schemas uses data types specified in the XML Primitive Data types schema. In addition, UBL has other schemas that extend the XML Schema Language specification to include special data types and codes. It is important to realize that XML document validation is complex and occurs on many different levels and that validating software applications are not all created equally (some validate more thoroughly than others). Most validation processing will assure that an XML document is complete and properly structured according to its document schema, with appropriate data types in the data fields, and that it follows the specified business rules.

Unfortunately, not all XML processors are capable of validation. Currently available browsers do not validate. However, there are many XML validation packages available on the Web. One that the author uses is available from DecisionSoft at: *http://tools.decisionsoft.com/schemaValidate/* (an open source software application from Apache™). Be aware that URLs can and do change and you may need to search for this or another validation package. Figure 3-10 shows the initial DecisionSoft XML Schema Validator input form. Notice the two input boxes for identifying the location of the document schema and the corresponding instance document.

Figure 3-10: DecisionSoft XML Validation input form

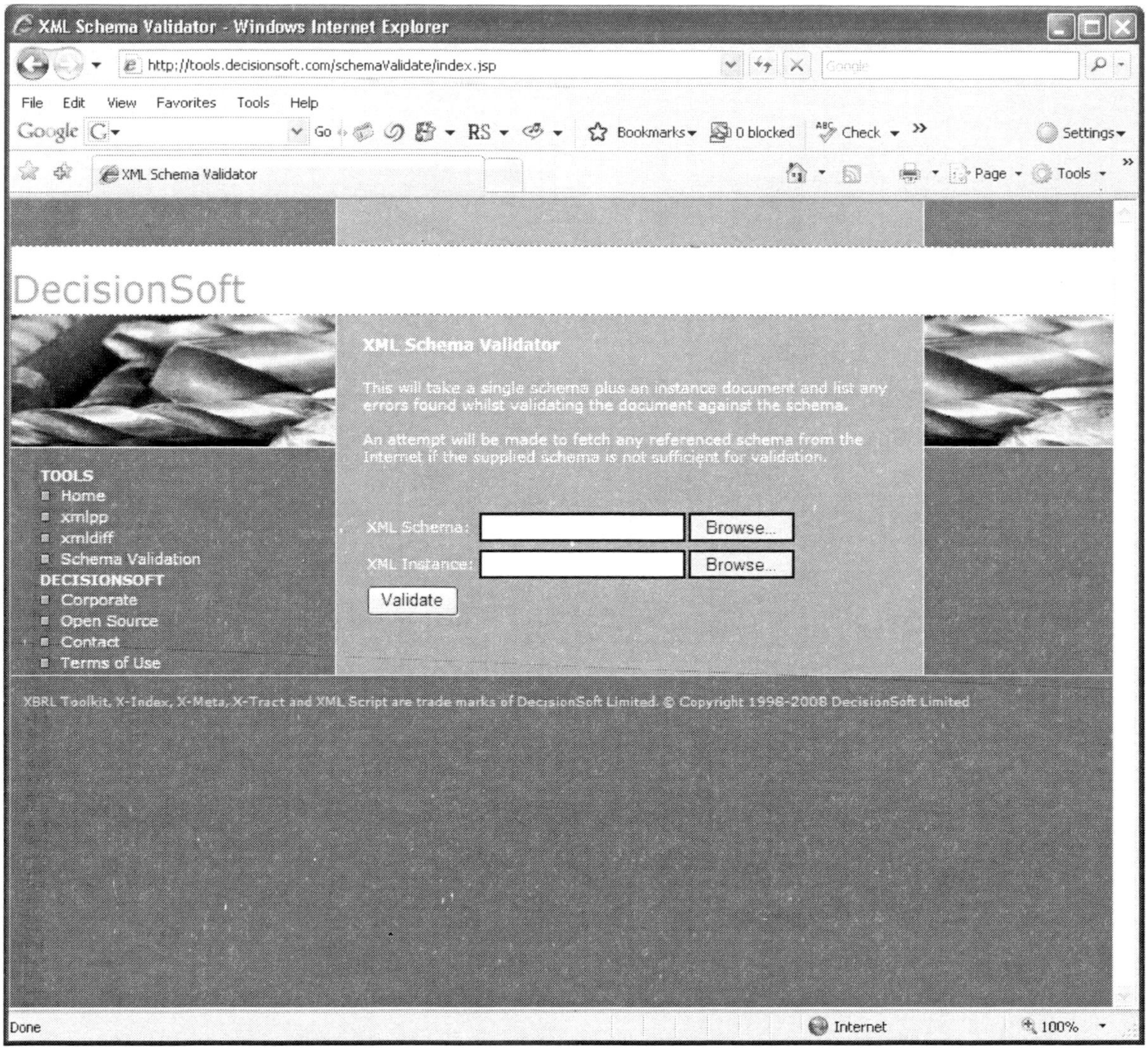

Interactive exercise 3-4: Download both the UBL Catalogue document (http://www.skipwhite.com/ Guide2008/Chapter3/OrderExampleWNS.xml) and the UBL Cataogue document schema (www.skipwhite.com/Guide2008/Chapter3/UBLCatalogueSchema.xml) and store them in the same folder. Point your browser to the DecisionSoft XML Schema Validator (http://tools.decisionsoft.com/schemaValidate/). On the initial Schema Validator screen, use the top browse button to point to the schema document you just downloaded and the lower browse button to point to the UBL Catalogue document in the same folder. After you click-through to the results screen, you should see a *Well Formed: VALID* and *Schema Validation: VALID* validation report.

XML document validation is particularly important for business processes executed over a computer network such as the Internet. XML documents are rapidly becoming the preferred method through which to exchange business-to-business information. When business partnerships are formed, they can use the non-proprietary XML standard to structure automated exchanges of such documents as purchase orders, confirmations, receipts, and invoices. Consider the situation where business A partners with business B in a supply chain arrangement. If A is the supplier of merchandise for B's inventory, B can regularly send agreed upon XML inventory-replenishment documents electronically to A. Supplier A will electronically validate and process the documents using XML-enabled software and send agreed upon XML receipt confirmation, shipping, and invoice documents electronically to B. Purchaser B will electronically validate and process each of these and send agreed upon XML receipt and payment documents to Supplier A. The obvious business-to-business advantage is that XML documents are based on open standards and can be processed, validated with schemas, and re-processed electronically with standard business software without a proprietary middleman, as is needed in EDI (Electronic Data Interchange) value-added networks. XBRL document validation is covered in the next chapter.

While the XML Schema language is quite technical and developing XML schemas can be tedious and error prone, a number of commercial XML schema generation software applications are available to aid in this work. Other Internet-based validation services include the WWW Consortium (W3C) (http://validator.w3.org/) and Scholarly Technology Group (http://www.stg.brown.edu/service/xmlvalid/). MS Visual Studio™ will both generate schemas from XML documents and validate.

XML Linking Language (XLink)

The XML Linking Language (XLink) is an important additional piece of the XML language foundation. The linking capability of HTML, as seen in Web pages, is referred to as "simple linking." Simple linking is unidirectional from a source document to a target document. This works well for Web pages but is inadequate for linking multiple documents and describing relationships between documents or elements within documents. The XLink language provides a method for using attributes to establish multi-directional relationships between elements in XML documents.

The XLink language defines a set of attributes that can be used with any XML element to create links, referred to as “explicit relationships,” between resources; resources are defined as “any addressable unit of information or service” (XLink V1.0 - http://www.w3.org/TR/xlink/). XLink links can be “simple” or “extended.” A simple link is unidirectional, similar to a link in an HTML document. Consider the situation in which a business wants to create a report containing inventory items with links to their approved vendor list for supplying those items. The following example shows how this can be accomplished using a simple XLink:

```
<InventoryItem xlink:type=“simple” xlink:href=“ApprovedVendorsList.xml”> .
```

In this line of code, the **InventoryItem** element has two **xlink** attributes, both of which are required for a “simple” link. The **xlink:type=“**simple**”** attribute identifies it as a simple link, and the **xlink:href=“**ApprovedVendorsList.xml**”** attribute indicates the location of the document to which to link. A simple link is always outbound from an XML element to another addressable resource, usually a target document or part of a document.

Now consider the situation in which a business wants to create a report reconciling a purchase order, a receiving report, and a voucher from a vendor prior to authorizing a payment. The following example shows how this can be accomplished using an extended XLink:

```
<OrderReconciliation xlink:type=“extended”>
   <PurchaseOrder id=“12345” xlink:type=“locator”
     xlink:href= “http://PurchaseOrders.xml”/>
  <ReceivingReport id=“34567” xlink:type=“locator”
     xlink:href= “http://ReceivingRpts.xml”/>
 <Voucher id=“456789” xlink:type=“locator” xlink:href= “http://Vouchers.xml”/>
 </OrderReconciliation>
```

In this block of code, the **OrderReconciliation** element contains the **xlink:type=“**extended**”** attribute that indicates its children elements will participate in an extended linking relationship. The **xlink:type="extended"** attribute tells the XML processor to look for XLink attributes on its children elements – **PurchaseOrder**, **ReceivingReport**, and **Voucher**. Each of these child elements contains the **xlink:type="locator"** attribute and a specific **xlink:href="xxx"** attribute indicating its URI. An XML processor that is XLink-capable recognizes that the **OrderReconciliation** element is an XLink extended-type element and looks for child elements with the **xlink:type="locator"** attribute that participate in the link. Each XLink locator-type element is a remote resource and has an **xlink:href** attribute that is used to locate it. The XLink-capable processor then follows the extended links participating in the **OrderReconciliation** element to assemble the set of resources and processes them to determine if a **Voucher** should be paid. Local resources can also participate in extended links and are identified with the XLink resource-type attribute **xlink:type="resource"**.

XBRL uses the XLink language for a variety of purposes, including simple links to footnotes necessary to properly understand an accounting item and extended links to describe the relationship between multiple items. Common accounting and financial relationships (such as "the items that make up Current assets") are defined using the XLink language in XBRL linkbases (covered in Chapter 4).

The XML Foundation and XBRL

Like all XML vocabularies, XBRL is built on the XML foundation. Figure 3-11 illustrates the relationship among XML, the XBRL Specification 2.1, XBRL Taxonomies, and XBRL instance documents. As you saw in the last two chapters, the XML foundation specifies a basic set of rules that all XML documents must follow and the rules for the creation of languages, like XML Schema, Namespaces, and XLink. These languages are used for processing XML documents and for the creation of XML vocabularies. The XBRL Specification 2.1 is one of those vocabularies. Written in the XML Schema language, it specifies a basic set of rules that all XBRL documents must follow and the rules for the creation of XBRL taxonomies and linkbases. XBRL taxonomies specify sets of elements and attributes to be used for specific financial reporting purposes, including U.S. GAAP for Commercial & Industrial companies (C&I),

Banking and Savings institutions, and Insurance companies. XBRL taxonomies are also written in the XML Schema language. XBRL linkbases specify sets of relationships necessary for understanding accounting and financial reporting concepts, such as Assets, Liabilities, and Equities. XBRL linkbases are written in the XLink language. XBRL instance documents are business reports that follow the rules specified in the XBRL 2.1 Specification and use elements defined in XBRL taxonomies. We will build on this foundation in Chapter 4.

Figure 3-11: The XML Foundation and XBRL

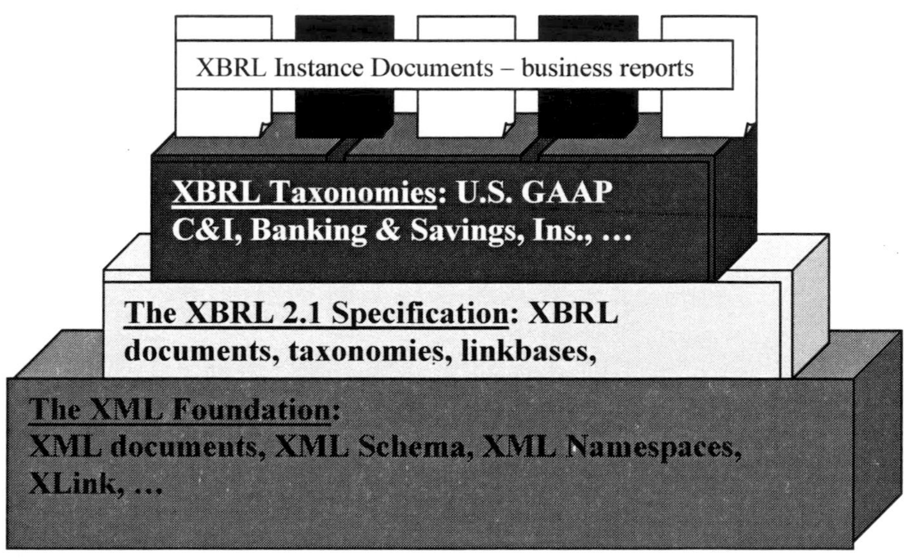

Summary

Several XML languages form the foundation for validating and processing XML documents and building XML vocabularies, such as UBL and XBRL. The XML Schema language is the language used to build XML schema documents and is the foundation language for all XML languages and vocabularies. XML schema documents define each element and attribute that can appear in a class of XML documents and the overall structure of such documents. XML schema documents are designed to be read by XML-enabled software applications and used to validate instances of the class of XML documents that they define. Because XML is a foundation language for the creation of other languages, XML vocabularies are being developed all around the world for a variety of purposes. XML Namespaces is a foundation language used to identify each XML vocabulary. XML namespaces are declared in the root element of an XML document, and each is assigned a unique prefix to be used to qualify elements and attributes that appear in an XML document. The XML Linking Language (XLink) is a foundation language to enable sophisticated linking capabilities in XML documents. It specifies a set of attributes to be used to create multidirectional links and relationships between elements in XML documents and other addressable resources.

The next Chapter introduces XBRL. A basic understanding of the XML foundation languages presented in this Chapter is necessary for understanding XBRL instance documents and taxonomies.

Glossary of new terms introduced in Chapter 3

Cardinality: A mathematical term referring to the number of elements in a set. In XML schemas, you define how many times an element can occur in an instance document using **minOccurs=**"xxx" and **maxOccurs=**"yyy".

Complex elements: XML elements that contain other elements nested within or elements with attributes. They must be defined with a complexType element in an XML schema.

Empty elements: XML elements that do not contain a data value or other elements nested within. An empty element always has a /> as a closing bracket.

Extended linking: A sophisticated link that can involve multiple documents and relationships. Extended links are used in building XML linkbases to describe complex relationships.

Namespace declaration: A namespace declaration in the form of xmlns:*prefix*="*URI of namespace*" that [to keep the grammar parallel with the other definitions]must appear as an attribute of an XML document's root element when elements from different namespaces are used in the document.

Primitive data type: A data type defined in the XML specification. Common primitive XML data types include string, integer, decimal, and date.

Reusable data components: XML elements that are defined once in an XML schema and then reused in other schemas and in instance documents as needed.

schema document: A computer-readable document created with the XML Schema language to define the contents and structure of a class of XML documents. Schema documents are used to validate their associated XML documents.

Simple elements: XML elements that do not contain other elements or attributes. They usually contain a data item and must be defined with a data type in an XML schema.

Simple linking: A unidirectional link between an XML element and an addressable resource. Simple links are similar to those found in HTML documents.

Valid XML document: An XML document that is well-formed and has been validated against the rules in its associated XML schema document.

XML namespace: A URI designating where additional information, such as a schema or a taxonomy, can be found. Each namespace in an XML document must be unique. They are used to designate specifically where elements and attributes are defined in order to avoid naming collisions.

XML Schema language: The XML language used to write other XML languages and vocabularies and to create XML schema documents.

XML vocabulary: An XML specification created for a particular purpose, such as the XBRL vocabulary for financial and business reporting. All XML vocabularies are written in the XML Schema language and define a specific set of elements and attributes and document structure for a particular purpose.

Exercises

Exercise 3-1: This exercise requires you to create a schema for the UBL Purchase Order document shown below (originally discussed in Chapter 2).

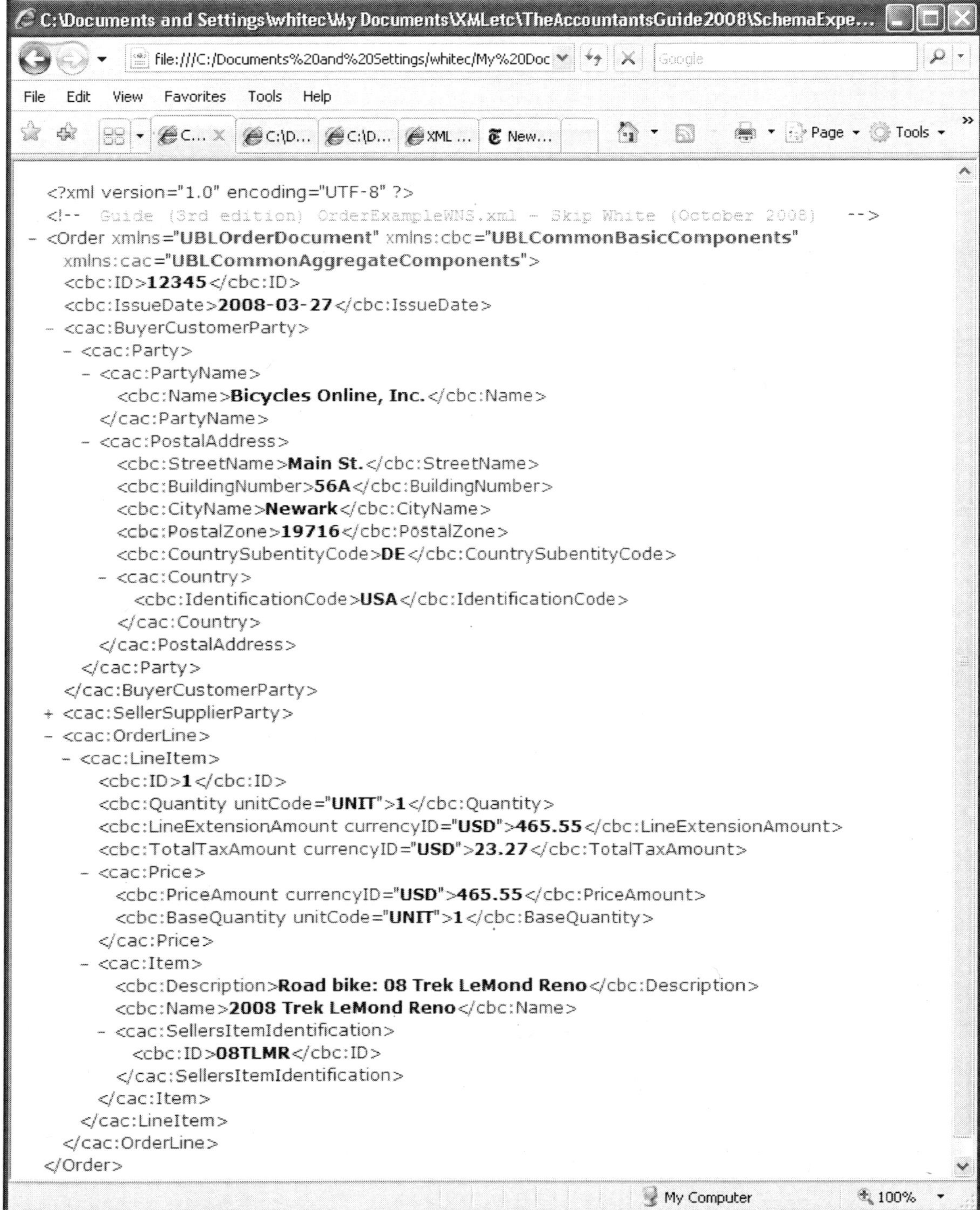

```
<?xml version="1.0" encoding="UTF-8" ?>
<!-- Guide (3rd edition) OrderExampleWNS.xml - Skip White (October 2008) -->
- <Order xmlns="UBLOrderDocument" xmlns:cbc="UBLCommonBasicComponents"
    xmlns:cac="UBLCommonAggregateComponents">
    <cbc:ID>12345</cbc:ID>
    <cbc:IssueDate>2008-03-27</cbc:IssueDate>
  - <cac:BuyerCustomerParty>
    - <cac:Party>
      - <cac:PartyName>
          <cbc:Name>Bicycles Online, Inc.</cbc:Name>
        </cac:PartyName>
      - <cac:PostalAddress>
          <cbc:StreetName>Main St.</cbc:StreetName>
          <cbc:BuildingNumber>56A</cbc:BuildingNumber>
          <cbc:CityName>Newark</cbc:CityName>
          <cbc:PostalZone>19716</cbc:PostalZone>
          <cbc:CountrySubentityCode>DE</cbc:CountrySubentityCode>
        - <cac:Country>
            <cbc:IdentificationCode>USA</cbc:IdentificationCode>
          </cac:Country>
        </cac:PostalAddress>
      </cac:Party>
    </cac:BuyerCustomerParty>
  + <cac:SellerSupplierParty>
  - <cac:OrderLine>
    - <cac:LineItem>
        <cbc:ID>1</cbc:ID>
        <cbc:Quantity unitCode="UNIT">1</cbc:Quantity>
        <cbc:LineExtensionAmount currencyID="USD">465.55</cbc:LineExtensionAmount>
        <cbc:TotalTaxAmount currencyID="USD">23.27</cbc:TotalTaxAmount>
      - <cac:Price>
          <cbc:PriceAmount currencyID="USD">465.55</cbc:PriceAmount>
          <cbc:BaseQuantity unitCode="UNIT">1</cbc:BaseQuantity>
        </cac:Price>
      - <cac:Item>
          <cbc:Description>Road bike: 08 Trek LeMond Reno</cbc:Description>
          <cbc:Name>2008 Trek LeMond Reno</cbc:Name>
        - <cac:SellersItemIdentification>
            <cbc:ID>08TLMR</cbc:ID>
          </cac:SellersItemIdentification>
        </cac:Item>
      </cac:LineItem>
    </cac:OrderLine>
</Order>
```

(File: *http://www.skipwhite.com/Guide2008/Chapter3/OrderExampleWNS.xml*)

As in the UBL Catalogue document schema, all UBL document schemas are created by reusing elements from the UBL Common Basic Components and the UBL Common Aggregate Components schema. Use the UBL Catalogue document schema as an example (*www.skipwhite.com/Guide2008/Chapter3/UBLCatalogueSchema.xml*).

The business rules for all UBL Purchase Orders are that each Purchase Order document must have the following elements in sequence:

1. One and only one **ID** with a unique order number.
2. One and only one **IssueDate**.
3. One and only one **BuyerCustomerParty**.
4. One and only one **SellerSupplierParty** (with the same structure as the **BuyerCustomerParty**).
5. And at least one **OrderLine**.

First, download the UBL Purchase Order document (*http://www.skipwhite.com/Guide2008/Chapter3/OrderExampleWNS.xml*) and save it in a folder. Second, download the UBL Catalogue schema document (*http://www.skipwhite.com/Guide2008/Chapter3/UBLCatalogueSchema.xml*) and save it in the same folder. Third, open the UBL Catalogue schema document in Notepad or your favorite text editor so that you can use it as an example and copy code from it. Fourth, open a new document in Notepad or your favorite text editor and copy and paste the XML version declaration, comment line, and the **xs:schema** element from the UBL Catalogue schema. Make the appropriate changes to the comment line to reflect the new schema (i.e. purchase order schema) and insert your name, and then make the following changes to the attributes in the **xs:schema** element:

- Change the **targetNamespace** to **targetNamespace=**"UBLOrderDocument".
- Change the default namespace to **xmlns=**"UBLOrderDocument".

Do not change the **xs:import** elements.

Fifth, starting with the Order document's root element name, make the appropriate changes to the UBL schema document and save it in the same folder as your UBL Purchase Order document with a **.xml** extension (possibly *PurchaseOrderSchema.xml*). After saving it: open your schema document in your browser to see if it is well-formed; then, validate the UBL Purchase Order document against your schema. When complete, be sure your name is in the comment line at the top of your schema document and turn it in on a flash drive. Your instructor may have additional instructions.

Exercise 3-2: After a business receives an Order, it must respond to the customer with an Order Response. This exercise requires you to create a schema for the UBL Order response document shown below.

Order Response document (part 1)

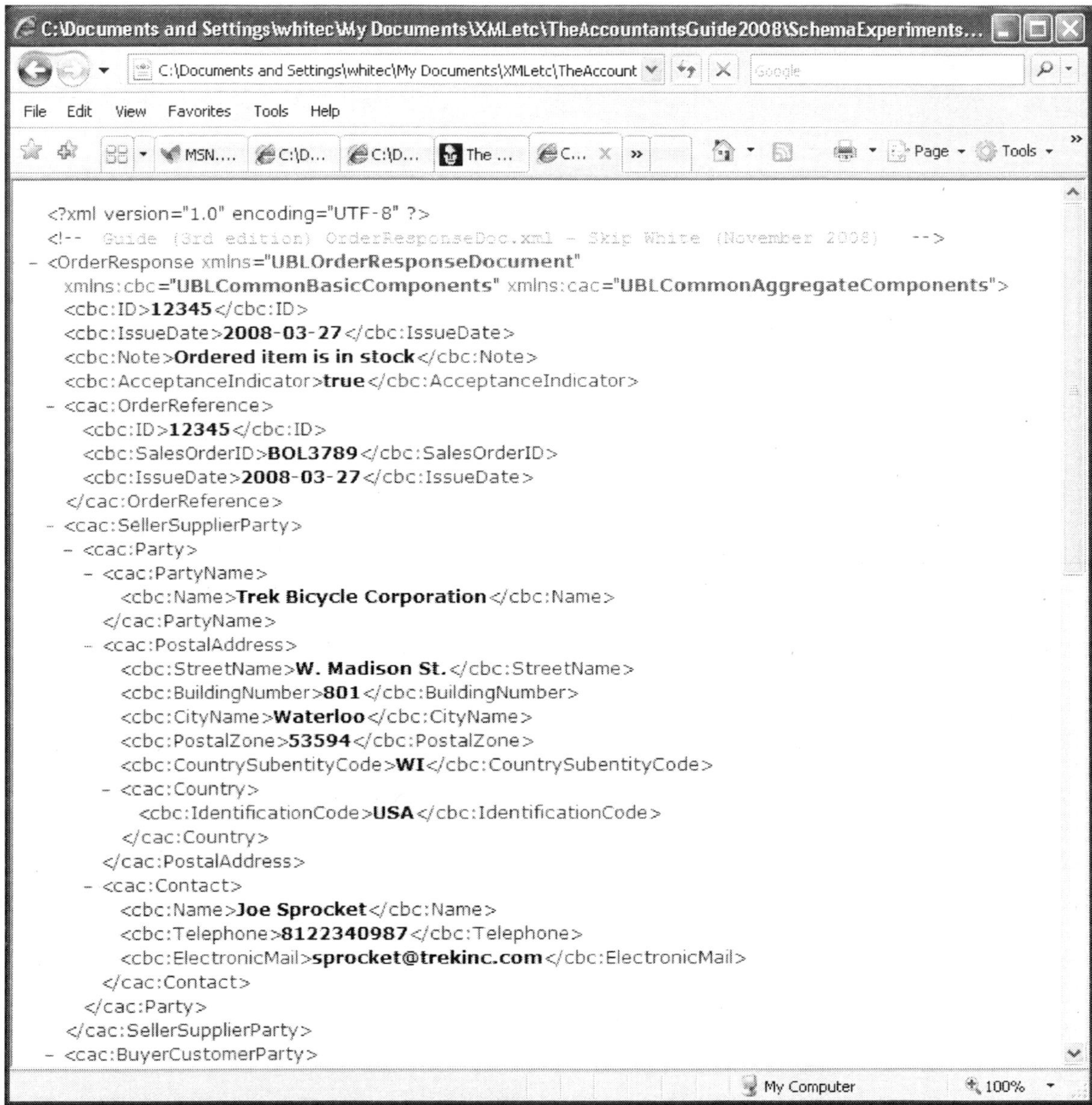

```
<?xml version="1.0" encoding="UTF-8" ?>
<!-- Guide (3rd edition) OrderResponseDoc.xml - Skip White (November 2008) -->
- <OrderResponse xmlns="UBLOrderResponseDocument"
    xmlns:cbc="UBLCommonBasicComponents" xmlns:cac="UBLCommonAggregateComponents">
    <cbc:ID>12345</cbc:ID>
    <cbc:IssueDate>2008-03-27</cbc:IssueDate>
    <cbc:Note>Ordered item is in stock</cbc:Note>
    <cbc:AcceptanceIndicator>true</cbc:AcceptanceIndicator>
  - <cac:OrderReference>
      <cbc:ID>12345</cbc:ID>
      <cbc:SalesOrderID>BOL3789</cbc:SalesOrderID>
      <cbc:IssueDate>2008-03-27</cbc:IssueDate>
    </cac:OrderReference>
  - <cac:SellerSupplierParty>
    - <cac:Party>
      - <cac:PartyName>
          <cbc:Name>Trek Bicycle Corporation</cbc:Name>
        </cac:PartyName>
      - <cac:PostalAddress>
          <cbc:StreetName>W. Madison St.</cbc:StreetName>
          <cbc:BuildingNumber>801</cbc:BuildingNumber>
          <cbc:CityName>Waterloo</cbc:CityName>
          <cbc:PostalZone>53594</cbc:PostalZone>
          <cbc:CountrySubentityCode>WI</cbc:CountrySubentityCode>
        - <cac:Country>
            <cbc:IdentificationCode>USA</cbc:IdentificationCode>
          </cac:Country>
        </cac:PostalAddress>
      - <cac:Contact>
          <cbc:Name>Joe Sprocket</cbc:Name>
          <cbc:Telephone>8122340987</cbc:Telephone>
          <cbc:ElectronicMail>sprocket@trekinc.com</cbc:ElectronicMail>
        </cac:Contact>
      </cac:Party>
    </cac:SellerSupplierParty>
  - <cac:BuyerCustomerParty>
```

(File: *http://www.skipwhite.com/Guide2008/Chapter3/OrderResponseDoc.xml*)

Order Response document (part 2)

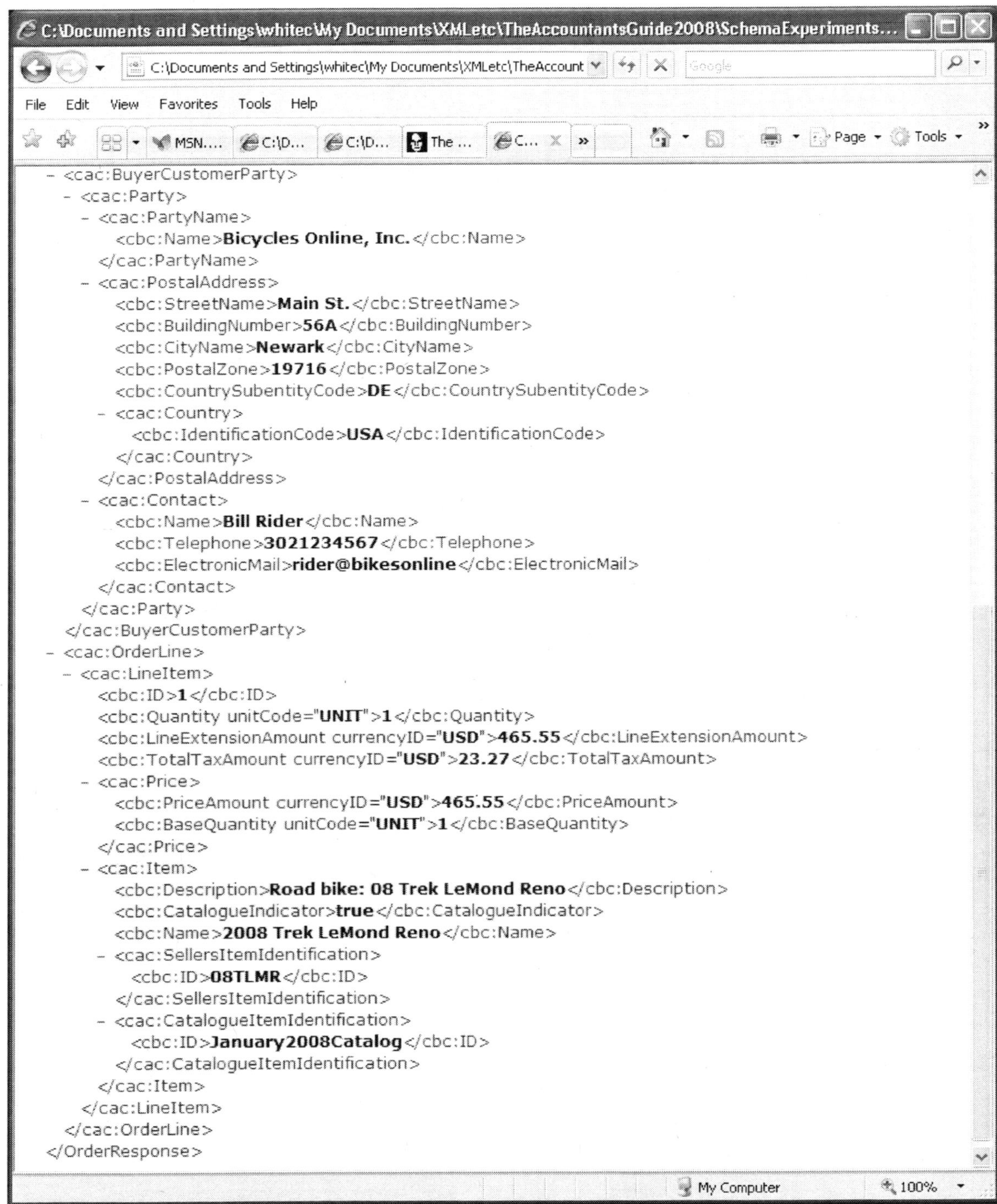

```
- <cac:BuyerCustomerParty>
  - <cac:Party>
    - <cac:PartyName>
        <cbc:Name>Bicycles Online, Inc.</cbc:Name>
      </cac:PartyName>
    - <cac:PostalAddress>
        <cbc:StreetName>Main St.</cbc:StreetName>
        <cbc:BuildingNumber>56A</cbc:BuildingNumber>
        <cbc:CityName>Newark</cbc:CityName>
        <cbc:PostalZone>19716</cbc:PostalZone>
        <cbc:CountrySubentityCode>DE</cbc:CountrySubentityCode>
      - <cac:Country>
          <cbc:IdentificationCode>USA</cbc:IdentificationCode>
        </cac:Country>
      </cac:PostalAddress>
    - <cac:Contact>
        <cbc:Name>Bill Rider</cbc:Name>
        <cbc:Telephone>3021234567</cbc:Telephone>
        <cbc:ElectronicMail>rider@bikesonline</cbc:ElectronicMail>
      </cac:Contact>
    </cac:Party>
  </cac:BuyerCustomerParty>
- <cac:OrderLine>
  - <cac:LineItem>
      <cbc:ID>1</cbc:ID>
      <cbc:Quantity unitCode="UNIT">1</cbc:Quantity>
      <cbc:LineExtensionAmount currencyID="USD">465.55</cbc:LineExtensionAmount>
      <cbc:TotalTaxAmount currencyID="USD">23.27</cbc:TotalTaxAmount>
    - <cac:Price>
        <cbc:PriceAmount currencyID="USD">465.55</cbc:PriceAmount>
        <cbc:BaseQuantity unitCode="UNIT">1</cbc:BaseQuantity>
      </cac:Price>
    - <cac:Item>
        <cbc:Description>Road bike: 08 Trek LeMond Reno</cbc:Description>
        <cbc:CatalogueIndicator>true</cbc:CatalogueIndicator>
        <cbc:Name>2008 Trek LeMond Reno</cbc:Name>
      - <cac:SellersItemIdentification>
          <cbc:ID>08TLMR</cbc:ID>
        </cac:SellersItemIdentification>
      - <cac:CatalogueItemIdentification>
          <cbc:ID>January2008Catalog</cbc:ID>
        </cac:CatalogueItemIdentification>
      </cac:Item>
    </cac:LineItem>
  </cac:OrderLine>
</OrderResponse>
```

(File: *http://www.skipwhite.com/Guide2008/Chapter3/OrderResponseDoc.xml*)

As in the UBL Catalogue document schema, all UBL document schemas are created by reusing elements from the UBL Common Basic Components and the UBL Common

Aggregate Components schema. Use the UBL Catalogue document schema as an example (*www.skipwhite.com/Guide2008/Chapter3/UBLCatalogueSchema.xml*).

The business rules for all UBL Order Responses are that each Order Response document must have the following elements in sequence:

1. One and only one **ID** with a unique order number.
2. One and only one **IssueDate**.
3. One and only one **AcceptanceIndicator**.
4. One and only one **OrderReference**.
5. One and only one **SellerSupplierParty**.
6. One and only one **BuyerCustomerParty** (with the same structure as the **SellerSupplierParty**)..
7. And at least one **OrderLine**.

First, download the UBL Order Response document (*http://www.skipwhite.com/Guide2008/Chapter3/OrderResponseDoc.xml*) and save it in a folder. Second, download the UBL Catalogue schema document (*http://www.skipwhite.com/Guide2008/Chapter3/UBLCatalogueSchema.xml*) and save it in the same folder. Third, open the UBL Catalogue schema document in Notepad or your favorite text editor so that you can use it as an example and copy code from it. Fourth, open a new document in Notepad or your favorite text editor and copy and paste the XML version declaration, comment line, and the **xs:schema** element from the UBL Catalogue schema. Make the appropriate changes to the comment line to reflect the new schema (i.e. order response schema) and insert your name, and then make the following changes to the attributes in the **xs:schema** element:

- Change the **targetNamespace** to **targetNamespace="** UBLOrderResponseDocument **"**.
- Change the default namespace to **xmlns="** UBLOrderResponseDocument **"**.

Do not change the **xs:import** elements.

Fifth, starting with the Order Response document's root element name, make the appropriate changes to the UBL schema document and save it in the same folder as your UBL Purchase Order document with a **.xml** extension (possibly *OrderResponse-Schema.xml*).

After saving it: open your schema document in your browser to see if it is well-formed; then, validate the UBL Order Response document against your schema. When complete, be sure your name is in the comment line at the top of your schema document and turn it in on a flash drive. Your instructor may have additional instructions.

Downloadable files:

Available from: www.SkipWhite.com/Guide2008/Chapter3/ *file name*:

- File name: CatalogueItemExampleWNS (Figure 3-1)
  http://www.skipwhite.com/Guide2008/Chapter3/CatalogueItemExampleWNS.xml
- File name: UBLCatalogueSchema (Figure 3-2)
  http://www.skipwhite.com/Guide2008/Chapter3/UBLCatalogueSchema. xml
- File name: UBLCommonBasicComponentsSchema (Figure 3-4)
  http://www.skipwhite.com/Guide2008/Chapter3/UBLCommonBasicComponentsSchema. xml
- File name: UBLCommonAggregateComponentsSchema (Figure 3-6)
  http://www.skipwhite.com/Guide2008/Chapter3/UBLCommonAggregateComponentsSchema. xml
- File name: OrderExampleWNS.xml (Exercise 3-1)
  http://www.skipwhite.com/Guide2008/ Chapter3/OrderExampleWNS.xml
- File name: OrderResponseDoc.xml (Exercise 3-2)
  http://www.skipwhite.com/Guide2008/ Chapter3/OrderResponseDoc.xml

References and more information:

XML Schema, W3C, 2005-09-12 (http://www.w3.org/2001/XMLSchema)

XML Schema Primer, W3C, 2004-10-28 (http://www.w3.org/TR/xmlschema-0/)

XML Schema Tutorial, W3Schools (http://www.w3schools.com/schema/default.asp)

Answers:

Question 3-1: What type of element (simple or complex) is each of the following?

Country - complex because it has an **IdentificationCode** nested within it

Price - complex because it has elements nested within it

Item - complex because it has elements nested within it

LineExtensionAmount - complex because it has an attribute

Interactive exercise 3-2: Using the XML Schema language, how would you define each of the following two elements appearing in an instance document?

1. **<AccountantName>**Skip White**</AccountantName>**

```
<xs:element name="AccountantName" type="xs:string"/>
```

2. **<AccountantFee units=“USD”>**10000**</AccountantFee>**

```
<xs:element name="AccountantFee ">
<xs:complexType>
<xs:simpleContent>
   <xs:extension base="xs:decimal">
   <xs:attribute name="units" type="xs:string" use="required"/>
   </xs:extension>
</xs:simpleContent>
</xs:complexType>
</xs:element>
```

Interactive exercise 3-3: To answer these questions, you should open the UBL Catalogue document (*http://www.skipwhite.com/Guide2008/Chapter3/CatalogueItem-ExampleWNS.xml*) and the UBL Common Aggregate Components schema (*http://www.skipwhite.com/Guide2008/Chapter3/UBLCommonAggregateComponentsSchema.xml*) in side by side browser windows.

1. What are the child elements of the **cac:CatalogueLine** element? (Hint: A child element has one and only one parent element.)

   cdc:ID
   cac:RequiredItemLocationQuantity
   cac:Item

2. What are the child elements of the **cac:Item** element?

   cbc:Description
   cbc:Name
   cac:SellersItemIdentification

The Accountant's Guide to XBRL

Chapter 4: XBRL Instance Documents and Taxonomies

Overview

This chapter describes valid XBRL (eXtensible Business Reporting Language) instance documents and XBRL taxonomies and their role in reporting financial and business operations information.

As you have read, XML is a set of rules and syntax that provides a foundation with which to create XML documents and other languages and specifications that extend the XML family of technologies. Like UBL, XBRL is an XML vocabulary. While UBL defines the structure and contents of common business documents and their reusable data components, XBRL defines the structure and contents of common financial and business operations reports and their reusable components. The XBRL Specification 2.1 (XBRL International, 2005-11-07) is a set of rules and syntax to follow to create ***XBRL instance documents*** and ***XBRL taxonomies*** and extensions. XBRL documents are referred to as "instance documents" because each one is an instance of a class of documents described in the XBRL Specification. The XBRL Specification includes a schema which defines the structure of all XBRL instance documents and schemas defining XBRL taxonomies; which can be thought of as dictionaries defining elements to be used in XBRL instance documents. Like all XML specifications, the XBRL specification is quite complex and XBRL instance documents look complex to the uninformed user. The goal of this Chapter is to help you understand, use, and interpret XBRL instance documents and taxonomies.

To help you understand and build XBRL instance documents, we will first enumerate and illustrate the rules for valid XBRL instance documents. Note that we will not validate our XBRL instance documents using validation software because as of this point in time XBRL validation software packages are not free. We will discuss the levels and complexities of XBRL validation and several validation tools. Also in this Chapter, we will discuss the framework for U.S. financial reporting using XBRL instance documents and conclude with illustrations of financial reporting using the new U.S. GAAP v1.0 taxonomies.

The Rules for Valid XBRL Instance Documents

The XBRL Specification 2.1 is made up of two major parts: the rules for XBRL instance documents and the guidelines for XBRL taxonomies. XBRL instance documents are computer-readable files in a prescribed format that carry data items tagged with predefined elements representing accounting and financial reporting concepts. XBRL taxonomies define the elements and their relationships representing the accounting and financial concepts to be reported in XBRL instance documents. Each XBRL taxonomy includes a schema defining elements for a particular reporting purpose (e.g., commercial and industrial companies reporting under US GAAP) written in the XML Schema language, referred to as a ***taxonomy schema***, and ***linkbases*** defining relationships between elements written in the XLink language. Both are discussed later in this Chapter.

To help illustrate the basic connection between XBRL instance documents and XBRL taxonomies, we can start with the example of a business entity that wants to report a balance in accounts payable of $34,250,000. In XBRL terminology, "accounts payable" is a financial reporting concept defined in an XBRL taxonomy schema as a monetary item with the name "AccountsPayable." In very simplified format, the business entity would report the following **<AccountsPayable>**34250000**</AccountsPayable>**. XBRL reporting is much more complex than this because we are required to include attributes indicating what entity is doing the reporting, what period of time is involved, what currency it is in, what precision applies, and in which taxonomy this concept is defined. As you should remember from our discussion of UBL, such attributes add meaning to an element in order to be able to fully interpret the meaning of the data item it contains.

It is important to realize that XBRL instance documents carry "facts" being reported by a specific entity, for a specific time period, and in a specific currency if monetary items are being reported. Each fact is surrounded with this context information expressed according the rules for valid XBRL instance documents. Figure 4-1 illustrates the format that a valid XBRL instance document reporting a single monetary item at a specific instant in time must follow. It is a shell in which the author has highlighted in **bold** the required XBRL elements and in *underlined italic* the information to be input for a specific reporting instance.

Figure 4-1: An abstract XBRL instance document

```
<xbrli:xbrl xmlns:prefix="a specific xbrl namespace"  xmlns:prefix="others" >

  <link:schemaRef  xlink:type="simple"
     xlink:href="the URI of a specific xbrl taxonomy" />

  <xbrli:context  id="a unique context identifier" >
      <xbrli:entity>
        <xbrli:identifier  scheme= "a scheme identifier"> a unique entity identifier
          </xbrli:identifier>
       </xbrli:entity>
       <xbrli:period>
         <xbrli:instant> a specific date </xbrli:instant>
       </xbrli:period>
  </xbrli:context>

  <xbrli:unit  id="a unique unit identifier" >
      <xbrli:measure> a specific unit of measure </xbrli:measure>
  </xbrli:unit>

  <prefix:xbrl element name from taxonomy  contextRef="id" unitRef="id"
      decimal="value"> xbrl item being reported
   </prefix:xbrl element name from taxonomy>

</xbrli:xbrl>
```

(File: *http://www.skipwhite.com/Guide2008/Chapter4/XbrlShell.xml*)

To illustrate the construction of XBRL instance documents, we will walk through this shell and build an XBRL instance document to report that United Technologies, Inc. had "accrued liabilities" in the amount of $12,304,000,000 in U.S. dollars as of June 30, 2008. Each sub-heading in this section will require you to build a portion of the document. The end result will be a valid XBRL instance document reporting United Technologies' "accrued liabilities."

The root element and its namespace declarations

All XBRL instance documents must be well-formed and valid XML documents because they must follow the rules for all XML documents, as well as the rules for XBRL instance documents. The required root element name of an XBRL instance document is **xbrl**. As mentioned in Chapters 2 and 3, a root element's name should reflect the contents and purpose of the document. The XBRL root element also contains all of the necessary XBRL and XML namespace declarations to be used to support the document. Remember that namespace declarations always appear as attributes of the root element and use the keyword **xmlns**. They are necessary to identify the namespaces that support the contents of an XML document. Since United Technologies, Inc. (UTX) reports as a Commercial & Industrial company under U.S. GAAP, they must include a namespace declaration identifying this taxonomy: **xmlns:us-gaap="**http://xbrl.us/us-gaap/2008-03-31". Remember that a namespace identifier has to be a unique URI (i.e., a Web address or a local identifier). If you go to this URI with your browser, you will get a "page not found" error message because it is not intended to be accessed by a browser. If however, you go to the XBRL.org financial reporting taxonomies home page, http://www.xbrl.org/FRTaxonomies/, and scroll down and click on "XBRL US GAAP Taxonomy 1.0," you will see the taxonomy's summary page (see Figure 4-2). A taxonomy summary page provides basic information about an XBRL taxonomy including its unique namespace identifier, its preferred namespace prefix, and links to other resources we will cover later in this chapter. Near the bottom of Figure 4-2, notice that the US GAAP Taxonomy 1.0 Namespace identifier for all elements is http://xbrl.us/us-gaap/2008-03-31 (i.e., all elements refers to all U.S. GAAP taxonomies, including those for Commercial & Industrial companies, Banking & Savings institutions, Brokers & Dealers, Insurance companies, and Real Estate companies), its preferred Namespace prefix is **us-gaap**, and its core taxonomy schema is Physically located at http://xbrl.us/us-gaap/1.0/elts/us-gaap-std-2008-03-31.xsd; if you point your browser to this URL, you will find an actual schema.

Figure 4-2: XBRL US GAAP Taxonomy 1.0 Summary Page

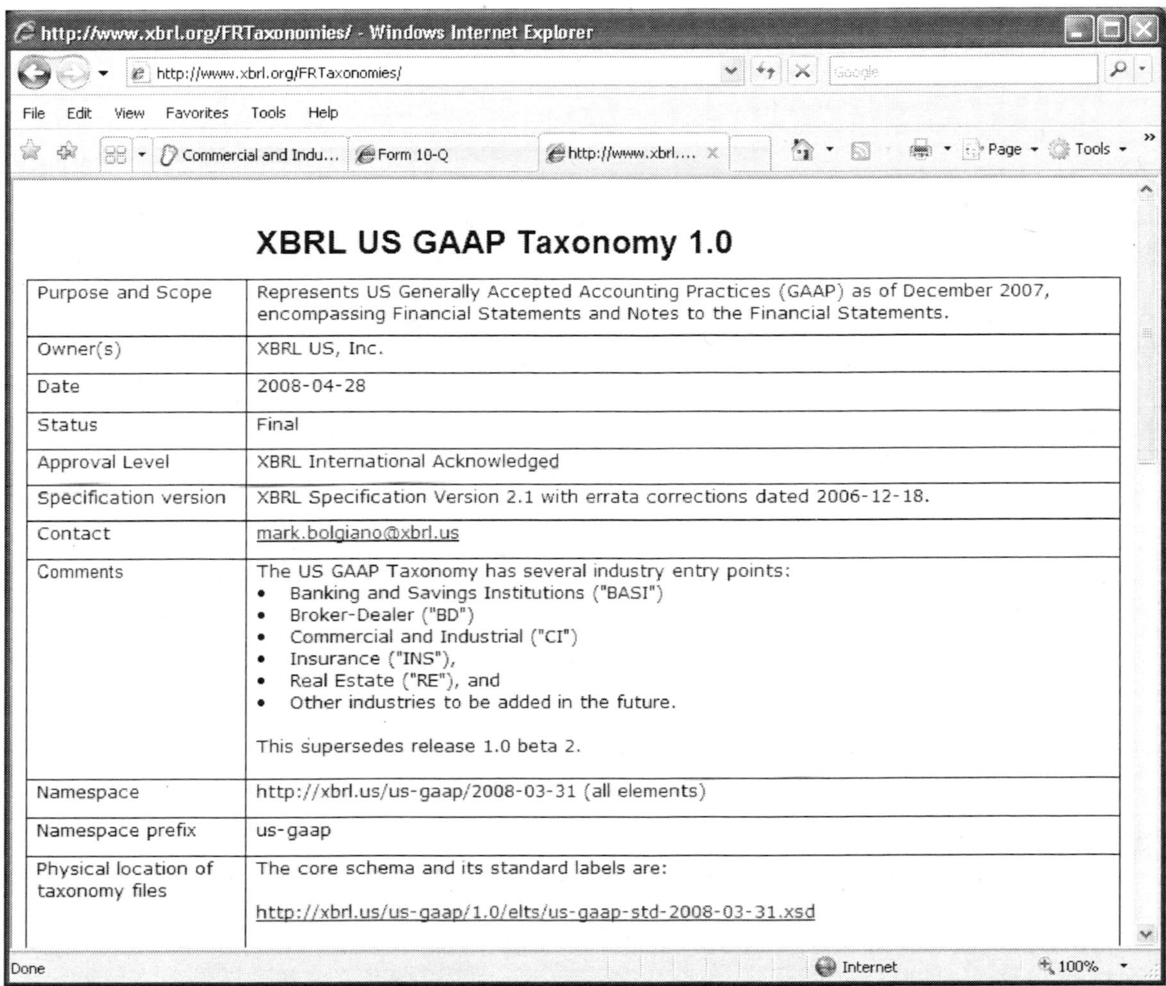

XBRL US GAAP Taxonomy 1.0

Purpose and Scope	Represents US Generally Accepted Accounting Practices (GAAP) as of December 2007, encompassing Financial Statements and Notes to the Financial Statements.
Owner(s)	XBRL US, Inc.
Date	2008-04-28
Status	Final
Approval Level	XBRL International Acknowledged
Specification version	XBRL Specification Version 2.1 with errata corrections dated 2006-12-18.
Contact	mark.bolgiano@xbrl.us
Comments	The US GAAP Taxonomy has several industry entry points: • Banking and Savings Institutions ("BASI") • Broker-Dealer ("BD") • Commercial and Industrial ("CI") • Insurance ("INS"), • Real Estate ("RE"), and • Other industries to be added in the future. This supersedes release 1.0 beta 2.
Namespace	http://xbrl.us/us-gaap/2008-03-31 (all elements)
Namespace prefix	us-gaap
Physical location of taxonomy files	The core schema and its standard labels are: http://xbrl.us/us-gaap/1.0/elts/us-gaap-std-2008-03-31.xsd

The structure and format for all XBRL instance documents is defined by a schema which can be accessed from the **xbrli** namespace: http://www.xbrl.org/2003/instance. If you point your browser to this namespace, you will find a link to the physical location of the XBRL instance document schema. This namespace declaration should appear in all XBRL instance documents.

Interactive exercise 4-1: Open **Notepad** or your favorite text editor and enter the **xbrl** root element and these two namespace declarations in a new file. It should appear as follows (I have bolded all element and attribute names for illustration only):

<**xbrli:xbrl xmlns:us-gaap**="http://xbrl.us/us-gaap/2008-03-31"
xmlns:xbrli="http://www.xbrl.org/2003/instance"

This is the root element and the first two namespace declarations in an XBRL instance document for a company (e.g. UTX) reporting financial information under U.S. GAAP. Remember that a namespace prefix (e.g. **xbrli**) simply identifies the namespace in which a specific element is defined (e.g. **xbrl** as the root element of an XBRL instance document). Two other namespace declarations that appear in most XBRL instance documents are the following:

- **link**="http://www.xbrl.org/2003/linkbase" (the namespace which defines XBRL linkbases)
- **xlink**="http://www.w3.org/1999/xlink" (the namespace in which the XML XLink language is defined).

Interactive exercise 4-2: Starting with the root element and the first two namespace declarations you created in Interactive exercise 4-1, open Notepad and enter the above two additional namespace declarations in your file. That is, create a complete XBRL root element with namespace declarations for this reporting application.

The schemaRef element

The next required element in an XBRL instance document is the ***schemaRef element***. The **schemaRef** element is required to appear as the first child element of the **xbrl** root element. The **schemaRef** element is used to "link" an XBRL taxonomy schema to an instance document and is defined in the XBRL **link** namespace. The **link:schemaRef** element always has two attributes defined in the XML **xlink** namespace: **xlink:type**="simple" and **xlink:href**="*URL of an XBRL taxonomy schema*". This should look familiar to you as it was covered in Chapter 3 (XML Linking Language XLink). Since we are creating this XBRL instance document to report financial information for UTX under U.S. GAAP, the **link:schemaRef** element would link it to this XBRL taxonomy schema. It would appear as follows:

<link:schemaRef xlink:type="simple" **xlink:href=** "http://xbrl.us/us-gaap/1.0/elts/us-gaap-std-2008-03-31.xsd "/> . Notice that this URL identifies the Physical location of the US GAAP taxonomy files (see Figure 4-2).

Interactive exercise 4-3: Starting with the complete root element you created in Interactive exercise 4-2, open Notepad and enter the **link:schemaRef** element in your XBRL instance document as the first child of the root element.

Notice that the **link:schemaRef** element is an empty element (i.e., it has attributes but does not have a data value or other elements nested within it).

The context element

The next required element in an XBRL instance document is the ***context element***. The **context** element is defined in the **xbrli** namespace. Its purpose is to establish the "reporting context" of the XBRL instance document by identifying the entity doing the reporting and the instant or duration of time that applies to the data items reported. At least one is required in every XBRL instance document and it can appear anywhere in the document; though it is common practice to place the **xbrli:context** element(s) immediately after the **link:schemaRef** element. Each **xbrli:context** element must have an ***id attribute*** that must be unique in the instance document because it is used for reference purposes. In addition, an **xbrli:context** element always contains an ***entity element*** and a ***period element*** nested within it; both are defined in the **xbrli** namespace. The choice of an **id** attribute value is up to the XBRL document creator but should make sense to a human reader and it must start with a letter, not a number or special character. The **xbrli:entity** element always contains an ***identifier element***, with a ***scheme attribute***, that uniquely identifies the entity reporting the facts in the instance document. The **xbrli:context** element also always contains a **xbrli:period** element containing elements that precisely identify the instant or interval of time that applies to the facts being reported.

Since we are creating an XBRL instance document to report that United Technologies, Inc. had "accrued liabilities" of a certain amount as of June 30, 2008, we need to create an **xbrli:context** element reflecting this "reporting context." It turns out that UTX uses a **xbrli:context id** naming convention that represents the date at which the facts in its XBRL instance documents are being reported (e.g. As_of_Jun30_2008). This is a convention used by many entities reporting information in XBRL instance documents. Remember that the choice of **id** value is up to the document creator, but it must start with a letter. The beginning of UTX's **xbrli:context** element is **<xbrli:context id**="As_of_Jun30_2008">.

The next part of UTX's **xbrli:context** element in this instance document is the **xbrli:entity** element. An **xbrli:entity** element always starts with **<xbrli:entity>**. Nested within the **xbrli:entity** element is the **xbrli:identifier** element with its **scheme** attribute, both of which depend on the entity's reporting purpose. If an entity is reporting to the SEC, the identifier element would use the following pattern:
<xbrli:identifier scheme="http://www.sec.gov">*SEC identifier*<**/xbrli:identifier>.**
In UTX's case, it would be **<xbrli:identifier scheme**="http://www.sec.gov"> 0000101829<**/xbrli:identifier**>. If an entity is reporting to its stock exchange, it would likely use the following pattern: **<xbrli:identifier scheme**="*stock exchange URL*">*ticker symbol* <**/xbrli:identifier**>. For UTX, it would be **<xbrli:identifier scheme**="http:// www.nyse.com">UTX<**/xbrli:identifier**>. The point is, the **xbrli:entity identifier** will differ depending on the reporting purpose.

Interactive exercise 4-4: Starting with the complete root element and **link:schemaRef** element you created in Interactive exercise 4-3, open Notepad and enter the beginning **xbrli:context** element and the **xbrli:entity** element that UTX would use if it were creating this instance document for reporting to the SEC.

The next part of UTX's **xbrli:context** element in this instance document is the **xbrli:period** element. An **xbrli:period** element always starts with **<xbrli:period>** and contains either an **xbrli:instant** element for reporting a specific date or an

xbrli:startDate and an **xbrli:endDate** element combination for reporting a duration of time. Dates in XBRL instance documents are required to be in the international date format, yyyy-mm-dd. Since we are creating an instance document to report UTX's "accrued liabilities" and since this accounting concept is always reported as of a specific date, we would use the **xbrli:instant** element as follows:
<xbrli:instant>2008-06-30**</xbrli:instant>**.

Interactive exercise 4-5: Starting with the context element you created in Interactive exercise 4-4, open Notepad and enter the beginning **xbrli:period** element, with its nested **xbrli:instant** element and finish the **xbrli:context** element by adding its ending tag.

Interactive exercise 4-6: Write a complete **xbrli:context** element for UTX to use in an instance document to report income statement items (e.g. net income) for the period of time January 1, 2008 to June 30, 2008. Use a unique **xbrli:context id** and for the **xbrli:entity identifier** use their NY Stock Exchange identifier.

Answer:

____

____

____

____

____

____

____

____

An **xbrli:entity** element can also contain an optional ***segment element***; also defined in the **xbrli** namespace. The **xbrli:segment** element is used to report business segment information; such as, the operating activities of a division of a business entity. The **xbrli:segment** element always appears nested within the **xbrli:entity** element after the **xbrli:identifier** element. The **xbrli:segment** element will be covered in more detail later in this Chapter.

The unit element

The next element in an XBRL instance document is the ***unit element***. The **unit** element is also defined in the **xbrli** namespace. Its purpose is to identify the units in which a numeric item is measured. All monetary items, such as "accrued liabilities," "cost of goods sold," or "net income," are measured in a currency, whereas shares of stock or ratios are measured in "pure" numbers. At least one **xbrli:unit** element is required in every XBRL instance document that reports numeric items and it can appear anywhere in the document; though it is common practice to place the **xbrli:unit** element(s) immediately after the **xbrli:context** element(s). Each XBRL **xbrli:unit** element must have an ***id attribute*** that must be unique in the instance document because it is used for reference purposes. In addition, an **xbrli:unit** element always contains a ***measure element*** nested within it. The choice of an **id** attribute value is up to the XBRL document creator but should make sense to a human reader. For a **xbrli:unit** element to be used for a monetary item, a common practice is to use the International Standards Organization (ISO) three-letter currency abbreviation for its **id** attribute value; as in the following example.

```
<xbrli:unit  id="USD" >
  <xbrli:measure>iso4217:USD</xbrli:measure>
</xbrli:unit>
```

This a standard **xbrli:unit** element that any company reporting monetary items measured in US dollars would use in their instance document. Notice that the **xbrli:unit** element's **id** attribute is easily understood by a human. In addition, the value of the **xbrli:measure** element, iso4217:USD, refers to the ISO document numbered 4217 which defines a three-letter abbreviation for every currency in the world. A few other common currency abbreviations are EUR (Euros), JPY (Japanese Yen), CAD (Canadian Dollars), and CNY (Chinese Yuan Renminbi).

Interactive exercise 4-7: Open Notepad and enter this **xbrli:unit** element after your **xbrli:context** element.

As mentioned above, another common measure appearing in financial reports is "shares," which indicates a numeric measurement of the number of shares of stock. The standard way to indicate shares in an **xbrli:measure** element is "**xbrli:shares**." It would appear as follows:

```
<xbrli:unit id="shares" >
   <xbrli:measure>xbrli:shares</xbrli:measure>
</xbrli:unit>
```

Again, the **xbrli:unit** element's **id** attribute value, shares, is humanly understandable and the **xbrli:measure** element value, xbrli:shares, indicates that "shares" is defined in the **xbrli** namespace.

Also related to reporting stock information in financial reports, it is common to report the per share value of stock and/or the earnings per share. Both of these require an **xbrli:unit** element that defines a numerator measured in currency by a denominator measured in shares. The following example shows how this is done.

```
<xbrli:unit id= "EPS" >
    <xbrli:divide>
        <xbrli:unitNumerator>
            <xbrli:measure>iso4217:USD</xbrli:measure>
        </xbrli:unitNumerator>
        <xbrli:unitDenominator>
            <xbrli:measure>xbrli:shares</xbrli:measure>
        </xbrli:unitDenominator>
    </xbrli:divide>
</xbrli:unit>
```

Though this looks complex, it is easy to understand. Within the **xbrli:unit** element is a **xbrli:divide** element containing an **xbrli:unitNumerator** element and a **xbrli:unitDenominator** element. Together, this provides sufficient information for a human or a computer application to unambiguously interpret the EPS being reported. It is common for companies to use the **id** attribute value "EPS" or "PerShare," but remember it is up to the document creator.

XBRL items

The last element required in an XBRL instance document is at least one ***XBRL item***. An XBRL **item** is a "fact" reported in an XBRL instance document by an entity for a specific period of time. All XBRL instance documents are required to report at least one fact. So far in building this instance document we have linked it to the US GAAP v1.0 taxonomy with the **link:schemaRef** element, identified the entity and the instant of time with the **xbrli:context** element, and identified the unit of measure with the **xbrli:unit** element. All of this is metadata to be used to correctly tag the fact being reported. In the example we are building, the fact to be reported is that UTX had "accrued liabilities" of $12,304,000,000, in US dollars, as of June 30, 2008. To report this item in our XBRL instance document, we must first look up the standard element name for this accounting concept in the US GAAP taxonomy. The XBRL US home page is http://xbrl.us/Pages/default.aspx. Click US GAAP Taxonomies and you should see the US GAAP Taxonomies 1.0 and Supporting Documentation page as shown in Figure 4-3.

Figure 4-3: US GAAP Taxonomies and Supporting Documentation

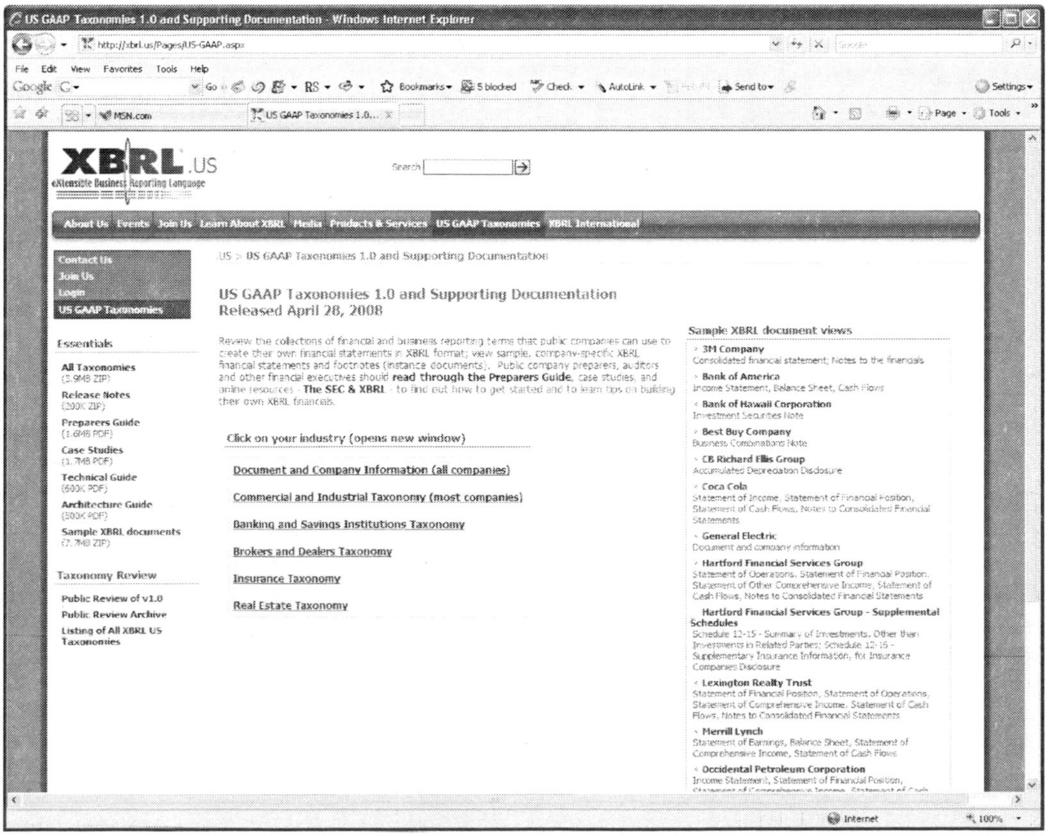

(http://xbrl.us/Pages/US-GAAP.aspx)

Since most US companies, including UTX, report under the US GAAP for Commercial and Industrial category, click the link to this taxonomy and your browser should load the new taxonomy viewer; as in Figure 4-4.

Figure 4-4: US GAAP v1.0 taxonomy viewer

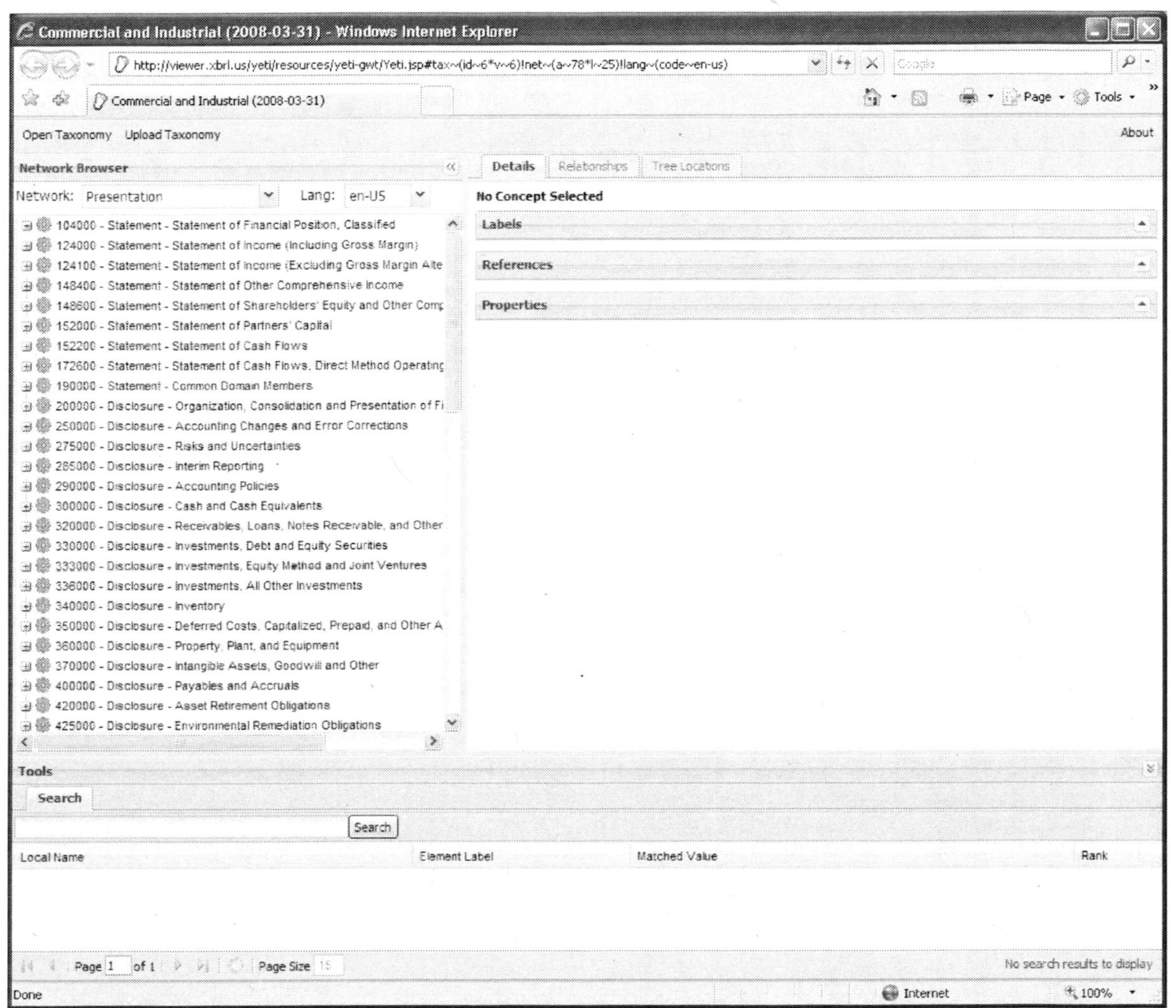

To find the specific standard element name for a concept, you can type its general name (e.g. accrued liabilities) in the search block or open the financial statement in which it is found and work your way down the hierarchy until you find it.

Interactive exercise 4-8: If you have access to a computer with an Internet connection, open the US GAAP taxonomy viewer and then type *accrued liabilities* in the search block and then click the first item in the response area. You should now see the details of this US GAAP financial reporting concept as shown in Figure 4-5.

Figure 4-5: US GAAP Accrued Liabilities

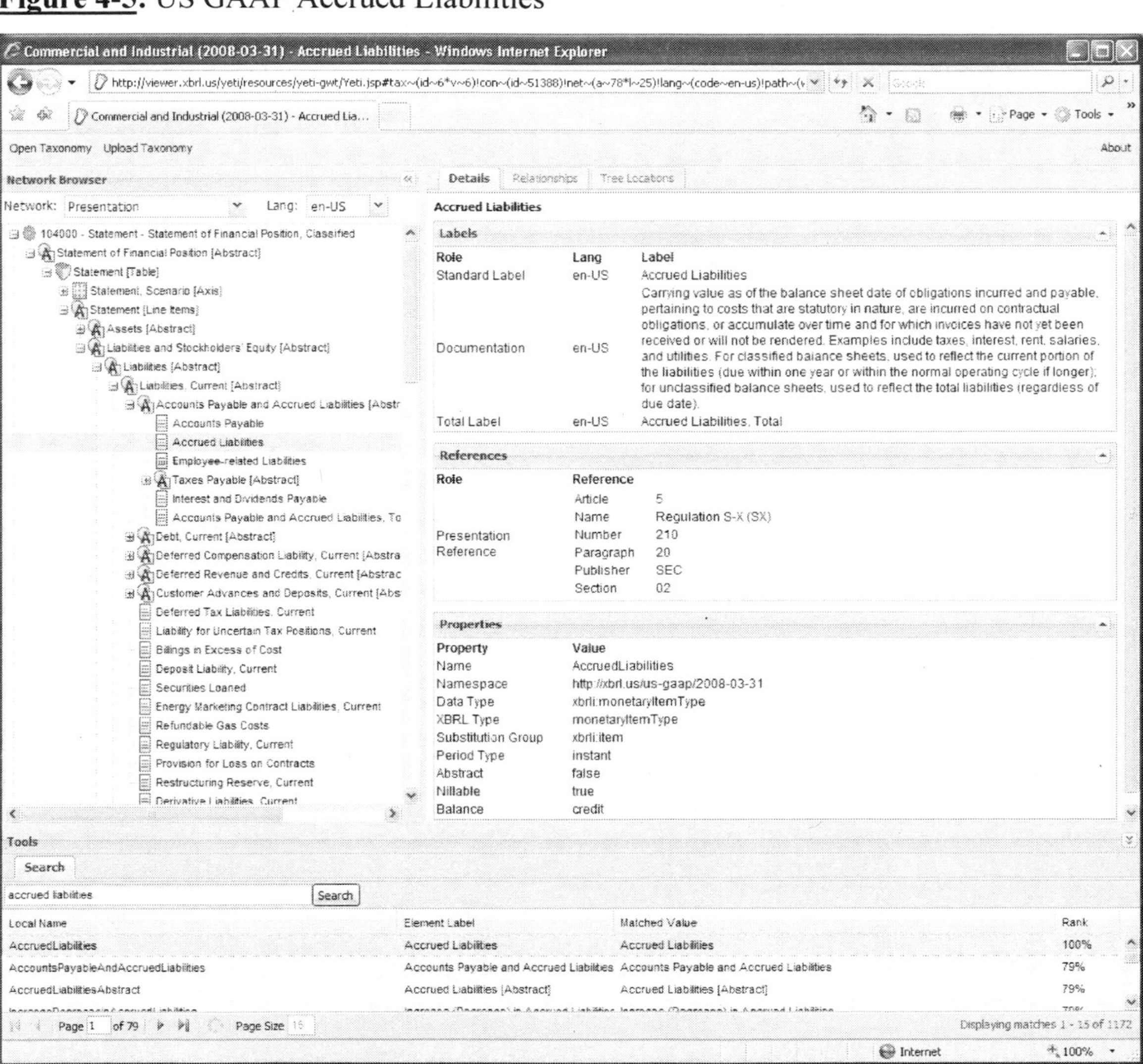

The taxonomy viewer has a left panel that shows the financial statement hierarchy in which an item is found (e.g. Accrued Liabilities is reported as a Current Liability in the Statement of Financial Position). This hierarchy looks complex because there are many sub-classifications. Notice that the majority of sub-classifications are marked with a red A in a green oval. These are referred to as "abstract" items and are used only for classification purposes (i.e. they are not element names and they are only used for classification purposes in XBRL taxonomies).

The taxonomy viewer has a right panel divided into 3 windows containing the details of the XBRL item highlighted in the left panel. The Labels window shows the Standard Label, the Documentation (also referred to as the "description"), and the Total Label for the item. The Standard Label is the standard line item text that would appear on a financial statement reporting the item and the Total Label is the standard line item text that would be used to indicate that an accumulated total is being reported. As you will see later, companies are free to use, but are not required to use, these standard labels. The Documentation describes in a sentence the detailed meaning of the financial reporting concept that the item represents. This is the most important thing to consider before deciding to use a specific element name in an XBRL instance document. Use it to decide if a specific element is appropriate for reporting a specific fact in your XBRL instance document. Below the Labels window is the References window. Here you will find references to the official accounting/financial reporting documents in which this element is defined. Below the References window is the Properties window. Here you will find the specific information necessary to use this element in an XBRL instance document. The Properties window includes the element's predefined Name, **AccruedLiabilities**, to be used in an XBRL instance document, the Namespace in which it is defined, http://xbrl.us/us-gaap/2008-03-31, and other information such as, it is a monetary item reported as of an instant in time, it is not abstract, and it normally has a credit balance. Now that we have found the element name representing this financial reporting concept, we can create the element as it would appear in this instance document.

Interactive exercise 4-9: Open Notepad and enter the following in your XBRL instance document after your **xbrli:unit** element:
<us-gaap:AccruedLiabilities contextRef="As_of_Jun30_2008" **unitRef**="USD" **decimals**="-6"> 12304000000**</us-gaap:AccruedLiabilities>**

This is a complete element reporting a business "fact" in an XBRL instance document. It looks complex but is easy to understand and is unambiguously interpretable by a human or a software application. The individual parts are as follows:

- The element name **us-gaap:AccruedLiabilities** means **AccruedLiabilities** as defined in the **us-gaap** taxonomy schema. Remember that this instance document is linked to this taxonomy schema through its **link:schemaRef** element.
- The **contextRef=**"As_of_Jun30_2008**"** attribute means that the **xbrli:context** element with **id="**As_of_Jun30_2008**"** applies to this item (e.g. **contextRef** is short for "context reference").
- The **unitRef="**USD**"** attribute means that the **xbrli:unit** element with **id="**USD**"** applies to this item (e.g. **unitRef** is short for "unit reference").
- The **decimals=**"-6" attribute means that this item is being reported "as correct to the nearest million" (i.e., count 6 spaces to the left). Each numeric item in an XBRL instance document must have a **decimals** attribute indicating the arithmetic precision of the value of the item being reported.

Figure 4-6 shows the complete XBRL instance document, with the standard version instruction and several comments added, as it would appear when processed by a browser. With the standard element name representing this accounting concept and all of the metadata surrounding the value being reported, either a human or a software application would be able to unambiguously interpret it as: "UTX Inc. is reporting that its 'accrued liabilities' is $12,304,000,000 in U.S. dollars as of June 30, 2008." In addition, a software application would be able to validate that **us-gaap:AccruedLiabilities** is defined in the US GAAP taxonomy and that the instance document follows the basic rules for all XBRL instance documents.

Figure 4-6: A complete XBRL instance document

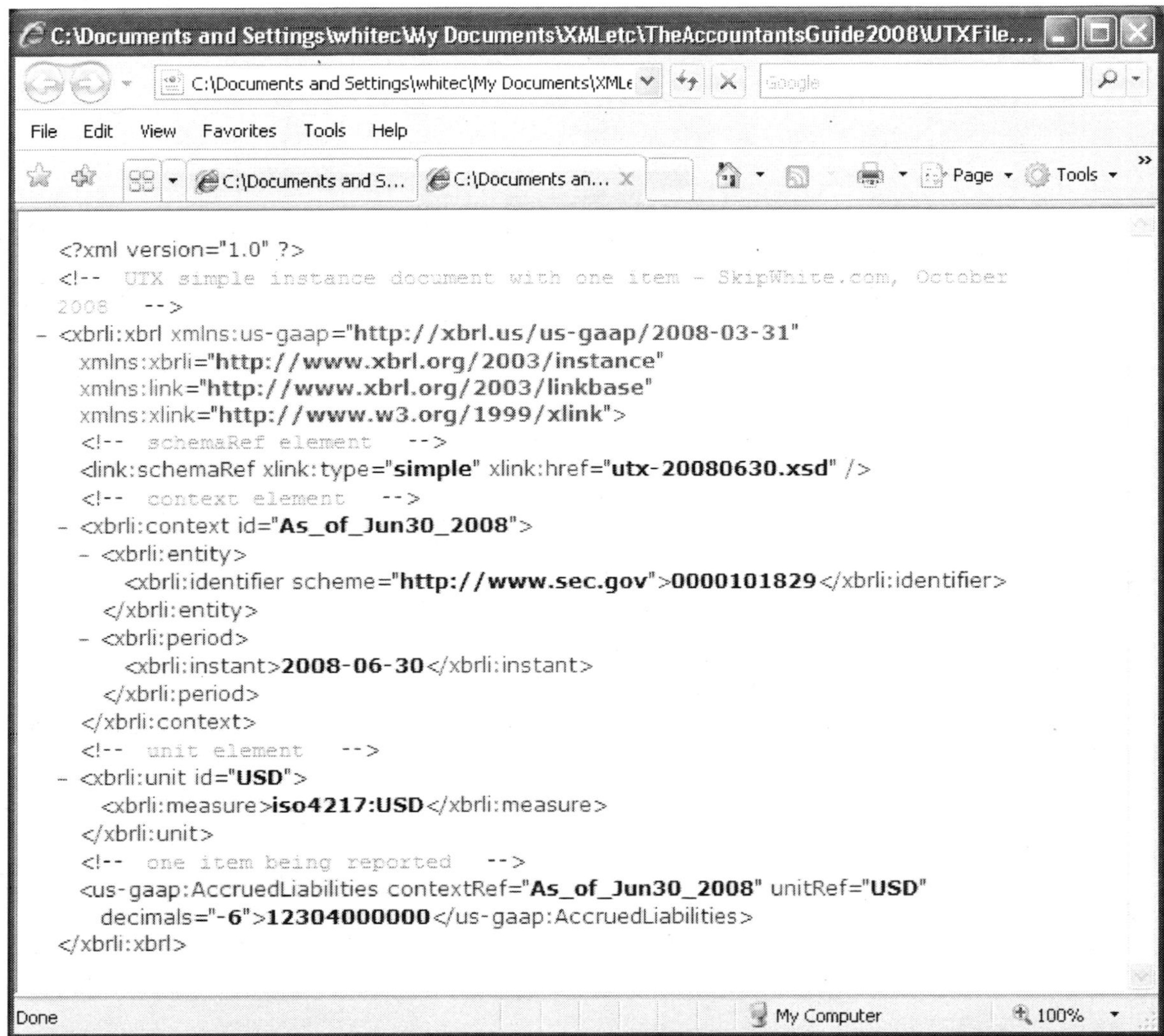


```
<?xml version="1.0" ?>
<!--  UTX simple instance document with one item - SkipWhite.com, October
2008   -->
- <xbrli:xbrl xmlns:us-gaap="http://xbrl.us/us-gaap/2008-03-31"
    xmlns:xbrli="http://www.xbrl.org/2003/instance"
    xmlns:link="http://www.xbrl.org/2003/linkbase"
    xmlns:xlink="http://www.w3.org/1999/xlink">
    <!--  schemaRef element   -->
    <link:schemaRef xlink:type="simple" xlink:href="utx-20080630.xsd" />
    <!--  context element   -->
  - <xbrli:context id="As_of_Jun30_2008">
    - <xbrli:entity>
        <xbrli:identifier scheme="http://www.sec.gov">0000101829</xbrli:identifier>
      </xbrli:entity>
    - <xbrli:period>
        <xbrli:instant>2008-06-30</xbrli:instant>
      </xbrli:period>
    </xbrli:context>
    <!--  unit element   -->
  - <xbrli:unit id="USD">
      <xbrli:measure>iso4217:USD</xbrli:measure>
    </xbrli:unit>
    <!--  one item being reported   -->
    <us-gaap:AccruedLiabilities contextRef="As_of_Jun30_2008" unitRef="USD"
      decimals="-6">12304000000</us-gaap:AccruedLiabilities>
  </xbrli:xbrl>
```

Interactive exercise 4-10: UTX also has "current assets" of $24,779,000,000 as of the same date. In the US GAAP taxonomy, find the standard element name for "current assets" then open Notepad and add this element to your UTX instance document (you can outline your answer in the space below).

Answer:

Since you are now familiar with general XML documents, UBL documents, and XBRL instance documents, you should realize that there is a pattern and a set of rules to follow when creating XBRL instance documents. The pattern and rules are as follows:

1. The instance document must start with the root element name **xbrl**. Since it is defined in the **xbrli** namespace, it will usually appear as **xbrli:xbrl**.
2. The **xbrli:xbrl** root element must contain the namespace declaration attributes necessary to support the document. The namespaces found in most current XBRL instance documents are the following:
   - **xmlns:xbrli**="http://www.xbrl.org/2003/instance" (for XBRL instance documents)
   - **xmlns:link**="http://www.xbrl.org/2003/linkbase" (for XBRL linkbases)
   - **xmlns:xlink**="http://www.w3.org/1999/xlink" (for XML XLink)
3. The **xbrli:xbrl** root element must also contain a namespace declaration attribute for at least one XBRL taxonomy (e.g. **xmlns:us-gaap**="http://xbrl.us/us-gaap/2008-03-31" - for companies reporting under US GAAP).
4. There must be at least one **xbrli:schemaRef** element as the first child element, in the following format:
   - **<link:schemaRef xlink:type=**"simple" **xlink:href="***URI of XBRL taxonomy schema***"/>**
5. There must be at least one **xbrli:context** element; by convention the **xbrli:context** element(s) appear immediately after the **link:schemaRef** element(s). It will have a unique **id** attribute starting with a letter and must contain an **xbrli:entity** element and a **xbrli:period** element. The **xbrli:entity** element must contain an **xbrli:identifier** element with a **scheme** attribute. The **xbrli:period** element must contain an **xbrli:instant** element or a **xbrli:startDate/xbrli:endDate** pair with dates in the international date format *yyyy-mm-dd.*
6. If numeric items are to being reported in the instance document, there must be at least one **xbrli:unit** element; by convention the **xbrli:unit** element(s) appear immediately after the **xbrli:context** element(s). It must have a unique **id** attribute

and <u>must</u> contain a **xbrli:measure** element in the proper format (e.g. iso4217:*currency abbreviation* <u>or</u> xbrli:shares).

7. There <u>must</u> be at least one XBRL item in the appropriate format. To find the appropriate element name to use, do the following:
   - Access the appropriate taxonomy for the entity reporting the financial information (e.g. US GAAP for any company reporting under US GAAP).
   - Locate an appropriate element name representing <u>each</u> accounting/ financial reporting concept to be reported and <u>verify</u> that it is the appropriate element to use by first reading its <u>documentation/description</u> and then looking for additional information, such as its location in a financial statement hierarchy, its reporting period type (i.e. instant or duration), its balance (i.e. debit or credit), and its data type and abstract value (i.e. abstract must be false).
   - Input the item with the appropriate **contextRef**, **unitRef**, and **decimals** attributes that apply and the value to be reported.

Every time you create an XBRL instance document, you will follow this pattern and these rules. As you will see, actual XBRL instance documents, such as SEC filings, are very complex so keeping these rules in mind will provide a foundation for understanding and interpreting them. The remainder of this Chapter is devoted to understanding the US GAAP taxonomies in more depth and the need for <u>***extension taxonomies***</u> when creating financial statements.

Understanding the US GAAP Taxonomies v1.0

The US GAAP Taxonomies v1.0 contain over 12,000 XBRL elements each representing an accounting or financial reporting concept. These are divided between elements that appear on the face of financial statements and those that appear as disclosures. Physically, the US GAAP Taxonomies v1.0 are one large file that any entity reporting under US GAAP can use to tag financial information in XBRL format. Logically, they are first subdivided into US GAAP and non-GAAP taxonomies. The US GAAP taxonomies are further subdivided into industry folders that bring together sets of related financial concepts commonly used in five industry groups; including, Banking and Savings Institutions, Brokers and Dealers, Commercial and Industrial, Insurance, and Real Estate. Each of these is referred to as an "industry entry point" because an entity reporting under US GAAP would start the preparation of their financial statements by viewing the statements, elements, and disclosures in their own specific industry. As illustrated in Figure 4-7, a bank or savings institution would "enter" the US GAAP taxonomies through the Banking and Savings Institutions folder. Here they would look for elements relevant to their type of reporting. As shown in Figure 4-7, companies in this industry use a Statement of Financial Position that is unclassified and based on deposit operations and has elements unique to their operations (e.g. **FederalHome-LoanBankStock**).

Figure 4-7: Banking and Savings Institutions entry point

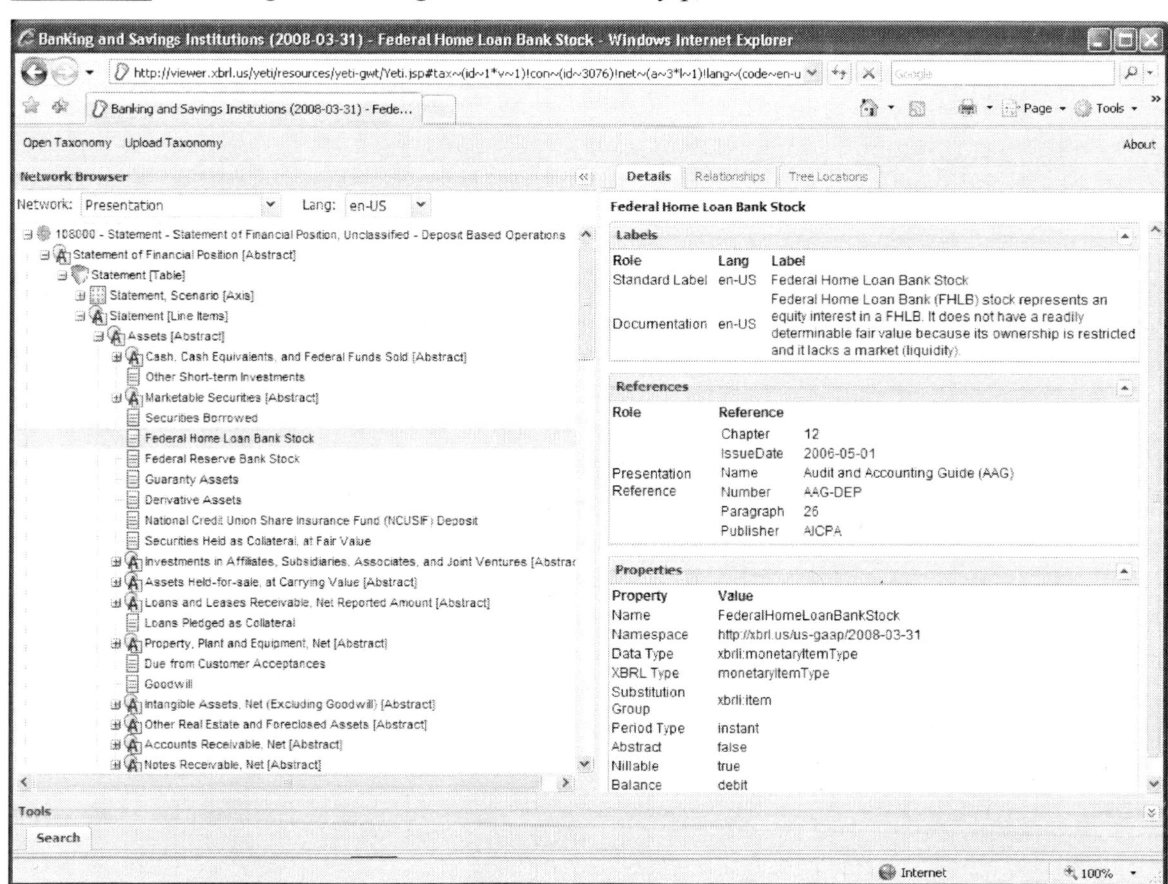

The non-GAAP taxonomies are further subdivided into the following five special purpose taxonomies:

- The Document and Entity Information taxonomy containing elements for capturing entity details such as contact names and addresses, legal entity names, and Web sites and document information such as the name and type of an instance document and periods of time that apply.
- Four report taxonomies containing elements to tag information found in each of the following reports:
    - The Accountants' Report
    - The Management Report on Internal Controls
    - The Management Discussion and Analysis
    - The SEC Officers' Certifications

A convenient way to think about the complete set of US GAAP v1.0 taxonomies is that it contains elements representing concepts for all US GAAP and SEC financial reporting disclosure requirements. Each major industry category has elements unique to its financial reporting and conventions collected in industry entry points. In addition, a single XBRL financial report may contain the primary financial statements, footnotes disclosures, an accountant's report, SEC-specific information in the form of a management report, a MD&A, and an officers' certification, and additional information about the entity and the instance document. Elements for all of these are found in the complete set of US GAAP v1.0 taxonomies.

XBRL taxonomies include schemas which define elements representing financial reporting concepts and ***linkbases*** which define the relationships between financial reporting concepts. Linkbases are written in the XLink language and describe the various relationships between accounting and financial reporting concepts. They are necessary because software applications require explicit computer-readable descriptions of how the elements in financial reports relate to each other (e.g. the presentation and calculation of Gross Profit on an Income Statement). In XBRL, there are a number of linkbases each of which describe a specific set of relationships between financial concepts; including, labels, calculation, presentation, authoritative references, and dimensions. The three most important linkbases are the Presentation, Calculation, and Dimensions linkbases. The

Presentation linkbase describes the relationships between elements as they would typically appear in published financial statements (e.g. Current assets are presented before Long-term assets in a balance sheet). The Calculation linkbase describes the mathematical relationships between elements in a taxonomy by defining how a series of elements sum up to another element (e.g. Gross profit = Revenue minus Cost of good sold). The Dimensions linkbase describes detailed information about the horizontal and vertical axes of a table in a note to the financial statements. It does this by defining tables with axes, domains, members, and line items.

The concept of dimensions is somewhat difficult to understand. It can best be explained through an example. What if MyBikes.com needs to report “Current deferred revenue” of $100,000 and “Noncurrent deferred revenue” of $40,000 on its balance sheet as of September 30, 2008, and wants to disclose in the footnotes that the “Current deferred revenue” is made up of $80,000 in “Layaway sales” and $20,000 in “Subscription arrangements” and that the “Noncurrent deferred revenue” is all “Layaway sales?” If you go to Liabilities in the Statement of Financial Position in the US GAAP taxonomy, you will find an element named **DeferredRevenueCurrent** and another named **DeferredRevenueNoncurrent** which would be used in the MyBikes.com’s instance document to report the total amounts, as in the following partial instance document:

```
<xbrli:context id="Sept30-2008">
   <xbrli:entity>
      <xbrli:identifier  scheme="www.nasdaq.com">MYBK</xbrli:identifier>
   </xbrli:entity>
   <xbrli:period>
      <xbrli:instant>2008-09-30</xbrli:instant>
   </xbrli:period>
</xbrli:context>
<us-gaap:DeferredRevenueCurrent  contextRef="Sept30-2008" unitRef="USD"
   decimals="0">100000</us-gaap:DeferredRevenueCurrent>
<us-gaap:DeferredRevenueNoncurrent  contextRef="Sept30-2008" unitRef="USD"
   decimals="0">40000</us-gaap:DeferredRevenueNoncurrent>
```

As you would expect, reporting current and noncurrent deferred revenue is straight-forward (i.e., find the appropriate element names in the US GAAP taxonomy and use them to tag the data values using a standard **context** element and **contextRef** attribute).

The footnote disclosure, however, is more complex. It involves the creation of separate **context** elements each containing a **segment** element to identify the two dimensions of deferred revenue to be reported (i.e., "Layaway sales" and "Subscription arrangement sales"). The first step is to look for predefined members of a dimension in the US GAAP taxonomy. There are approximately 60 "Disclosure" taxonomies within the US GAAP taxonomy v1.0 and one of those is Disclosure - Deferred Revenue. If you have access to a computer with an Internet connection, go to the US GAAP taxonomy viewer and find and click Disclosure – Deferred Revenue. As shown in Figure 4-8, in the Disclosure – Deferred Revenue section of the taxonomies you will find a Deferred Revenue, by Arrangement, Disclosure [Text Block] element.

Figure 4-8: Deferred Revenue, by Arrangement, Disclosure

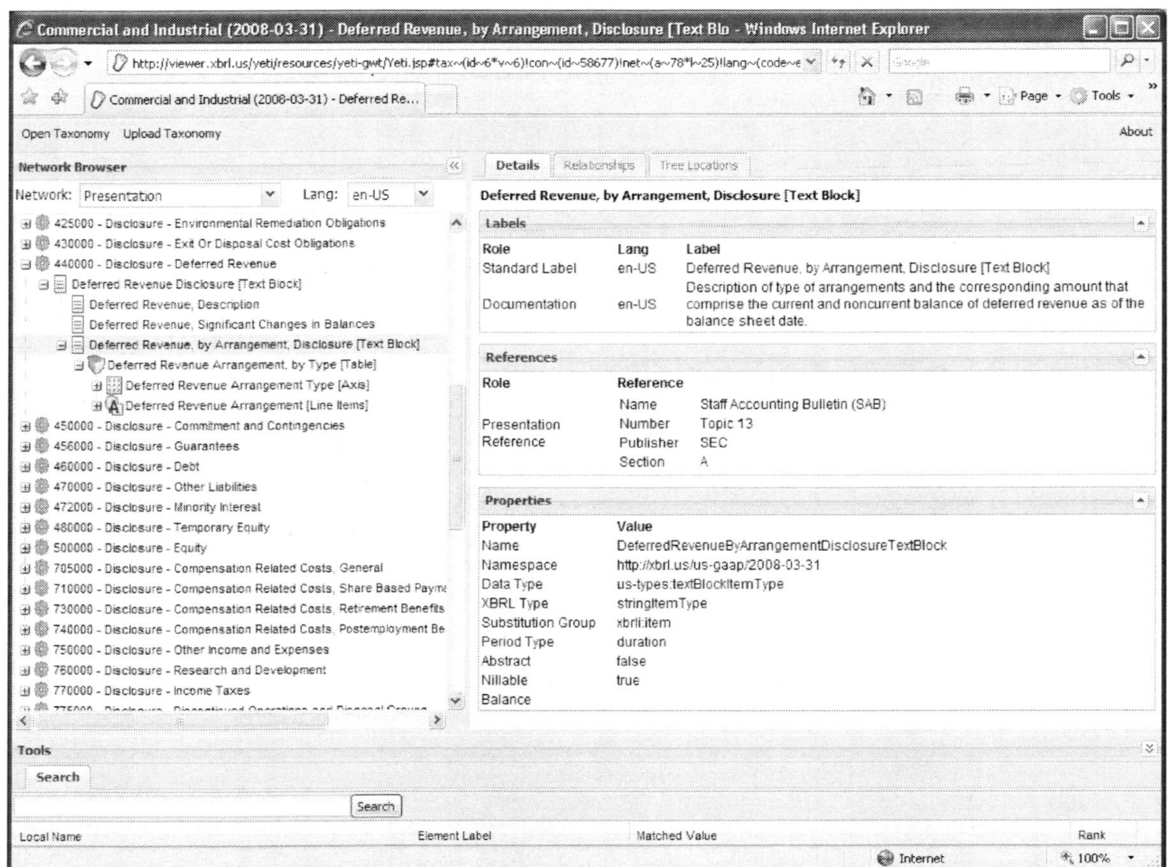

A text block is a special type of XBRL element used for grouping purposes that can appear in an instance document; it does not have a balance and is not abstract. The first child of this element is an abstract element, Deferred Revenue Arrangement, by Type

[Table], which defines a table; also referred to as a "schedule." A table/schedule is a special type of XBRL element which defines multiple dimensions that are used together to report facts in instance document disclosures. In this example, MyBikes.com wants to report that Current Deferred Revenue is made up of two dimensions, Layaway sales and Subscription arrangements and that Noncurrent Deferred Revenue is made up totally of Layaway sales. A table/schedule always has an axis, also known as a "dimension," and line items. If you click Deferred Revenue Arrangement Type [Axis] then click Deferred Revenue Arrangement Type [Domain], you will see a number of elements referred to as "Members;" meaning "members of a domain." You should now see a number of predefined domain members including Layaway Sale [Member] and Subscription Arrangement [Member] (as in Figure 4-9).

Figure 4-9: Deferred Revenue Arrangement Domain Members

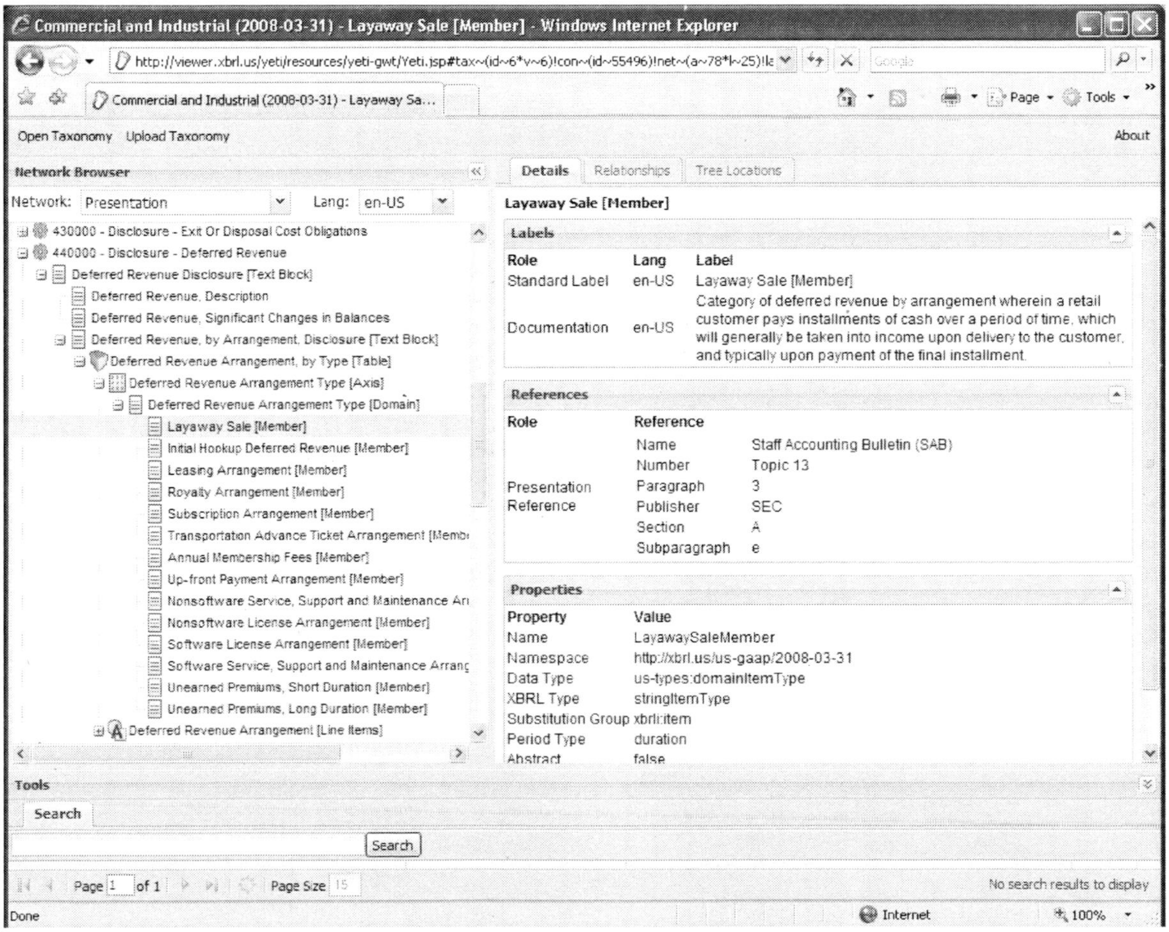

In XBRL terminology, "Deferred Revenue Arrangement Type [Axis]" is the dimension and the items we want to report values for, "Layaway Sales [Member]" and "Subscription Arrangement [Member]," are "members" which appear as column headers across the horizontal axis of a table. The vertical axis of the table is referred to as the "Line Items" and consist of Current, Noncurrent, and Total Deferred Revenue. Figure 4-10 is a rendering of the disclosure table that MyBikes.com wants to include in its footnotes.

Figure 4-10: Deferred Revenue disclosure/table (rendered in a Web browser)

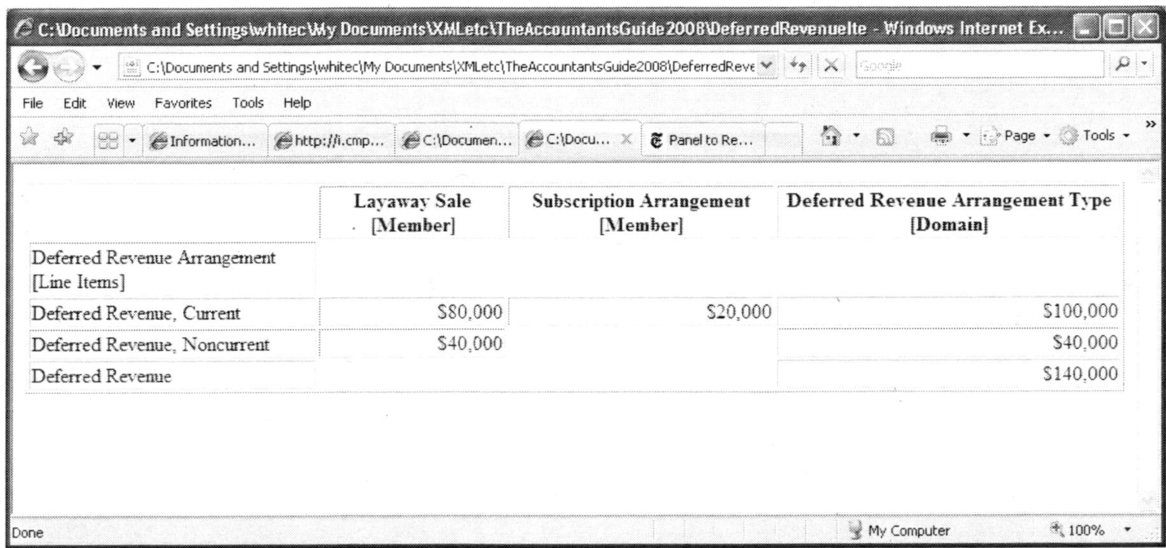

	Layaway Sale [Member]	Subscription Arrangement [Member]	Deferred Revenue Arrangement Type [Domain]
Deferred Revenue Arrangement [Line Items]			
Deferred Revenue, Current	$80,000	$20,000	$100,000
Deferred Revenue, Noncurrent	$40,000		$40,000
Deferred Revenue			$140,000

To include this information in their instance document, MyBikes.com must set up two additional **context** elements each with a **segment** element to identify each of the domain members. The following **context** element illustrates how this would be done for the first domain member, Layaway sales.

```
<xbrli:context id="LayawaySaleSept30-2008">
    <xbrli:entity>
        <xbrli:identifier  scheme="www.nasdaq.com">MYBK</xbrli:identifier>
        &lt;xbrli:segment&gt;
            <xbrldi:explicitMember
              dimension="us-gaap:DeferredRevenueArrangementTypeAxis">
              us-gaap:LayawaySaleMember</xbrldi:explicitMember>
         &lt;/xbrli:segment&gt;
    </xbrli:entity>
    <xbrli:period>
        <xbrli:instant>2008-09-30</xbrli:instant>
   </xbrli:period>
</xbrli:context>
```

The **xbrli:context** element has an **id** with a unique identifier, "LayawaySaleSept30-2008", that differentiates it from the more standard **xbrli:context id**="Sept30-2008" used earlier. Note that as the author of this instance document, I chose these **id** values – there is no standard rule except that it must start with a letter. Next, the **xbrli:context** element has a standard **xbrli:identifier** element and an **xbrli:segment** element with an **xbrli:explicitMember** child element. This element is where the dimension and member are defined through the **dimension**="us-gaap:DeferredRevenueArrangementTypeAxis" attribute and the **xbrli:explicitMember** value "us-gaap:LayawaySaleMember". Notice that both of these are predefined in the US GAAP taxonomy (see Figure 4-9) and we simply chose to use them.

After creating this **xbrli:context** element we can use it's id to report current and noncurrent deferred revenue from Layaway sales as follows:

```
<us-gaap:DeferredRevenueCurrent  contextRef="LayawaySaleSept30-2008"
  unitRef="USD"  decimals="0">80000</us-gaap:DeferredRevenueCurrent>
<us-gaap:DeferredRevenueNoncurrent  contextRef="LayawaySaleSept30-2008"
  unitRef="USD" decimals="0">40000</us-gaap:DeferredRevenueNoncurrent>
```

These items can be unambiguously interpreted by a human or software as MyBikes.com is reporting that "current deferred revenue from layaway sales as of September 30, 2008 is $80,000" and "noncurrent deferred revenue from layaway sales as of September 30, 2008 is $40,000."

Xbrli:segment elements and their **xbrli:explicitMember** elements are somewhat complex because they are designed to be flexible so that companies can use them to report financial and performance information for any and all segments of their business and so that the reported information can be put into tables and used to analyze dimensional performance. As with deferred revenue, there are many predefined dimensions in the US GAAP taxonomy. In addition, there are predefined segments in which entities are expected to add their own unique information, see the Disclosure – Segment Reporting taxonomy in the US GAAP taxonomy for example. This taxonomy provides structure which would be used by an entity to report information for identifiable reporting segments no matter how the entity is organized (i.e. by products, geographic regions, regulatory environments, or operating segments).

<u>Interactive exercise 4-11</u>: Open the US GAAP taxonomy viewer and go to Disclosure – Deferred Revenue (as in Figure 4-9). Using as examples the **xbrli:context** element with **id=**"LayawaySaleSept30-2008**"** and the reported **us-gaap:DeferredRevenueCurrent** with the **contextRef=**"LayawaySaleSept30-2008**"**, write an **xbrli:context** and item to set up the Subscription arrangement domain member and use it to report that **us-gaap:DeferredRevenueCurrent** from Subscription arrangement is $20,000.

____

____

____

____

____

____

____

____

____

____

____

____

____

____

Extension Taxonomies

There are over 12,000 elements representing accounting and financial reporting concepts in the US GAAP v1.0 taxonomy. However, the current state of development of the XBRL taxonomies is that they cannot be expected to meet the precise needs of every individual entity in every financial reporting situation. As such, XBRL is designed to be extensible, allowing instance document preparers to create extension taxonomies that add information to the publicly available US GAAP and other XBRL taxonomies. It is expected that extension taxonomies will need to be created by all companies filing financial statements with the SEC and that the extensions will be necessary for a variety of reasons. They are referred to as "extension taxonomies" because they "add to" the standard, publicly available taxonomies. As you will see, some extensions will not create comparability and reuse issues while others will.

The first rule that every US GAAP XBRL instance document author is expected to follow is to use elements from the XBRL US GAAP taxonomy whenever possible. In other words, if a financial reporting concept in the US GAAP taxonomy is similar to one that you are going to report, use it. In reporting to the SEC, companies have been known to define new elements in an extension taxonomy schema simply because the wording did not meet their expectations; they defined a new element named **OtherCurrentPrepaid-Expenses**, instead of using **us-gaap:OtherPrepaidExpensesCurrent**. This should be avoided at all costs because it affects the comparability of financial reports between different companies. Remember that the most important thing to consider when determining whether to use an existing element from the US GAAP taxonomy is its description/definition.

The second rule that every US GAAP XBRL instance document author should follow is that if you have a commonly reported item, such as "Cash and cash equivalents," use the element defined in the US GAAP taxonomy even if the element name and/or standard label are not exactly what you like. For example, in the US GAAP taxonomy "Cash and cash equivalents" is defined with the element name, **CashAndCashEquivalentsAt-**

CarryingValue, with the standard label, "Cash and Cash Equivalents, at Carrying Value." The appropriate solution is to use the standard element name in your instance document but change the "preferred" label to be used when rendering the information. Standard labels are contained in the "Labels linkbase" and are easily changed using an XBRL taxonomy tool such as Rivet Dragon Tag or Fujitsu XWand; tools will be discussed in more detail in Chapter 6. Doing so means that the reported item in an instance document is comparable to the same item in other instance documents and that you can render it with your own preferred label.

The third rule that every US GAAP XBRL instance document author should follow is that if you do not find an element where you would expect to find it in the US GAAP taxonomy, look for it in the appropriate disclosure section. For example, under inventory in the US GAAP taxonomy you will find the elements **InventoryFinishedGoods** and **InventoryWorkInProcess** but not **InventoryFinishedGoodsAndWorkInProcess**. If you typically report this combination on your balance sheet, you might think that you will have to define a new element for this purpose. However, if you look in the Disclosure – Inventory section of the US GAAP taxonomy, you will find the element **Inventory-FinishedGoodsAndWorkInProcess** defined. With an XBRL taxonomy tool, it is trivial to move this item from the disclosure section to the balance sheet section of the US GAAP taxonomy. The tool will take care of changing the calculation and presentation relationships in the associated linkbases and the resulting extension taxonomy will still contain comparable items to the standard US GAAP taxonomy. This will be demonstrated in Chapter 6.

The fourth rule that every US GAAP XBRL instance document author should follow is that when dimensional reporting is called for, use the existing predefined dimensions whenever possible. As was demonstrated with deferred revenue in the last section, many predefined dimensions exist for commonly reported items. In addition, the US GAAP taxonomy has predefined dimension structures to be used for common entity-specific dimensional reporting.

The fifth rule that every US GAAP XBRL instance document author should follow is that when an entity creates an extension taxonomy, it should be named properly and it's taxonomy schema should be referenced in the **link:schemaRef** element in the instance document that it supports. As with the standard US GAAP XBRL v1.0 taxonomy, an extension taxonomy always consist of several files; including a taxonomy schema and its linkbases (i.e., labels, presentation, calculation, dimensions, and references linkbases). These files should all be accessible by way of a unique namespace. For US SEC filings, the following namespace naming convention has been adopted: http://xbrl.*CompanyName*.com/*year* (e.g. http://xbrl.*MyBikes*.com/*2008)*. The namespace should also have a preferred prefix that indicates the company's name; a ticker symbol is often used. In addition, an extension taxonomy should import at least one US GAAP entry point taxonomy schema. Further, the extension taxonomy schema should be named as follows: *tickerSymbolMoreLetters-FilingPeriodDate*.xsd (e.g. mbkcorp-20081231.xsd). For SEC filings, always check the latest version of the SEC's EDGAR Filing Manual for the latest information on files and naming conventions.

Summary

XBRL instance documents are a class of XML documents that follow the basic rules of XML and the rules described in the XBRL Specification 2.1. XBRL instance documents are reports that contain facts, generically referred to as "items," reported by a specific entity at a specific point in time. XBRL instance documents have a prescribed set of elements and a prescribed format:

- The root element is **xbrl**. The root element will contain all applicable namespace declaration attributes.
- The first child element is a **link:schemaRef** element. It is required to have two attributes: **xlink:type="**simple**"** and **xlink:href="**the URI of a taxonomy schema**"**. There can be more than one **link:schemaRef** element and they can be followed by **link:linkbaseRef** elements.
- It must have at least one **xbrli:context** element that must contain an **xbrli:entity** element and a **xbrli:period** element. It can optionally contain a **xbrli:segment** element.

- If numeric items are being reported, it must contain a **xbrli:unit** element with an appropriate measure element.
- It must have at least one **item**. The name of the item must be defined as an element in one of the taxonomy schemas identified in a **link:schemaRef** element. The **item** must also have a **contextRef** attribute and if it is numeric, a **unitRef** and a **decimals** attribute.

In this Chapter, we introduced and used the US GAAP XBRL v1.0 taxonomy. Physically it is one large file which defines over 12,000 elements each representing an accounting or financial reporting concept. Logically, it is divided into US GAAP taxonomies for financial reporting and non-GAAP taxonomies for accountants' report, management discussion and analysis, report on internal controls reporting, and SEC officer certifications. The US GAAP taxonomies are logically subdivided into industry "entry points;" including Banking and Savings Institutions, Brokers and Dealers, Commercial and Industrial, Insurance, and Real Estate. As of this writing, December 2008, XBRL US has released for review and public discussion a new draft of the XBRL US GAAP taxonomies. The public comment period ends January 15, 2009 and it is expected that the new taxonomies will be available in February 2009.

Since XBRL instance documents are designed to hold data in a specific context and be processed by software applications, they make possible electronic reporting of financial performance in a standardized format using standardized, predefined terms. When adopted by a critical mass of business entities, the result will be more easily understandable and comparable financial performance reports. From an efficiency perspective, XBRL reporting has major benefits, including the reuse of information for a variety of purposes. Creating quarterly or annual financial statements in XBRL format, for example, allows them to be submitted to regulatory authorities like the SEC, posted to Web sites, and distributed to shareholders without re-entry or human processing. Such applications require transforming the XBRL instance documents into other forms, covered in Chapter 5.

Like all XML documents, XBRL instance documents can be validated. However, XBRL validation occurs on several levels and XBRL validation software tools are not free. As with UBL, XBRL instance documents can be validated against a specific document schema using an open source validation tool, such as the DecisionSoft Schema Validator. But this is only the first stage of XBRL validation. Full scale XBRL instance document validation requires the following additional steps:

- Following the link (i.e. **xlink:href=**"xxx") in the **link:schemaRef** element to verify that every element that appears in the instance document is defined in a valid XBRL taxonomy schema.
- Validating against the **xbrli** document schema.
- Validating relationships, calculations, and dimensions against the linkbases.

Together, these additional validation requirements make XBRL instance document validation a complex process requiring access to specialized validation software. There are now a number of XBRL document creation and validation software packages but none of them are free. Several are discussed in more detail in Chapter 6.

Glossary of new terms introduced in Chapter 4

context element: Sets the context for an XBRL instance document. At least one context element is required in each XBRL instance document. It must contain an id attribute for reference purposes, an entity element to identify the entity doing the reporting, and a period element to identify the period of time involved:

<context id= "*a unique context identifier*" >
<entity> <identifier> *a unique entity identifier*</identifier> </entity>
<period> <instant> *a specific date* </instant> </period>
</context>

entity element: Identifies the entity doing the reporting in an XBRL instance document. It must contain an identifier element with a scheme attribute:

<entity>
<identifier scheme="*a scheme identifier*"> *a unique entity identifier*</identifier>
</entity>

It can also contain a <scenario> element with values such as budgeted, restated, pro forma, etc.

Extension taxonomies: XBRL taxonomies created by an entity when necessary to add information and/or define elements representing accounting or financial reporting concepts not found in the standard XBRL taxonomies.

id attribute: Required on both the context and unit elements in an XBRL instance document. It is used for reference purposes on individual XBRL items reported in the instance document.

identifier element: Required child element of an entity element. It must contain a scheme attribute and a value that uniquely identifies the entity doing the reporting:
<identifier scheme= "*a scheme identifier*"> *a unique entity identifier* </identifier>

Instance documents: Well-formed XML documents that follow the rules for the class of documents known as XBRL instance documents as defined in the XBRL Specification.

Linkbases: Define presentation, calculation, and dimensions of XBRL financial statements. They are written in the XML XLink language.

measure element: Required child element of a unit element. It identifies a specific unit of measure for numeric items in an XBRL instance document and is required to have the form: <measure> *a specific unit of measure* </measure>.

period element: Identifies the period of time for which items are being reported in an XBRL instance document. It must contain either an instant element or elements to identify a duration of time:

<period>
<instant> *a specific date* </instant> </period>

Or

<period>
<startDate> *a specific date* </startDate>
<endDate> *a specific date* </endDate> </period>

Or – it can contain a <forever> element for long-lived items.

schemaRef element: First child element of the xbrl root element in an XBRL instance document. It must have two XLink attributes: <schemaRef xlink:type="simple" xlink:href="*the URI of an XBRL taxonomy schema*"/>

scheme attribute: A required attribute in the entity **identifier** element. It is used to identify the scheme associated with an **identifier** element's value and should reflect the reporting purpose (e.g. www.sec.gov).

segment element: An optional element used for reporting information specific to a segment of a business entity. It always appears in the **context** element after the **identifier** element.

Taxonomy schema: Taxonomy that lists elements used for a specific reporting purpose and written in the XML Schema language.

unit element: Identifies the unit of measure that applies to numeric items in an XBRL instance document. It must contain an id attribute for reference purposes and a measure element: <unit id= "*a unique unit identifier*"> <measure> *a specific unit of measure* </measure> </unit>

XBRL instance documents: XML documents that follow the rules specified in the XBRL Specification v2.1. They contain facts as values of accounting or financial reporting concepts and are reported by an entity at a specific point in time in a specific currency.

XBRL taxonomies: Define the accounting or financial reporting concepts used in XBRL instance documents to report facts. They are written in the XML Schema language.

XBRL item: Business fact reported in an XBRL instance document. Each item is defined in an XBRL taxonomy schema and appears in an instance document with meta-data attributes as follows:
<*prefix*:*xbrl element name from taxonomy* contextRef="*id*" unitRef="*id*" decimal="*value*" **or** precision="*a precision indicator*">
value of xbrl item being reported </*prefix*:*xbrl element name from taxonomy*>

Exercises

Exercise 4-1: MyBikes.com, MYBK on NASDAQ, must report to their bank at the end of each quarter their Current Asset and Liability information using the guidelines for U.S. GAAP Commercial & Industrial companies. Using the following information, create an XBRL instance document to report Current Assets and Liabilities for MyBikes as of 12/31/2007.

MyBikes.com – as of December 31, 2007 in U.S. Dollars:

Cash and cash equivalents	5,393,000
Short term investments	693,000
Accounts receivable, net	6,240,000
Inventory, net	7,954,000
Other current assets	947,000
Total current assets	$21,227,000
Accounts payable	5,481,000
Short-term loans and notes payable	971,000
Interest and dividends payable	78,000
Taxes payable	923,000
Other current liabilities	879,000
Total current liabilities	$8,332,000

Using Notepad or your favorite editor, build a complete XBRL instance document to report MyBikes.com Current Assets and Liabilities and save it with an appropriate name and a **.xml** extension. Test it to make sure it is well-formed by opening it in IE.

Hint: To complete this exercise you must go to the U.S. GAAP taxonomy and look up the appropriate element names (as demonstrated in the text).

Exercise 4-2: XBRL instance documents often have data from more than one time period and/or type of time period – instant versus duration. Each different time period requires a separate **context** element, with a unique **id** attribute, and you have to be careful that each reported item has the appropriate **contextRef** attribute. Starting with the XBRL instance document you created in Exercise 4-1, add the following information representing MyBikes.com's Operations information for 9/30/2007 to 12/31/2007.

Hint: it is common practice to add new context elements either directly before or after the existing context element(s). The actual items reporting the Operations information can appear anywhere in the document. Save it with an appropriate name and a **.xml** extension. Test it by opening it in IE to make sure it is well-formed.

MyBikes.com – for September 30, 2007 to December 31, 2007 in U.S. Dollars:

Sales from goods – net	$4,895,000
Sales from services – net	561,000
Operating revenue	5,456,000
Cost of goods and services	3,169,000
Gross profit	2,287,000
Selling and general admin exp.	657,000
Operating income	$1,630,000

Exercise 4-3: As of this writing, the SEC has proposed to require companies to include footnote disclosures by tagging blocks of text in XBRL instance documents. The US GAAP XBRL taxonomy includes many disclosure taxonomies which define elements to use for this purpose. In this exercise you will add footnotes related to revenue recognition to the instance document you created in Exercise 4-2. The following is the revenue recognition disclosure information that MyBikes.com needs to include with its operations income report.

General principles of revenue recognition:
The Company sells a wide range of products to a diversified base of customers around the world and has no material concentration of credit risk. Revenue is recognized when the risks and rewards of ownership have substantively transferred to customers. This condition normally is met when the product has been delivered or upon performance of services. Sales, use, value-added and other excise taxes are not recognized in revenue.

Revenue reduction policies:
The Company records estimated reductions to revenue for customer and distributor incentives, such as rebates, at the time of the initial sale. The estimated reductions are based on the sales terms, historical experience, trend analysis and projected market conditions in the various markets served.

Instructions: Starting with the XBRL instance document you created in Exercise 4-2, look up the appropriate element names and use them to tag the two revenue policies footnote disclosures. Hint: You will find the appropriate element names by looking for "Revenue Recognition, Policy" within the Disclosure – Accounting Policies taxonomy, which is part of the US GAAP Commercial & Industrial Taxonomy. Remember, these items are blocks of text so you need only the appropriate **contextRef** attribute in your instance document; you do not need a **unitRef** or **decimals** attribute

Downloadable files:

Available from: www.SkipWhite.com/Guide2008/Chapter4/ *file name*:

- File name: XbrlShell (Figure 4-1) http://www.skipwhite.com/Guide2008/Chapter4/XbrlShell.xml

References & more information:

XBRL International (http://www.xbrl.org/Home/)

XBRL Specification 2.1, 2005-11-07 (http://www.xbrl.org/Specification/XBRL-RECOMMENDATION-2003-12-31+Corrected-Errata-2005-11-07.htm)

XML Schema Tutorial, W3Schools (http://www.w3schools.com/schema/default.asp)

Answers:

Interactive exercise 4-2: Starting with the root element and the first two namespace declarations you created in Interactive exercise 4-1, open Notepad and enter the above two additional namespace declarations in your file. That is, create a complete XBRL root element with namespace declarations for this reporting application.

```
<xbrli:xbrl xmlns:us-gaap="http://xbrl.us/us-gaap/2008-03-31"
 xmlns:xbrli="http://www.xbrl.org/2003/instance"
 xmlns:link="http://www.xbrl.org/2003/linkbase"
 xmlns:xlink="http://www.w3.org/1999/xlink">
```

<u>Interactive exercise 4-4</u>: Starting with the complete root element and **link:schemaRef** element you created in Interactive exercise 4-3, open Notepad and enter the beginning **xbrli:context** element and the **xbrli:entity** element that UTX would use if it were creating this instance document for reporting to the SEC.

```
<xbrli:xbrl xmlns:us-gaap="http://xbrl.us/us-gaap/2008-03-31"
 xmlns:xbrli="http://www.xbrl.org/2003/instance"
 xmlns:link="http://www.xbrl.org/2003/linkbase"
 xmlns:xlink="http://www.w3.org/1999/xlink">
  <!-- schemaRef element -->
  <link:schemaRef xlink:type="simple" xlink:href= "http://xbrl.us/us-gaap/1.0/elts/
      us-gaap-std-2008-03-31.xsd"/>
  <!-- context element -->
  <xbrli:context id="As_of_Jun30_2008">
    <xbrli:entity>
      <xbrli:identifier scheme="http://www.sec.gov">0000101829</xbrli:identifier>
    </xbrli:entity>
```

<u>Interactive exercise 4-5</u>: Starting with the context element you created in Interactive exercise 4-4, open Notepad and enter the beginning **xbrli:period** element, with its nested **xbrli:instant** element and finish the **xbrli:context** element by adding its ending tag.

```
<xbrli:xbrl xmlns:us-gaap="http://xbrl.us/us-gaap/2008-03-31"
 xmlns:xbrli="http://www.xbrl.org/2003/instance"
 xmlns:link="http://www.xbrl.org/2003/linkbase"
 xmlns:xlink="http://www.w3.org/1999/xlink">
  <!-- schemaRef element -->
  <link:schemaRef xlink:type="simple" xlink:href= "http://xbrl.us/us-gaap/1.0/elts/
      us-gaap-std-2008-03-31.xsd"/>
  <!-- context element -->
  <xbrli:context id="As_of_Jun30_2008">
    <xbrli:entity>
      <xbrli:identifier scheme="http://www.sec.gov">0000101829</xbrli:identifier>
    </xbrli:entity>
    <xbrli:period
      <xbrli:instant>2008-06-30</xbrli:instant>
    </xbrli:period>
  </xbrli:context>
```

Interactive exercise 4-6: Write a complete **xbrli:context** element for UTX to use in an instance document to report income statement items (e.g. net income) for the period of time January 1, 2008 to June 30, 2008. Use a unique **xbrli:context id** and for the **xbrli:entity identifier** use their NY Stock Exchange identifier.

```
<xbrli:context id="From_Jan_1_to_Jun_30_2008">
  <xbrli:entity>
   <xbrli:identifier scheme="http://www.nyse.com">UTX</xbrli:identifier>
  </xbrli:entity>
  <xbrli:period
    <xbrli:startDate>2008-01-01</xbrli:startDate>
    <xbrli:endDate>2008-06-30</xbrli:endDate>
  </xbrli:period>
 </xbrli:context>
```

Interactive exercise 4-10: UTX also has “current assets” of $24,779,000,000 as of the same date. In the US GAAP taxonomy, find the standard element name for “current assets” then open Notepad and add this element to your UTX instance document (you can outline your answer in the space below).

```
<us-gaap:AssetsCurrent contextRef="As_of_Jun30_2008" unitRef="USD"
decimals="-6">24779000000</us-gaap:AssetsCurrent>
```

Interactive exercise 4-11: Open the US GAAP taxonomy viewer and go to Disclosure – Deferred Revenue (as in Figure 4-9). Using as examples the **xbrli:context** element with **id=**"LayawaySaleSept30-2008" and the reported **us-gaap:DeferredRevenueCurrent** with the **contextRef=**"LayawaySaleSept30-2008", write an **xbrli:context** and item to set up the Subscription arrangement domain member and use it to report that **us-gaap:DeferredRevenueCurrent** from Subscription arrangement is $20,000.

```
<!-- Context element -->
<xbrli:context id="SubscriptionArrangementSept30-2008">
    <xbrli:entity>
        <xbrli:identifier  scheme="www.nasdaq.com">MYBK</xbrli:identifier>
        &lt;xbrli:segment&gt;
            <xbrldi:explicitMember
              dimension="us-gaap:DeferredRevenueArrangementTypeAxis">
              us-gaap:SubscriptionArrangementMember</xbrldi:explicitMember>
         &lt;/xbrli:segment&gt;
    </xbrli:entity>
    <xbrli:period>
        <xbrli:instant>2008-09-30</xbrli:instant>
   </xbrli:period>
</xbrli:context>
<!-- Item -->
<us-gaap:DeferredRevenueCurrent  contextRef="SubscriptionArrangementSept30-
2008"  unitRef="USD"  decimals="0">20000</us-gaap:DeferredRevenueCurrent>
```

The Accountant's Guide to XBRL

Chapter 5: Transforming Documents with XSLT

Overview

This chapter describes the basics of the Extensible Stylesheet Language for Transformations (XSLT) and its role in processing XML documents for presentation and other business purposes.

As you know, XML documents are meant to be read by software applications. Though easily understood, they are tedious at best for humans to read. In fact, one of the major benefits of tagging data using standardized vocabularies like UBL and XBRL is that the instance documents can be read, validated, and transmitted over networks completely by software applications. Humans do not need to be involved. XML documents tend to be long-lived and are frequently "transformed" to serve any number of purposes, one of which is presentation for human consumption. Transformation means to change the structure and markup of an XML document so that it can serve another purpose, such as presentation as a Web page, without human intervention. The ***Extensible Stylesheet Language for Transformations (XSLT)*** is a subset of the XSL language that is used for performing transformations on XML documents. XSLT is one of the most useful pieces of the XML foundation because it can be used to transform any XML document into a presentation format, such as HTML or PDF, and to rearrange and combine any number of data items from any XML documents into other XML documents.

To help you become familiar with the basics of the XSLT language, we will first develop an example of XSLT instructions to transform an XML document into an ***XHTML*** Web page. HTML is the language used to create Web pages and an XHTML Web page is one that follows the basic rules of XML and is well-formed. We will then build on this example with more complex e-business examples of XSLT transformations using UBL instance documents to complete several typical e-business events.

The Basic XSLT Language

The basic XSLT language is a very simple "scripting" language used to create stylesheets to transform XML documents into another form. ***Stylesheet*** is an old term referring to the fact that XSLT scripts govern how an XML document is to be transformed (styled). A ***scripting language*** is one that is "interpreted" by a software processor at the time that it is being read by the processor rather than compiled ahead of time. So, an XSLT processor is an XML processor that can understand the XSLT language and can use an XSLT script to transform an XML document. An XSLT processor is software, such as the Internet Explorer or other current browser, that can take as input an XSLT document, also referred to as a "transformation script," and an XML document, referred to as a "source document," and create an output XML document, referred to as a "result document." Figure 5-1illustrates these relationships.

Figure 5-1: Transformation with XSLT

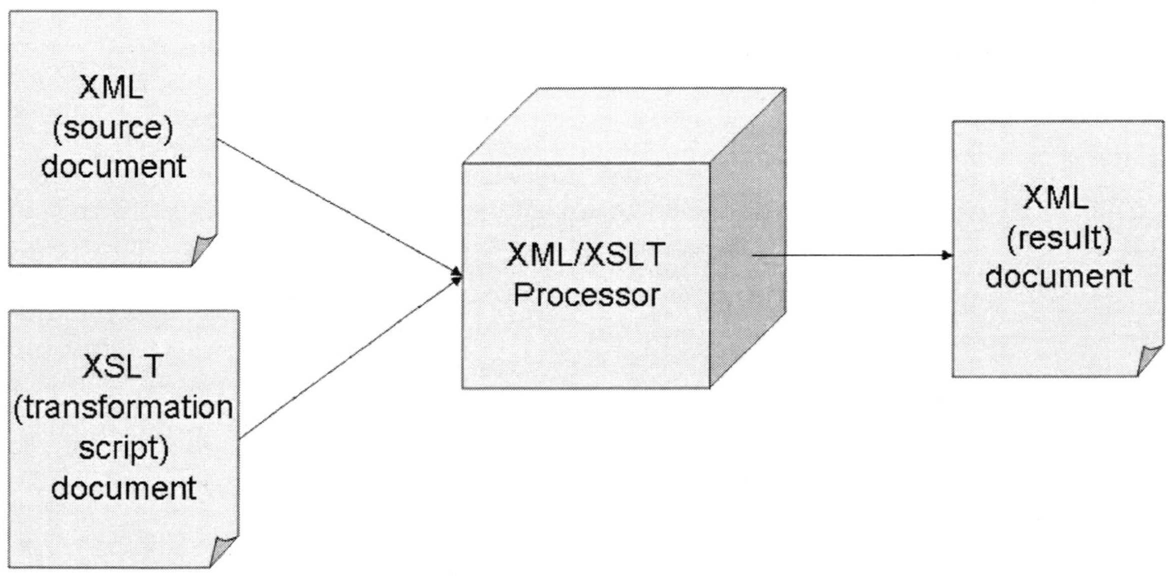

As you learned in Chapter 2, all XML documents must conform to a simple set of rules in order to be well-formed. The first rule is that every XML document must have one and only one root element. The second rule is that all other elements in an XML document must be properly nested. Starting with the root element, you can represent any XML document as a tree of nodes with each element being a node in the "node tree." The root node is at the base of the tree and its children and children's children are the branches of the tree. Figure 5-2B is a node tree representation of the collapsed UBL Catalogue in Figure 5-2A.

Figure 5-2A: A UBL Catalogue document (collapsed)

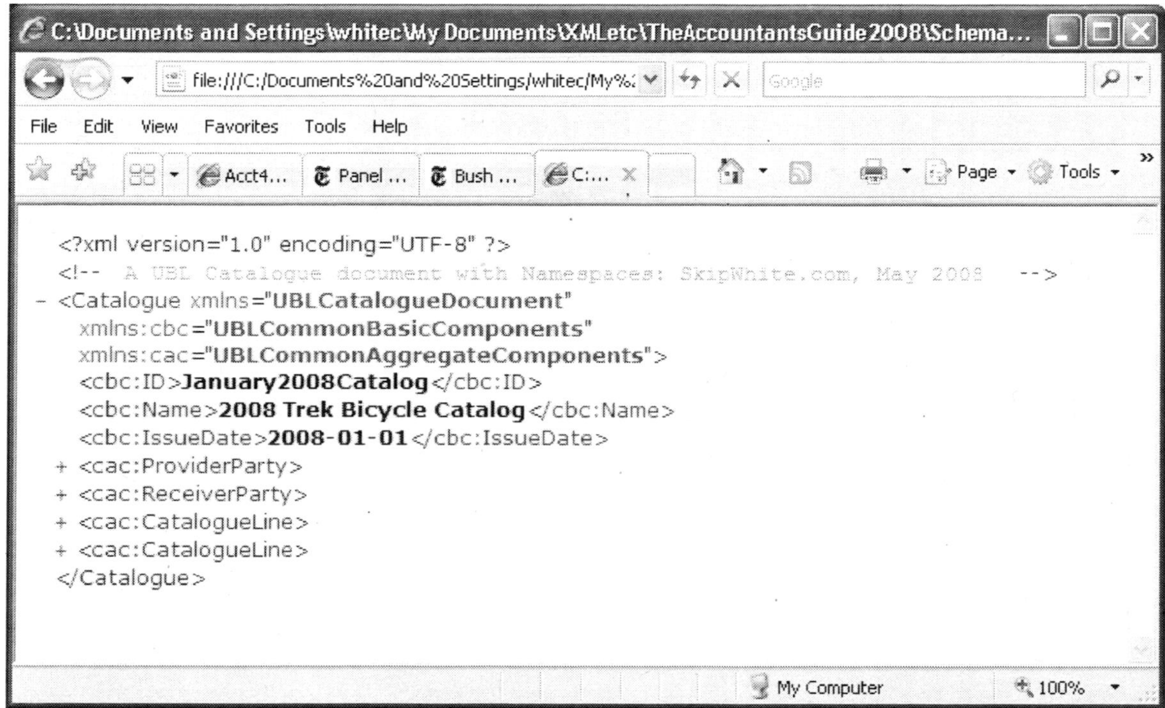

(File: *http://www.skipwhite.com/Guide2008/Chapter3/CatalogueItemExampleWNS.xml*)

Figure 5-2B: A UBL Catalogue document as a node tree

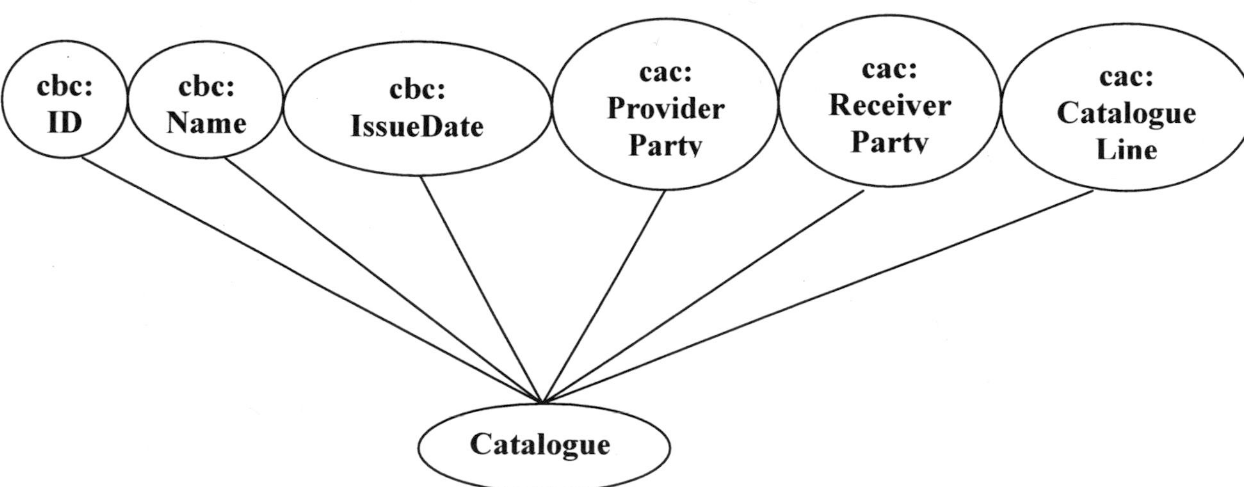

Comparing these two figures, you can see that each element in the UBL Catalogue instance document in Figure 5-2A is represented as a "node" in Figure 5-2B. The root element, **Catalogue**, contains three simple elements, **cbc:ID**, **cbc:Name**, and **cbc:IssueDate** (i.e. each has a value) and three complex elements, **cac:ProviderParty**, **cac:ReceiverParty**, and **cac:CatalogueLine** (i.e. each has other elements nested within it but are collapsed for viewing and illustration purposes). Since the **cbc:ID**, **cbc:Name**, and **cbc:IssueDate** elements each contain a value, they are referred to as "leaf nodes" (i.e. each is at the end of a branch). Likewise, the other three elements, **cac:ProviderParty**, **cac:ReceiverParty**, and **cac:CatalogueLine**, are referred to as "branch nodes" because each has other branches eventually ending in "leaf nodes." This simple illustration is important for two reasons. First, when an XML processor reads an XML document, it represents it as a node tree in memory. Second, the XSLT language is designed to navigate the node tree and perform transformations as per the instructions in an XSLT document. In the first example in this Chapter, we will transform a UBL Catalogue into a Web page.

Transforming a UBL Catalogue into a XHTML Web page

Figure 5-3 (Parts 1, 2, and 3) presents a simple example of how a business can use XSLT to transform a UBL Catalogue document into an XHTML Web page. It is divided into three parts: Part 1 (A and B) is the XML source document (*UBLCatalogueWStylesheet .xml*); Part 2 is an XSLT transformation script (*UBLCataloguePage.xsl*); and Part 3 is the resulting XHTML Web document. Part 1 (A and B), *UBLCatalogueWStylesheet.xml*, is the UBL Catalogue document discussed in Chapter 3, with a couple of comment statements and a processing instruction added to its prolog. Remember that the prolog comes before the root element and contains processing instructions and documentation. The comment statements are for documentation purposes and the instruction, **<?xml-stylesheet type="text/xsl" href="UBLCataloguePage.xsl"?>**, ties the source document to the stylesheet to be used for the document's transformation. It is interpreted as follows:

- **xml-stylesheet** is the reserved word for the stylesheet instruction.
- **type="text/xsl"** tells the processor to expect an XSL document.
- **href="UBLCataloguePage.xsl"** tells the processor the location and name of the XSLT document.

- The **.xsl** extension identifies the file as an XSL document.

When using a browser as your XML processor, an **xml-stylesheet** instruction is necessary to “call” a stylesheet for the XSLT transformation.

Figure 5-3 (Part 1A): UBL Catalogue with XSL instruction (same data content as Figure 3-1)

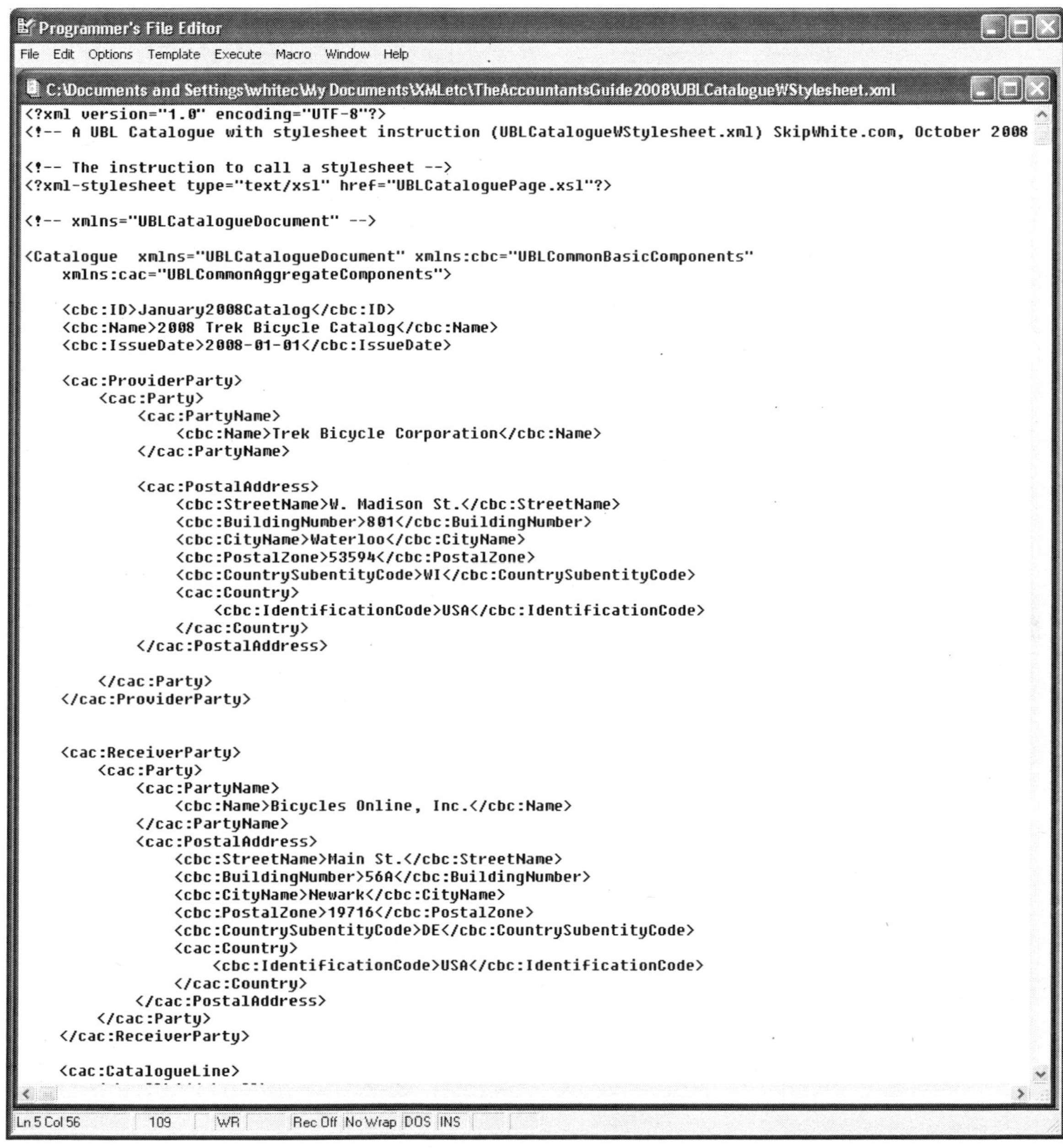

```
<?xml version="1.0" encoding="UTF-8"?>
<!-- A UBL Catalogue with stylesheet instruction (UBLCatalogueWStylesheet.xml) SkipWhite.com, October 2008

<!-- The instruction to call a stylesheet -->
<?xml-stylesheet type="text/xsl" href="UBLCataloguePage.xsl"?>

<!-- xmlns="UBLCatalogueDocument" -->

<Catalogue  xmlns="UBLCatalogueDocument" xmlns:cbc="UBLCommonBasicComponents"
    xmlns:cac="UBLCommonAggregateComponents">

    <cbc:ID>January2008Catalog</cbc:ID>
    <cbc:Name>2008 Trek Bicycle Catalog</cbc:Name>
    <cbc:IssueDate>2008-01-01</cbc:IssueDate>

    <cac:ProviderParty>
        <cac:Party>
            <cac:PartyName>
                <cbc:Name>Trek Bicycle Corporation</cbc:Name>
            </cac:PartyName>

            <cac:PostalAddress>
                <cbc:StreetName>W. Madison St.</cbc:StreetName>
                <cbc:BuildingNumber>801</cbc:BuildingNumber>
                <cbc:CityName>Waterloo</cbc:CityName>
                <cbc:PostalZone>53594</cbc:PostalZone>
                <cbc:CountrySubentityCode>WI</cbc:CountrySubentityCode>
                <cac:Country>
                    <cbc:IdentificationCode>USA</cbc:IdentificationCode>
                </cac:Country>
            </cac:PostalAddress>

        </cac:Party>
    </cac:ProviderParty>


    <cac:ReceiverParty>
        <cac:Party>
            <cac:PartyName>
                <cbc:Name>Bicycles Online, Inc.</cbc:Name>
            </cac:PartyName>
            <cac:PostalAddress>
                <cbc:StreetName>Main St.</cbc:StreetName>
                <cbc:BuildingNumber>56A</cbc:BuildingNumber>
                <cbc:CityName>Newark</cbc:CityName>
                <cbc:PostalZone>19716</cbc:PostalZone>
                <cbc:CountrySubentityCode>DE</cbc:CountrySubentityCode>
                <cac:Country>
                    <cbc:IdentificationCode>USA</cbc:IdentificationCode>
                </cac:Country>
            </cac:PostalAddress>
        </cac:Party>
    </cac:ReceiverParty>

    <cac:CatalogueLine>
```

Figure 5-3 (Part 1B): UBL Catalogue with XSL instruction (same data content as Figure 3-1)

```
Programmer's File Editor
File  Edit  Options  Template  Execute  Macro  Window  Help
C:\Documents and Settings\whitec\My Documents\XMLetc\TheAccountantsGuide2008\UBLCatalogueWStylesheet.xml
    <cac:CatalogueLine>
        <cbc:ID>1</cbc:ID>
        <cac:RequiredItemLocationQuantity>
            <cac:Price>
                <cbc:PriceAmount currencyID="USD">630.55</cbc:PriceAmount>
                <cbc:BaseQuantity unitCode="UNIT">1</cbc:BaseQuantity>
                <cbc:PriceTypeCode>Dealer price</cbc:PriceTypeCode>
            </cac:Price>
        </cac:RequiredItemLocationQuantity>
        <cac:Item>
            <cbc:Description>Road bike: 08 Trek 2.1 series</cbc:Description>
            <cbc:Name>Mens 2008 Trek 2.1</cbc:Name>
            <cac:SellersItemIdentification>
                <cbc:ID>08T2.1M</cbc:ID>
                <cac:PhysicalAttribute>
                    <cbc:AttributeID>Frame,Color,Fork</cbc:AttributeID>
                    <cbc:Description>Alpha black aluminum, Metalic silver, carbon</cbc:Description>
                </cac:PhysicalAttribute>
                <cac:MeasurementDimension>
                    <cbc:AttributeID>FrameSize</cbc:AttributeID>
                    <cbc:Measure>52 cm</cbc:Measure>
                </cac:MeasurementDimension>
            </cac:SellersItemIdentification>
        </cac:Item>
    </cac:CatalogueLine>


    <cac:CatalogueLine>
        <cbc:ID>2</cbc:ID>
        <cac:RequiredItemLocationQuantity>
            <cac:Price>
                <cbc:PriceAmount currencyID="USD">575.55</cbc:PriceAmount>
                <cbc:BaseQuantity unitCode="UNIT">1</cbc:BaseQuantity>
                <cbc:PriceTypeCode>Dealer price</cbc:PriceTypeCode>
            </cac:Price>
        </cac:RequiredItemLocationQuantity>
        <cac:Item>
            <cbc:Description>Mountain bike: 08 Trek 6700 series</cbc:Description>
            <cbc:Name>Womens 2008 Trek 6700</cbc:Name>
            <cac:SellersItemIdentification>
                <cbc:ID>08T6700W</cbc:ID>
                <cac:PhysicalAttribute>
                    <cbc:AttributeID>Frame,Color,Fork</cbc:AttributeID>
                    <cbc:Description>Alpha black aluminum, Sport blue, RockShox</cbc:Description>
                </cac:PhysicalAttribute>
                <cac:MeasurementDimension>
                    <cbc:AttributeID>FrameSize</cbc:AttributeID>
                    <cbc:Measure>14 in</cbc:Measure>
                </cac:MeasurementDimension>
            </cac:SellersItemIdentification>
        </cac:Item>
    </cac:CatalogueLine>

</Catalogue>
Ln 62 Col 17 | 109 | WR | Rec Off | No Wrap | DOS | INS
```

(File: *http://www.skipwhite.com/Guide2008/Chapter5/UBLCatalogueWStylesheet.xml*)

Figure 5-3 (Part 2): UBLCataloguePage.xsl (XSLT instructions)

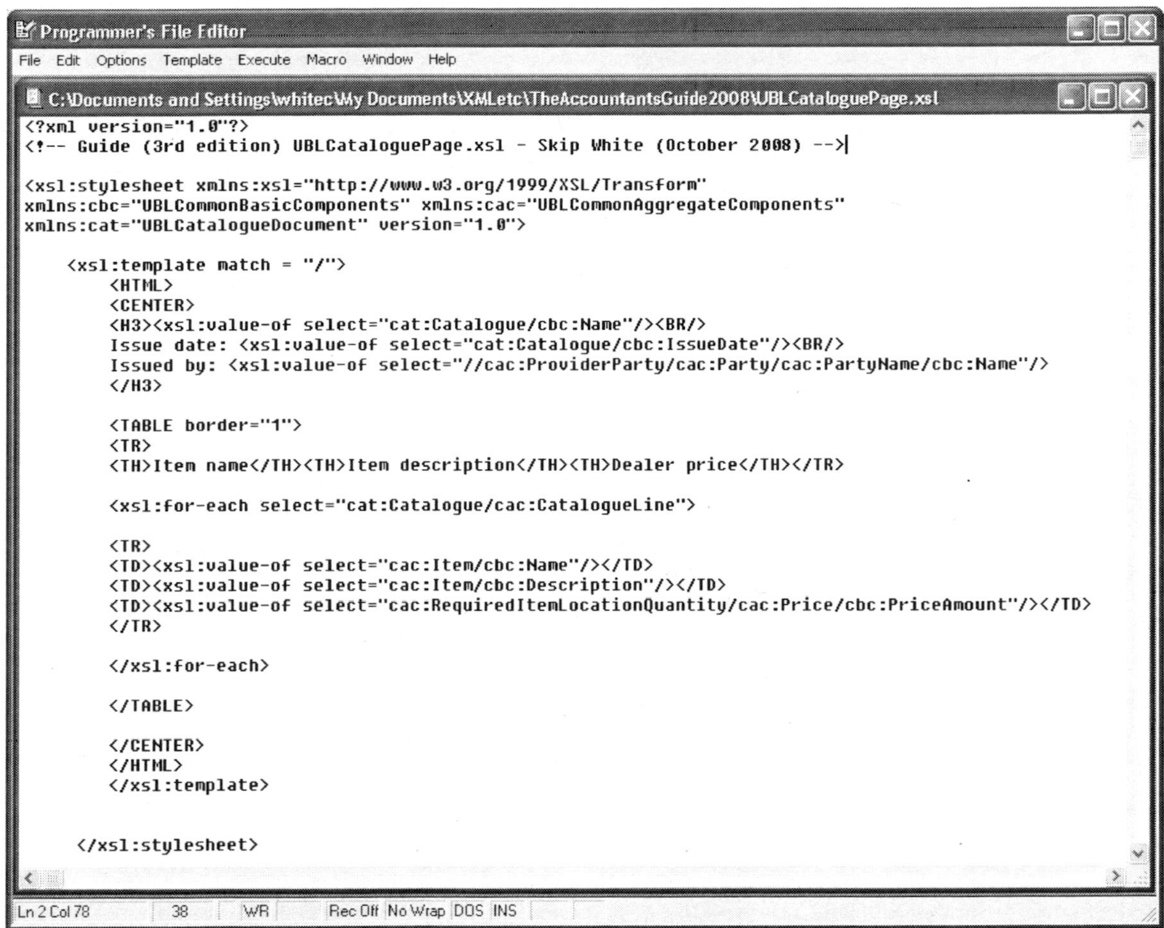

Programmer's File Editor

File Edit Options Template Execute Macro Window Help

C:\Documents and Settings\whitec\My Documents\XMLetc\TheAccountantsGuide2008\UBLCataloguePage.xsl

```
<?xml version="1.0"?>
<!-- Guide (3rd edition) UBLCataloguePage.xsl - Skip White (October 2008) -->

<xsl:stylesheet xmlns:xsl="http://www.w3.org/1999/XSL/Transform"
xmlns:cbc="UBLCommonBasicComponents" xmlns:cac="UBLCommonAggregateComponents"
xmlns:cat="UBLCatalogueDocument" version="1.0">

    <xsl:template match = "/">
        <HTML>
        <CENTER>
        <H3><xsl:value-of select="cat:Catalogue/cbc:Name"/><BR/>
        Issue date: <xsl:value-of select="cat:Catalogue/cbc:IssueDate"/><BR/>
        Issued by: <xsl:value-of select="//cac:ProviderParty/cac:Party/cac:PartyName/cbc:Name"/>
        </H3>

        <TABLE border="1">
        <TR>
        <TH>Item name</TH><TH>Item description</TH><TH>Dealer price</TH></TR>

        <xsl:for-each select="cat:Catalogue/cac:CatalogueLine">

        <TR>
        <TD><xsl:value-of select="cac:Item/cbc:Name"/></TD>
        <TD><xsl:value-of select="cac:Item/cbc:Description"/></TD>
        <TD><xsl:value-of select="cac:RequiredItemLocationQuantity/cac:Price/cbc:PriceAmount"/></TD>
        </TR>

        </xsl:for-each>

        </TABLE>

        </CENTER>
        </HTML>
        </xsl:template>


     </xsl:stylesheet>
```

Ln 2 Col 78 | 38 | WR | Rec Off | No Wrap | DOS | INS

(File: *http://www.skipwhite.com/Guide2008/Chapter5/UBLCataloguePage.xsl*)

Figure 5-3 (Part 3): The result - an XHTML Catalogue as viewed in a browser

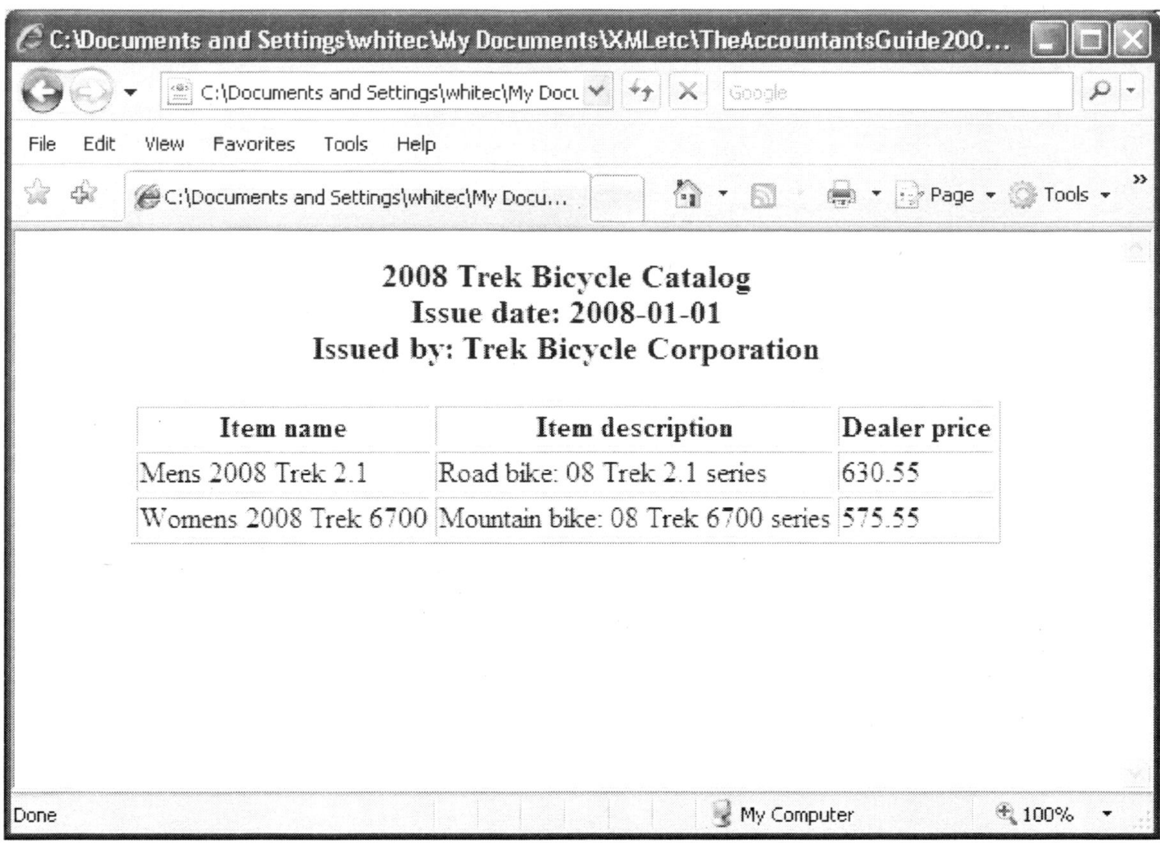

Though the XSLT code in *Part 2* looks complex, it is actually easy to understand. First, it is important to realize that XML source documents, *Part 1*, contain elements and data values and do not contain formatting information. To extract the data values and put them into a report you must reformat them into a form appropriate for the reporting purpose. In this example, specific data values in the XML source document need to be "selected" and reformatted so that they can be viewed by a Web browser. The XSLT code in *Part 2* accomplishes the transformation. The result is a document that is actually an XHTML document because it contains HTML codes that a Web browser can understand for display purposes and because it is a well-formed XML document.

The first line of the XSLT stylesheet (*Part 2*) is the same standard XML version instruction found in all XML documents. It is important to remember at this point that all XML documents (including XSLT stylesheets) follow the same basic rules enumerated previously: 1) one and only one root element (the root element "contains" all of the other elements nested within it); 2) matching beginning and ending element names; 3) all elements can contain attributes; and 4) all elements must be properly nested. The next line is a comment for documentation purposes:

- <!-- Guide (3rd edition) UBLCataloguePage.xsl - Skip White (October 2008) -->

The next line is the root element and its namespace declarations and version attributes.

- **<xsl:stylesheet xmlns:xsl=**"http://www.w3.org/1999/XSL/Transform"
- **xmlns:cbc=**"UBLCommonBasicComponents"
- **xmlns:cac=**"UBLCommonAggregateComponents"
- **xmlns:cat=**"UBLCatalogueDocument" **version=**"1.0">

"**xsl:stylesheet**" is the reserved root element name for all XSLT documents: "**xsl**" is the preferred namespace prefix for the Extensible Stylesheet Language of which XSLT is a subset, "**stylesheet**" is the required root element name for all XSL documents, and the first "**xmlns**" attribute identifies the URI of the XSL namespace. The "**xsl**" namespace prefix is then used throughout the XSLT document to identify XSLT instructions (also referred to as "rules"). The second and third namespace declarations for the UBL basic and aggregate components are the same as found in the UBL Catalogue source document; namespaces that appear in both documents <u>must</u> be exactly the same. The fourth namespace declaration, **xmlns:cat=**"UBLCatalogueDocument", needs a little explanation. The namespace "UBLCatalogueDocument" is the default namespace in the source document. Since default namespace declarations do <u>not</u> work in XSLT version 1.0 documents, we are required to add a namespace prefix to this declaration; I chose to use "**cat**". Finally, the attribute, **version=**"1.0", tells the processor that we are using this version of XSL. Note that XSL version 2.0 is now available but current Web browsers are not yet capable of processing it. In the remainder of this document, every line of code starting with "**xsl**" is an XSLT version 1.0 instruction (**bold** and in small letters).

<u>Processing XSLT instructions</u>

The XML processor reads all of the instructions/rules in the XSLT document and stores them in a table. It then reads the XML source document, stores it as a node tree, and looks in the table for rules to apply to the nodes. Sets of rules are referred to as “templates” and XSLT is known as a “template matching” language. The next line, **<xsl:template match="/">**, is the start of a template. It simply says “start the transformation process by matching to the entire source document.” The instruction uses the keyword “**xsl:template**” with the generic “**match="/"** ” attribute; the “/” is shorthand for “the entire source document.” Notice that all transformation instructions are contained within this initial template. Most XSLT documents contain multiple templates and **match** can be used to identify any node in the tree.

Since in this example we want the result document to be readable as a Web page, it must be formatted as an XHTML document. Focusing on the HTML codes, all CAPITALIZED for readability, the next lines of code tell the Web browser to set up the HTML output, as follows:

- <HTML> is the required HTML “container” element for an XHTML document (i.e. it contains all of the HTML formatting tags).
- <CENTER> is the HTML tag meaning “center” whatever follows in this document.
- <H3> is the HTML tag meaning display text using “**bold** font size three.”
- <TABLE border = "1"> is the HTML tag meaning set up a “table” with a small border.
- <TR> is the HTML tag meaning “table row” – all tables have rows.
- <TH> is the HTML tag meaning “table heading” and <TD> is the HTML tag meaning “table data” – all tables have rows and within each row are cells with data; the first row of a table usually contains column headings, <TH>, and the lower rows contain data, <TD>.

These lines of code tell a Web browser to center everything starting with a bold heading followed by a table with a small border. For tutorials and a summary of HTML codes, see: www.htmlhelp.com and http://www.w3schools.com.

The first XSLT instruction within the template, **<xsl:value-of select="cat:Catalogue/ cbc:Name"/>**, is known as a “**value-of select**” instruction. It is interpreted literally as “**select** whatever **value** you find at the end of the node tree path

cat:Catalogue/cbc:Name." Referring to the node tree in Figure 5-2B, start at the **Catalogue** root node and follow the path to the **cbc:Name** node and "select" its value. For obvious reasons, this is known as an **XPath** instruction. **XPath** is an XML specification used in the XSLT language. The <H3> at the beginning of the line tells the processor how to format and display whatever value is selected as the result of the "**value-of select**" instruction and the <BR/> at the end of the line tells the processor to break and start a new line before the next instruction (i.e., BR means "line break"). The next instruction, **<xsl:value-of select="cat:Catalogue/ cbc:IssueDate"/>**, is a similar **XPath** instruction to select the value found at the end of the node path **cat:Catalogue/cbc:IssueDate**. The "Issue date:" at the beginning of the line is text that the browser displays literally and the <BR/> at the end is the HTML line break tag. The next instruction, **<xsl:value-of select="//cac:ProviderParty/cac:Party/ cac:PartyName/cbc:Name"/>**, is a similar XPath instruction but it starts with // instead of **cat:Catalogue**. This is a shortcut in the XSLT language that is used to replace the initial part of a long **XPath** instruction (i.e., the // replaces **"cat:Catalogue"** in this XPath). Since there is only one **cat:Catalogue/cac:ProviderParty/cac:Party/ cac:PartyName/cbc:Name XPath** in this document, the // can be used at the beginning of the path. You have to be careful with your use of // because if the **XPath** is not unique the processor will get confused and only give you the value of the first one it finds! Once again, the "Issued by:" at the beginning of the line is text that the browser displays literally and the <BR/> at the end is the HTML line break tag. If you look at Figure 5-3 (Part 3), you will see the results of these instructions - "2008 Trek Bicycle Catalog", "2008-01-01", and "Trek Bicycle Corporation" are the values found at the leaf nodes in the source document located with the corresponding **XPath** instructions and each is formatted according to the HTML tags.

As mentioned previously, <TABLE border="1"> is the HTML tag and border attribute to tell a browser to set up a table with a small border, <TR> sets up the first row of the table, and the <TH> tags contain the column headings – Item name, Item description, and Dealer price. After the table is set up, we want to select values nested within each of the **cac:CatalogueLine** elements. To do this we set up a "**for-each** loop" and point to the first **cac:CatalogueLine** element with the **<xsl:for-each select="cat:Catalogue/ cac:CatalogueLine">** instruction. Literally, this instruction tells the processor to go to each node in the source document with this node path and perform whatever instructions are found within the **for-each** loop; which ends with the closing **for-each** tag (i.e., **</xsl:for-each>**). The <TR> tag sets up a row and each of the <TD>**<xsl:value-of select="..." />** </TD> instructions directs the processor to find a specific value and enter it in a cell. Since we are in a **for-each** loop that points to a **cac:CatalogueLine** element, the first instruction, <TD>**<xsl:value-of select="cac:Item/cbc:Name"/>**</TD> tells the processor to select the value found at this leaf node and put it into the first cell. The other two instructions do the same according to their specified path. Refer to Figure 5-3 (Part 3) for the results.

The remainder of the tags in the XSLT document, see Figure 5-3 (Part 2), are necessary to close the open tags in order to make it a well-formed XHTML document. With this simple example, you have been exposed to the basics of the XSLT language and its power to transform XML documents to other forms; in this case a Web page.

Interactive exercise 5-1: We are now ready to run the transformation. First, download the source document file, *http://www.skipwhite.com/Guide2008/Chapter5/ UBLCatalogueWStylesheet.xml*, and save it in a folder (you can rename it if you so desire). Second, download the XSLT file, *http://www.skipwhite.com/Guide2008/ Chapter5/UBLCataloguePage.xsl*, and save it in the same folder (do not change its name because it is the name used in the source document's **xml-stylesheet** instruction: **<?xml-stylesheet type="text/xsl" href="UBLCataloguePage.xsl"?>** . Next, open your browser and double-click the source document's name. Note that in some computer labs, because of security precautions, you may have to right-click the source document's name and select open-with and choose IE or your favorite browser. The result should be the same as Figure 5-3 (*Part 3*).

When you use a browser as your XML processor to open an XML source document that contains an **xml-stylesheet** instruction, it reads the **xml-stylesheet** instruction and opens both the source file and the XSLT file. It checks both documents to make sure they are well-formed and understandable and then puts all of the instructions found in the XSLT document in a table. It then processes the nodes in the source document according to the XSLT instructions and creates the result document which your browser displays as a table in a Web page.

XSLT Processing

XSLT is a conceptually simple yet powerful scripting language for XML document processing. Since it is part of the XML foundation, any up-to-date XML processor can be used to transform XML documents with XSLT instructions. The current version of XSLT is version 2.0 but as of this writing, Web browsers can only process XSLT version 1.0 instructions. XSLT creates several compelling business reasons for using it: you do not need additional, proprietary software or powerful hardware to process XML documents; data tagged in an XML document can be reused without human intervention or data re-entry; and transformations can become part of business processes to efficiently process information surrounding business events. In this section, we will extend the basics of XSLT processing by building more sophisticated business examples.

The Catalogue XHTML document that we created in the previous section is quite simple and the price amounts could use better formatting. Since XML documents do not contain any formatting, we have to use XSLT to format numbers. We do this by placing a **format-number** function in the **value-of select** instruction as follows:

<xsl:value-of select="format-number (cac:RequiredItemLocationQuantity/ cbc:Price/cbc:PriceAmount, '$#,##0.00')"/>

The **format-number** function starts with the **format-number** key word and uses the following format: **format-number(** *the item to be selected* **,** '*the format pattern*'). It can be used on any numeric items. The format-number pattern must be within 'small quotes'.

Interactive exercise 5-2: Open Notepad or your favorite text editor and open the XSLT document *UBLCataloguePage.xsl* that we have been working with in this Chapter. Change the **value-of select** clause for the **cbc:PriceAmount** element to include a

format-number instruction as illustrated above. Save the file and run the transformation by opening your source document *UBLCatalogueWithStylesheet.xml* with your browser. The result should look like the report in Figure 5-4. If you get an error, you have not used the correct **format-number** syntax.

Figure 5-4: UBL Catalogue Report (with number formatting)

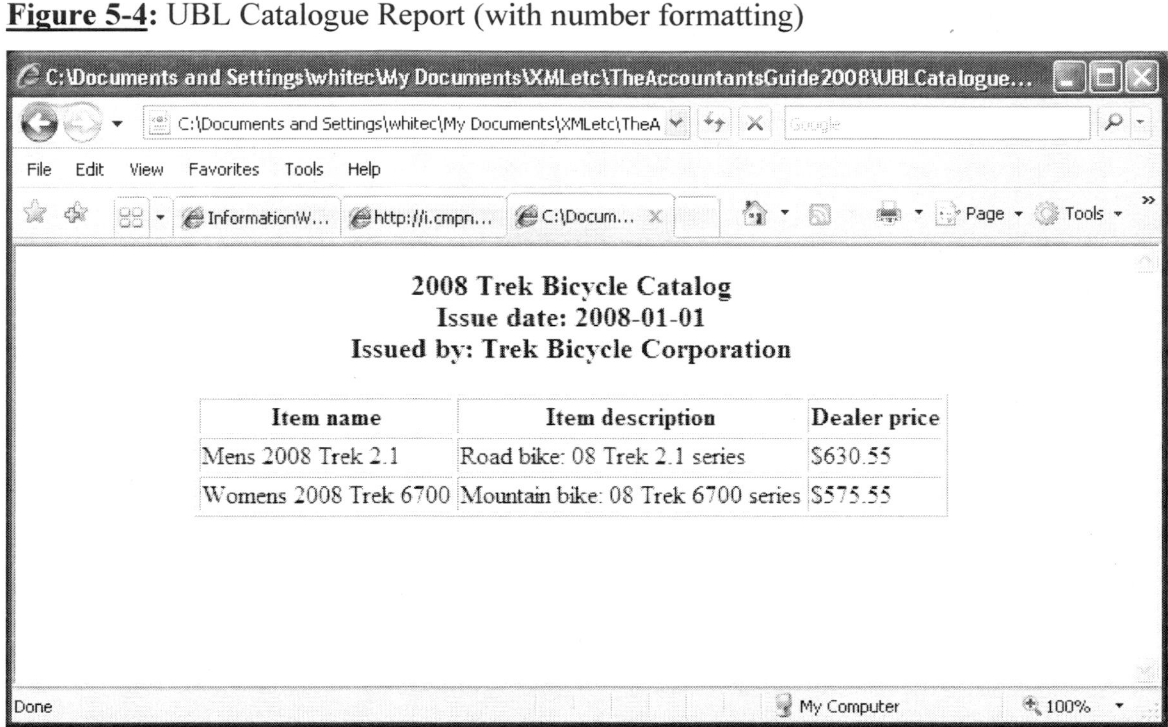

2008 Trek Bicycle Catalog
Issue date: 2008-01-01
Issued by: Trek Bicycle Corporation

Item name	Item description	Dealer price
Mens 2008 Trek 2.1	Road bike: 08 Trek 2.1 series	$630.55
Womens 2008 Trek 6700	Mountain bike: 08 Trek 6700 series	$575.55

As covered in Chapters 2 and 3, the UBL vocabulary includes a library of XML documents designed to facilitate e-business document exchanges. After an entity receives a Catalog from a business partner, the next step in the procurement process is to create a Purchase Order. XSLT is the perfect tool to use to extract data from a UBL Catalogue and use it to create a UBL Purchase Order. This requires more complex XSLT programming and a more robust XML processor. Since this is beyond the scope of this book, we will instead continue to work with XSLT to render documents as XHTML Web pages.

In the transformation of the UBL Catalogue into a Web page, we created the XSLT document and then added a stylesheet instruction, **<?xml-stylesheet type="text/xsl" href="UBLCataloguePage.xsl"?>** to our Catalogue source document. This was done to simplify opening the source document with a browser and have it read this instruction and access the XSLT document with the transformation instructions. In business processes, writing an instruction to a source document is often impractical and has limited generalizability. In a procurement process using UBL, a business entity would want to receive a Catalogue and use it for many different purposes. Instead of repeatedly writing **xml-stylesheet** instructions to source documents, a better solution is to write any number of XML reporting documents to "call" XSLT documents containing instructions to access and reuse the information in one or more remote XML source documents. As covered in Chapter 2, the next step in the procurement process is to create a Purchase Order using the information in the Catalogue source document (Figure 2-4 shows both side-by-side). After creating a Purchase Order, it is likely we would want to render it as a Web page. Instead of writing an **xml-stylesheet** instruction to the Purchase Order source document, we will create an "XML shell document" to access the Purchase Order and reuse it's information in a Web page (see Figure 5-5).

Figure 5-5: An XML shell document for processing remote XML documents

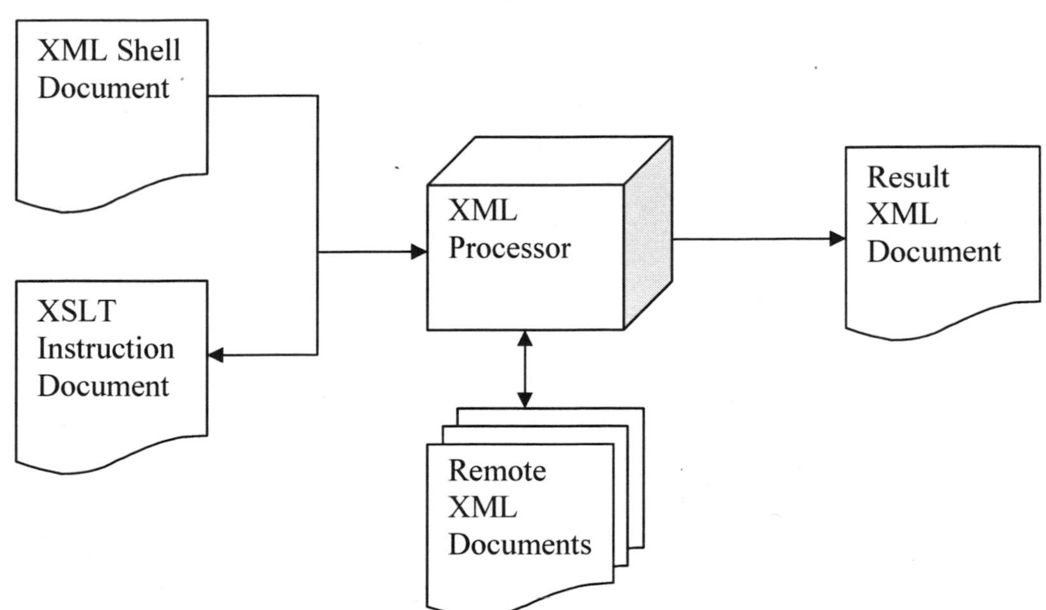

The *CreatePurchaseOrderPage.xml* shell document has two purposes – to provide a title for the Purchase Order Web page and to execute the **xml-stylesheet** instruction to call the XSLT document containing the instructions to access information in the Purchase Order and reuse it in an XHTML Web page (see Figure 5-6).

Figure 5-6: The *CreatePurchaseOrderPage.xml* shell

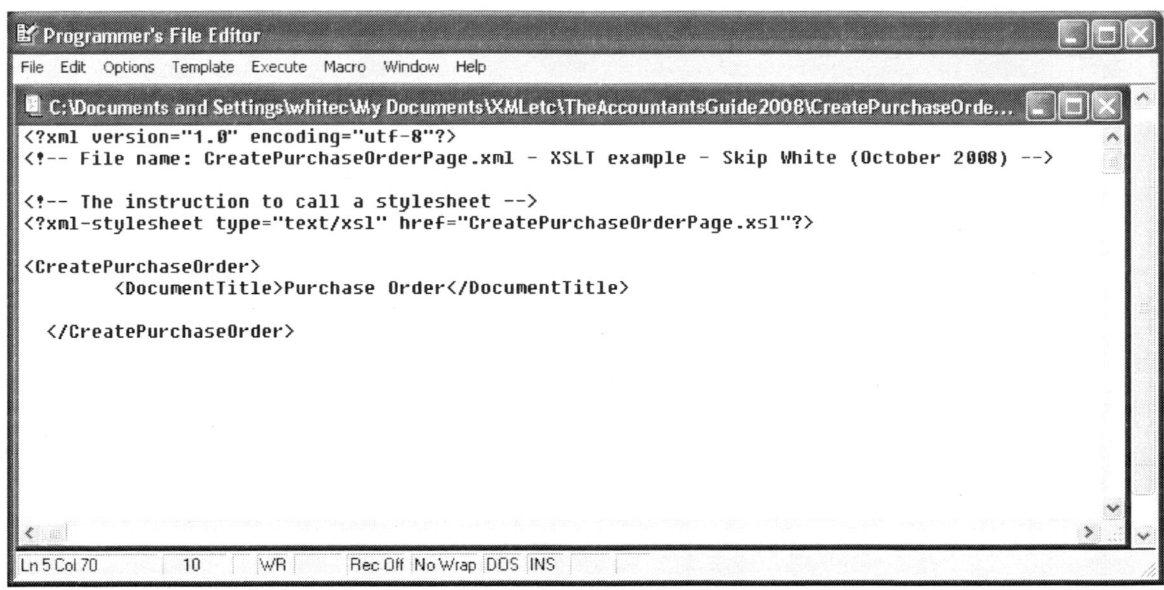

```
<?xml version="1.0" encoding="utf-8"?>
<!-- File name: CreatePurchaseOrderPage.xml - XSLT example - Skip White (October 2008) -->

<!-- The instruction to call a stylesheet -->
<?xml-stylesheet type="text/xsl" href="CreatePurchaseOrderPage.xsl"?>

<CreatePurchaseOrder>
        <DocumentTitle>Purchase Order</DocumentTitle>

  </CreatePurchaseOrder>
```

(File: *http://www.skipwhite.com/Guide2008/Chapter5/CreatePurchaseOrderPage.xml*)

This is a simple XML file that would be opened in a Web browser whenever someone wants to render the UBL Purchase Order as a Web page. Notice that it contains an **xml-stylesheet** instruction to call a file named *CreatePurchaseOrderPage.xsl*. **xml-stylesheet** instructions always appear in the "prolog" (i.e., before the root element) of an XML document and exist to tell an XML processor where to find an XSLT instruction document. The complete UBL Purchase Order that the *CreatePurchaseOrderPage.xsl* file will use for the source of the purchase information, is shown in Figure 5-7 parts 1 and 2. Notice that it does not contain an **xml-stylesheet** instruction.

Figure 5-7: UBL Purchase Order (Part 1)

Programmer's File Editor

File Edit Options Template Execute Macro Window Help

C:\Documents and Settings\whitec\My Documents\XMLetc\TheAccountantsGuide2008\CreatePOE...

```
<?xml version="1.0" encoding="UTF-8"?>
<!-- Guide (3rd edition) PurchaseOrder.xml - Skip White (November 2008) -->

<Order xmlns="UBLOrderDocument" xmlns:cbc="UBLCommonBasicComponents"
    xmlns:cac="UBLCommonAggregateComponents">

    <cbc:ID>12345</cbc:ID>
    <cbc:IssueDate>2008-03-27</cbc:IssueDate>
    <cac:BuyerCustomerParty>
        <cac:Party>
            <cac:PartyName>
                <cbc:Name>Bicycles Online, Inc.</cbc:Name>
                </cac:PartyName>
            <cac:PostalAddress>
                <cbc:StreetName>Main St.</cbc:StreetName>
                <cbc:BuildingNumber>56A</cbc:BuildingNumber>
                <cbc:CityName>Newark</cbc:CityName>
                <cbc:PostalZone>19716</cbc:PostalZone>
                <cbc:CountrySubentityCode>DE</cbc:CountrySubentityCode>
                <cac:Country>
                    <cbc:IdentificationCode>USA</cbc:IdentificationCode>
                    </cac:Country>
                </cac:PostalAddress>
            </cac:Party>
        </cac:BuyerCustomerParty>

    <cac:SellerSupplierParty>
        <cac:Party>
            <cac:PartyName>
                <cbc:Name>Trek Bicycle Corporation</cbc:Name>
                </cac:PartyName>
            <cac:PostalAddress>
                <cbc:StreetName>W. Madison St.</cbc:StreetName>
                <cbc:BuildingNumber>801</cbc:BuildingNumber>
                <cbc:CityName>Waterloo</cbc:CityName>
                <cbc:PostalZone>53594</cbc:PostalZone>
                <cbc:CountrySubentityCode>WI</cbc:CountrySubentityCode>
                <cac:Country>
                    <cbc:IdentificationCode>USA</cbc:IdentificationCode>
                    </cac:Country>
                </cac:PostalAddress>
            </cac:Party>
        </cac:SellerSupplierParty>


    <cac:OrderLine>
```

Ln 35 Col 9 | 66 | WR | Rec Off | No Wrap | DOS | INS

Figure 5-7: UBL Purchase Order (Part 2)

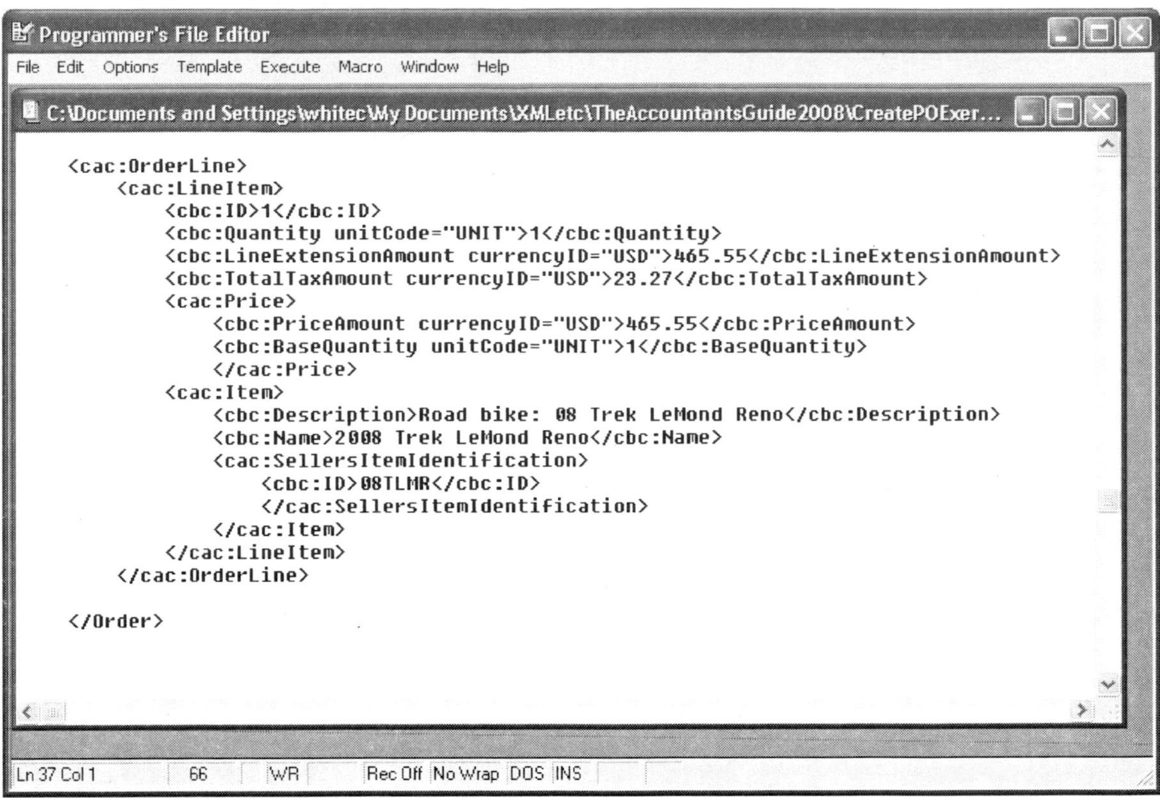


```xml
<cac:OrderLine>
    <cac:LineItem>
        <cbc:ID>1</cbc:ID>
        <cbc:Quantity unitCode="UNIT">1</cbc:Quantity>
        <cbc:LineExtensionAmount currencyID="USD">465.55</cbc:LineExtensionAmount>
        <cbc:TotalTaxAmount currencyID="USD">23.27</cbc:TotalTaxAmount>
        <cac:Price>
            <cbc:PriceAmount currencyID="USD">465.55</cbc:PriceAmount>
            <cbc:BaseQuantity unitCode="UNIT">1</cbc:BaseQuantity>
            </cac:Price>
        <cac:Item>
            <cbc:Description>Road bike: 08 Trek LeMond Reno</cbc:Description>
            <cbc:Name>2008 Trek LeMond Reno</cbc:Name>
            <cac:SellersItemIdentification>
                <cbc:ID>08TLMR</cbc:ID>
                </cac:SellersItemIdentification>
            </cac:Item>
        </cac:LineItem>
    </cac:OrderLine>

</Order>
```

(File: *http://www.skipwhite.com/Guide2008/Chapter5/PurchaseOrder.xml*)

Interactive exercise 5-3: Together we are going to write the XSLT instructions to create the *CreatePurchaseOrderPage.xsl* file which will render the UBL Purchase Order source document as a Web page (the result is shown in Figure 5-8). First, download the UBL Purchase Order document, *PurchaseOrder.xml* (Figure 5-7) and the Create Purchase Order Page document, *CreatePurchaseOrderPage.xml* (Figure 5-6) and save them in the same folder on your computer or storage device and do not change their names.

Setting up your **.xsl** file: Open Notepad or your favorite text editor, start a new file, and enter the following:

```
<?xml version="1.0"?>
<!-- File name: CreatePurchaseOrderPage.xsl – enter your name and date -->
<xsl:stylesheet  xmlns:xsl="http://www.w3.org/1999/XSL/Transform"
```

Figure 5-8: UBL Purchase Order rendered as a Web page

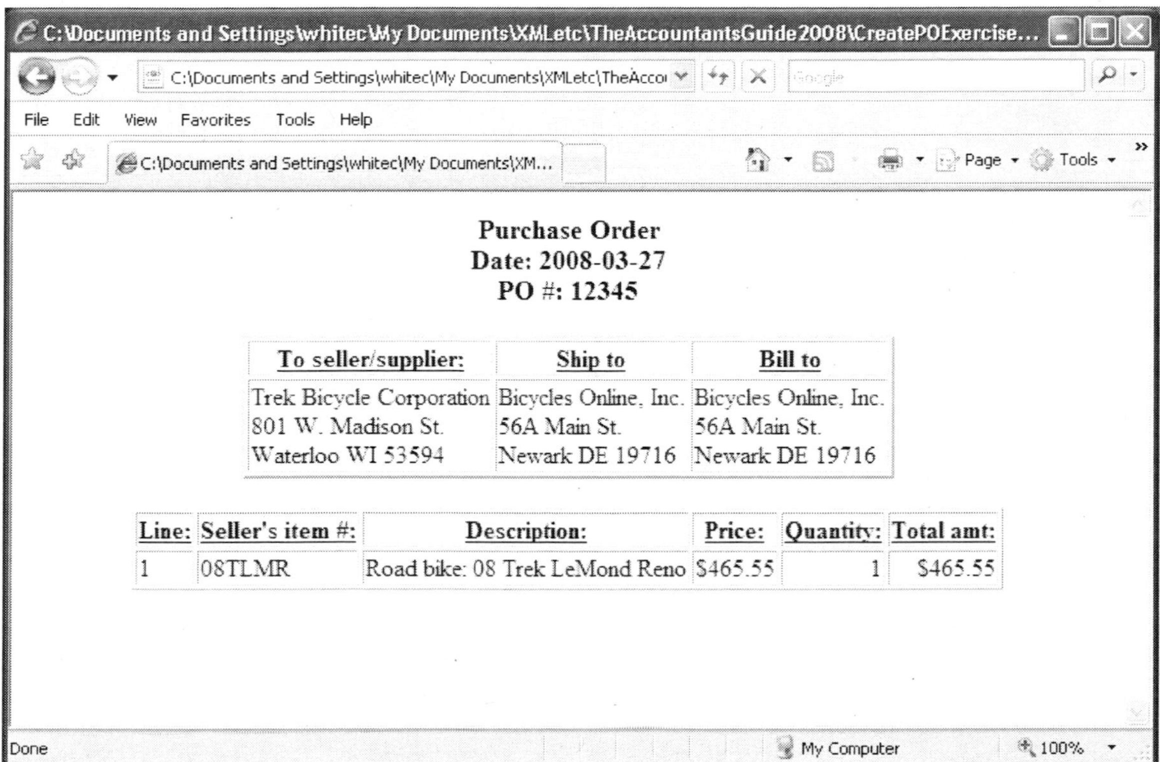

Purchase Order
Date: 2008-03-27
PO #: 12345

To seller/supplier:	Ship to	Bill to
Trek Bicycle Corporation 801 W. Madison St. Waterloo WI 53594	Bicycles Online, Inc. 56A Main St. Newark DE 19716	Bicycles Online, Inc. 56A Main St. Newark DE 19716

Line:	Seller's item #:	Description:	Price:	Quantity:	Total amt:
1	08TLMR	Road bike: 08 Trek LeMond Reno	$465.55	1	$465.55

The first line is the XML version instruction, the second is a comment line to document the file name and you as the author, and the third line is the **xsl:stylesheet** root element and the namespace declaration for the XSLT language. You should start all of your XSLT documents with this code. Next, copy the three namespaces from the *PurchaseOrder.xml* file, our source document for Purchase Order information, and paste them into your new file/XSLT document. Notice that one is a default namespace (**xmlns=**"UBLOrderDocument"). Since default namespaces are not allowed in XSLT v1.0, you must add a namespace prefix to it in your XSLT document; as in **xmlns:ord=**"UBLOrderDocument" ; I chose "**ord**" for my prefix. Next, finish your **xsl:stylesheet** element by including a **version=**"1.0"> declaration. Your XSLT document should look like the following (with your name and date):

```
<?xml version="1.0"?>
<!-- Guide (3rd edition) CreatePurchaseOrderPage.xsl - Skip White 11/15/2008 -->

<xsl:stylesheet xmlns:xsl="http://www.w3.org/1999/XSL/Transform"
xmlns:cbc="UBLCommonBasicComponents"
xmlns:cac="UBLCommonAggregateComponents"
```

xmlns:ord="UBLOrderDocument" version="1.0">

I always copy my namespace declarations from a source document to my XSLT file because they must be exactly the same in both documents or the transformation will not work (i.e., you will not get any output); this can be a very frustrating error. You should save your file as *CreatePurchaseOrderPage.xsl* – this is the file name used in the *CreatePurchaseOrderPage.xml* document.

Setting up your result document heading: Start your **xsl:template** and HTML document with the following code:

```
<xsl:template match = "/">
        <HTML>
        <CENTER>
        <H3> <xsl:value-of select="//DocumentTitle"/> <BR/>
        Date: <xsl:value-of select="document('PurchaseOrder.xml')/
                ord:Order/cbc:IssueDate"/> <BR/>
        PO #: <xsl:value-of select="document('PurchaseOrder.xml')/
                ord:Order/cbc:ID"/> <BR/>
        </H3>
```

You usually start an XSL template with **<xsl:template match = "/">**; remember that the **"/"** refers to the entire source document and you can change this to an appropriate **XPath** if you only want to work with part of a document. The <HTML> tag is necessary if you want to create a Web page as your result page and the <CENTER> and <H3> tags start formatting the output. The **<xsl:value-of select="//DocumentTitle"/>** instruction "selects" the data value found at this leaf node in the source "shell" document and sends it to the result document and the <BR/> tag provides a line break. The text "Date:" is a literal sent directly to the result document. The next instruction **<xsl:value-of select= "document('PurchaseOrder.xml')/ord:Order/cbc:IssueDate"/>** needs some explanation because it shows how we access a remote document using the **document('*URI*')/*xpath*** instruction. Actually, it is quite simple: the **xsl:value-of select** instruction is the same but it is followed by the key word **document** and the *URI* of the document that we want to select from inside parentheses, in single quotation marks. After the closing parenthesis, you simply designate the **XPath** to the leaf node from which you want to select a value (i.e. the **/ord:Order/cbc:IssueDate** is the **XPath** in the remote *OrderExample.xml* document). Note that with the **xsl document(‘*URI*’)/*xpath*** function, we can access any information in any addressable xml document. The remainder of this code follows the same pattern (i.e.
 for line break, “PO #:” is a literal, the **xsl:value-of select** instruction finds the next piece of data in the remote document, followed by a line break and the closing </H3> tag). Enter this code and save your file.

Setting up the first table in your result document: Set up the first table with headings and select the first data item from the Purchase Order for output in your result document with the following code:

```
<TABLE border="2">
        <TR>
        <TH><U>To seller/supplier:</U></TH> <TH><U>Ship to</U></TH>
           <TH><U>Bill to</U></TH>
        </TR>
        <TR>
        <TD><xsl:value-of select="document('PurchaseOrder.xml')//
               cac:SellerSupplierParty/cac:Party/cac:PartyName/cbc:Name"/><BR/>
```

To create a table in a HTML result document, you always use the <TABLE> tag. If you want a border around it, you use a border attribute with a value (i.e., border="2" provides a wider border than border="1"). The first <TR> tag sets up a row and each of the three <TH> tags (“table header” tags) contains a literal value within the <U> (meaning “underline”) tag. The next <TR> sets up the first row and the first <TD> tag contains a **xsl:value-of select** clause containing the **document(‘*URI*’)/*xpath*** function to select the name of the seller/supplier for output in the result document. Remember that a // is simply a shortcut at the beginning of an **XPath**. As always, the <BR/> tag gives a line break. We now want to write **value-of select** instructions for the rest of the seller/supplier’s address (i.e. the building number, street name, city, etc.) from the Purchase Order. Try writing this code on your own. Note that to get a blank space between selected values (e.g. the building number and the street name), include the ASCII code * * between them – literally this means “blank space” to a Web browser. When finished, be sure to include the closing TD tag, </TD>.

Testing your transformation code: At this point, it is time to test your XSLT document to be sure you are on the right track. To do so, you must have a well-formed document so you must close all open tags. The following will do the job:

```
</TR>
</TABLE>
</CENTER>
</HTML>
</xsl:template>
</xsl:stylesheet>
```

After entering this code and saving your file, open the *CreatePurchaseOrderPage.xml* document in your browser. The result should look like Figure 5-9.

Figure 5-9: Partial Purchase Order test

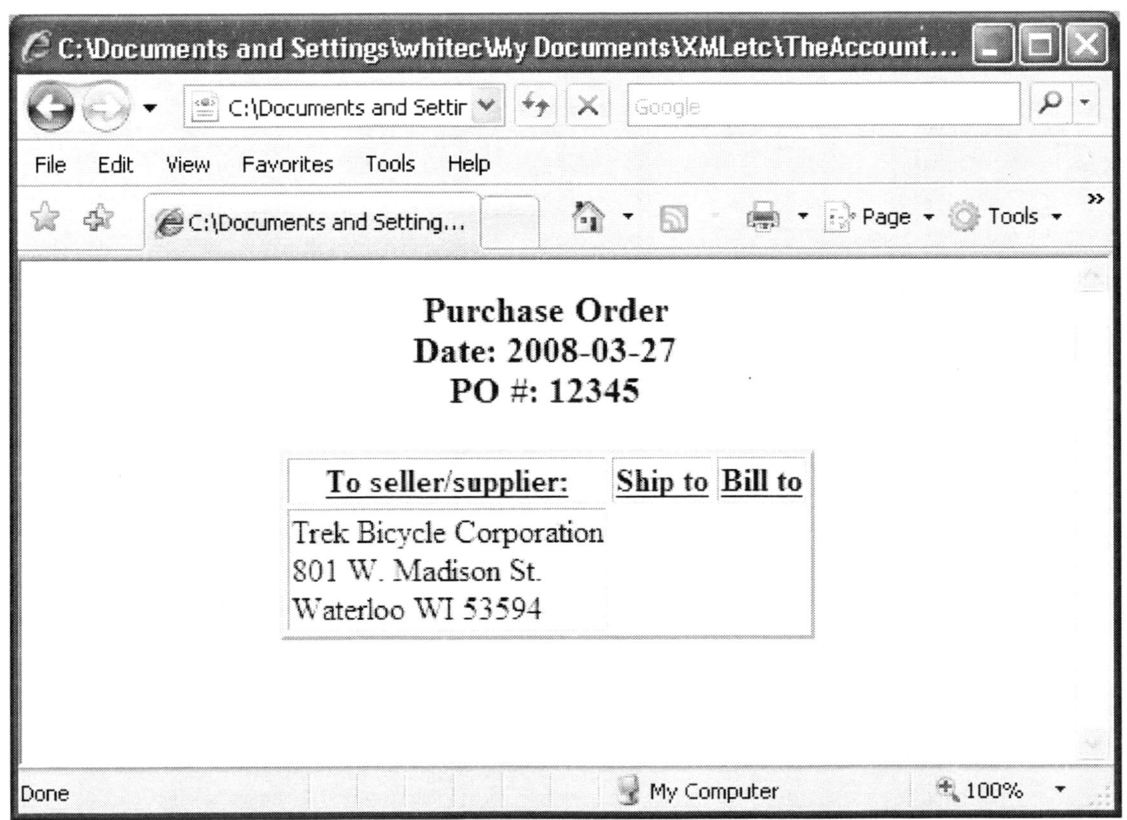

Completing the Ship to and Bill to information: If you get this result, it is time to complete this table by setting up two more <TD> cells and selecting the appropriate information from the Purchase Order. The easiest way to do this is to copy and paste your initial <TD> block of code in its entirety and then make the appropriate changes. Since we are working with a UBL Purchase Order, which has identical **cac:Party** structures for sellers and buyers, all you have to do is change each **cac:SellerSupplierParty** to **cac:BuyerCustomerParty**. After making the changes and saving your file, be sure to test your code.

Setting up the second table in your result document: Set up the second table with headings and an **xsl:for-each** loop with the following code:

```
<P/>
<TABLE border="1">
<TR>
<TH><U>Line:</U></TH> <TH><U>Seller's item #:</U></TH>
<TH><U>Description:</U></TH> <TH><U>Price:</U></TH>
<TH><U>Quantity:</U></TH> <TH><U>Total amt:</U></TH>
<xsl:for-each select="document('PurchaseOrder.xml')//cac:OrderLine">
```

The <P/> is a "paragraph break" tag (i.e., it provides a bigger break than a <BR/>) separating the second table from the first. Be careful to insert this code in your file after the closing table tag, </TABLE>, and before the closing center tag, </CENTER> (i.e., we want to close the first table, have a break, and start the second table still centered on the Web page). The beginning <TABLE> tag and the header row are functionally the same as in the first table and this table has a smaller border. As explained earlier, the **xsl:for-each select** instruction sets up a "**for-each**" loop by selecting a set of nodes in a source document and processing them according to the instructions contained within the "**for-each**" instruction. In this case, the **select** instruction uses the same **document('*URI*')/*xpath*** structure, discussed earlier, and points to each **cac:OrderLine** found in the Purchase Order document.

Populating the order line data table: The following code selects the appropriate values from leaf nodes for each **cac:OrderLine** element and inserts each in an individual cell (i.e., between a set of <TD> tags) in a row in the data table:

```
<TR>
<TD align="left"> <xsl:value-of select="./cac:LineItem/cbc:ID"/> </TD>
<TD> <xsl:value-of select="./cac:LineItem/cac:Item/cac:SellersItemIdentification/
        cbc:ID"/> </TD>
<TD> <xsl:value-of select="./cac:LineItem/cac:Item/cbc:Description"/> </TD>
<TD align="right"> <xsl:value-of select="format-
number(./cac:LineItem/cac:Price/cbc:PriceAmount,'$##.00')"/> </TD>
<TD align="right"> <xsl:value-of select="./cac:LineItem/cbc:Quantity"/> </TD>
<TD align="right"> <xsl:value-of select="format-number(./cac:LineItem/
        cbc:LineExtensionAmount,'$##.00')"/> </TD>
</TR>
</xsl:for-each>
</TABLE>
```

Notice that the **XPath** in each **value-of select** instruction starts with a **./** - the period at the beginning of the **XPath** literally means "start the **XPath** at the element designated in the **for-each select** instruction". It is necessary here because we want to select data from a remote document, not the shell document (i.e., since we started this XSLT processing by way of a shell document, and are now working with a remote document inside a **for-each** loop, the period is necessary so that the processor knows which document to select from). Notice also that many of the <TD> tags have an align attribute; as in <TD align="left">. An align attribute is necessary when you want your data to be justified right or left in a cell. After the <TD> **value-of select** instructions, we need to close the table row, </TR>, and the **for-each** loop, **</for-each>**, and this data table, </TABLE>.

Save your file and process it by opening the *CreatePurchaseOrderPage.xml* document in your browser. The result should look like Figure 5-8. Note that if there had been more than one **cac:OrderLine** element in the *PurchaseOrder.xml* document, each one would have been processed and its data entered on a row in the data table.

Transforming using the apply-templates instruction

We have now used several basic XSLT instructions to transform XML documents. As with most programming languages, there is more than one way to accomplish a task. In the interactive exercise just completed we used the "**for-each**" loop instruction to process the **cac:OrderLine** elements. Another method to accomplish the same thing is the "**apply-templates**" instruction. As mentioned earlier, XSLT is referred to as a "template matching" language. Remember that the first child element after the **xsl:stylesheet** root element is **<xsl:template match** = **"/">** which starts a template by "matching" the entire source document. Within this template, it is often desirable to apply other templates to specific documents or pieces of documents. For example, to create the Purchase Order in the previous exercise, we could have applied a template to the remote document which would have accomplished the same result as the **for-each** loop. The general rule in the XSLT language is that you start your transformation with a main template (i.e., one that matches the entire source document) and then "apply" other templates as needed. In the example we have been working with, you would replace the **<xsl:for-each select= "document('PurchaseOrder.xml')//cac:OrderLine">** with **<xsl:apply-templates select="document('PurchaseOrder.xml')//cac:OrderLine"/>**. Notice that the **select** instruction is exactly the same in both but the **xsl:apply-template** instruction is an empty element. The **xsl:apply-templates** instruction literally tells the processor to go find a template that matches **cac:OrderLine**, the last node in the **XPath**. This template is identified with the template instruction **<xsl:template match="cac:OrderLine">**. It contains the instructions to apply to all "**cac:OrderLine**" nodes. Notice that they are exactly the same instructions as in the "**for-each**" loop. The complete template is:

```
<xsl:template match="cac:OrderLine">
<TR>
<TD align="left"> <xsl:value-of select="./cac:LineItem/cbc:ID"/> </TD>
<TD> <xsl:value-of select="./cac:LineItem/cac:Item/cac:SellersItemIdentification/
        cbc:ID"/> </TD>
<TD> <xsl:value-of select="./cac:LineItem/cac:Item/cbc:Description"/> </TD>
<TD align="right"> <xsl:value-of select="format-
number(./cac:LineItem/cac:Price/cbc:PriceAmount,'$##.00')"/> </TD>
<TD align="right"> <xsl:value-of select="./cac:LineItem/cbc:Quantity"/> </TD>
<TD align="right"> <xsl:value-of select="format-number(./cac:LineItem/
        cbc:LineExtensionAmount,'$##.00')"/> </TD>
</TR>
```

</xsl:template>

Remember that XSLT is a "template matching" language. The first instruction following the **xsl:stylesheet** root element in an XSLT document is **<xsl:template match= "/">**. Within this overall template, it is common to call other templates using the **<xsl:apply-templates select= "xxx"/>** and **<xsl:template match= "xxx">** instructions. The advantage to using this technique, as opposed to a "**for-each**" loop, is that you can call a template multiple times without rewriting the code. You can even call a previously written and archived template.

Summary

XSLT documents are XML documents that contain instructions to apply to nodes in one or more XML source documents to transform them into an XML result document. An XSLT processor reads both the XSLT document and the XML source document(s), interprets the XSLT instructions, and then applies them to the source document(s) to create an XML result document. Since all documents being processed are XML documents, XSLT transformations can be accomplished by any up-to-date XML-enabled software, eliminating the need for proprietary software and expensive hardware.

Although the XSLT language is quite powerful, its basics are easy to understand. It is a scripting language that contains instructions that are interpreted at the same time they are being processed. Sets of instructions are grouped in "templates" that "match" nodes in source document(s). The templates tell the XSLT processor how to find and "select" nodes and node values in the source document(s) and transform them into nodes in a result document. The result document can then be processed for whatever purpose it is designed: display as a Web page, storage in a database, or further processing as an XML document. In the following end-of-chapter exercises, you will use the basic XSLT language to write scripts to transform XML documents, including XBRL instance documents, into Web pages.

In this Chapter, we have only scratched the surface of the XSLT language. For more information, there is an excellent tutorial at http://www.w3schools.com/xsl/ and for complete references see: *XSLT 2.0: Programmer's Reference* (3rd edition), by Michael Kay, Wrox Press, 2004; and *XPath 2.0: Programmer's Reference*, by Michael Kay, Wrox Press, 2004

Glossary of new terms introduced in Chapter 5

Extensible Stylesheet Language for Transformation (XSLT): An easily understood but very powerful scripting language for transforming XML documents from one form to another. Transformation is one of the most important aspects of working with XML documents. XSLT is a subset of XSL and is part of the XML foundation.

for-each loop: A block of code within a "for-each" element that is used to process multiple nodes with the same name. It is always used with a match attribute to identify the nodes in the source document to which it applies, as in <xsl:for-each select="*the path to a node set*">.

format-number: An XSLT instruction to format a number in a specific way in the result document. The format-number always takes two arguments as in the following: "format-number(*path to number*, *'format required'*)".

Node set: A set of nodes at the same level of a source document's hierarchy. They can be processed together as a set using XSLT instructions.

Rules: Another word for XSLT instructions. It refers to the fact that each XSLT instruction is a rule to be applied to an XML document to transform it into something different.

Stylesheet: A generic term used to describe XSLT documents. It refers to the original purpose of the XSLT language: to apply style to XML documents.

Scripting language: A programming language that is "interpreted" by a processor as the code is being processed.

Templates: Another word for a set of XSLT instructions. XSLT is referred to as a template matching language.

Transformation script: Another way to refer to an XSLT instruction set or an XSLT document. A transformation script is a set of rules or instructions to be used to transform a source document to a result document.

XHTML (Extensible Hypertext Markup Language):Well-formed HTML. HTML, the original language for creating Web pages, is a predefined tag set that tells a Web browser how to display Web pages. HTML documents do not have to be well-formed. XHTML is a set of rules to follow to create Web pages that are also well-formed XML documents.

xml-stylesheet: The reserved word for the instruction that ties an XML document to an XML stylesheet. As used with XSLT, it appears as follows in the prolog of an XML document: <?xml-stylesheet type="text/xsl" href="*URI of the stylesheet document*"?>.

xsl:stylesheet: The root element of an XSLT document. "**stylesheet**" is the key word for the root element, and "**xsl**" is its namespace identifier.

XSLT processor: A software package that can process XSLT instructions to transform XML documents.

xsl:apply-templates: An XSLT instruction to apply a new template to a node or node set and its children in a source document. It is often used to process multiple nodes with the same name and often has a select attribute, as in <xsl:apply-templates select="*path to node or node set*"/>. The processor then looks for <xsl:template match="*node or node set*"> and applies the rules found in this template.

xsl:template: The reserved word to identify the beginning of a template in an XSLT document. It is often used with a match attribute to identify the nodes in the source document to which it applies, as in <xsl:template match = "/">, which applies to the entire source document.

xsl:value-of select= "*a node*": An XSLT instruction to find "a node" and "select" its value for inclusion in a result document.

Exercises

<u>**Exercise 5-1**</u>: In this exercise you will write the XSLT instructions to create a Web page using the XBRL instance document created in Exercise 4-1 (I will refer to it as *MyBikesCurrentAssetsAndLiabilities.xml*) as the <u>source</u> document. When you created that XBRL instance document, you had to go to the **us-gaap v1.0** taxonomy to find the appropriate XBRL element name for each item. Each XBRL element in the **us-gaap** taxonomy also has a **standard label** in a label linkbase. Instead of writing complex XSLT instructions to access them, in this exercise we will modify the original XBRL instance document to include <u>a **label** attribute for each item</u>. For each item you will have to look up the Standard Label in the US GAAP taxonomy (i.e., for **CashAndCashEquivalents- AtCarryingValue** its standard label is "Cash and Cash Equivalents, at Carrying Value"). Open your *MyBikesCurrentAssetsAndLiabilities.xml* file in Notepad™ or your favorite text editor and add the appropriate **label** to <u>each XBRL item</u> in your instance document. This item should now be similar to the following: **<us-gaap:CashAndCash-EquivalentsAtCarryingValue contextRef="xxx" unitRef="USD" decimals="0" label="Cash and Cash Equivalents, at Carrying Value">**5393000**</us-gaap:Cash-AndCashEquivalentsAtCarryingValue** >.

Next add the **stylesheet** instruction **<?xml-stylesheet type="text/xsl" href="MyBikesCurrentAssetAndLiabReport.xsl"?>** to the prolog section of your *MyBikesCurrentAssetsAndLiabilities.xml.*

Next open a new file in Notepad™ or your favorite text editor and create your XSLT file named *MyBikesCurrentAssetAndLiabReport.xsl* (see Hints below). Your goal is to write the XSLT instructions to create a current asset and liability report similar to Figure 5-10.

Figure 5-10: Current Assets and liability report for MyBikes.com

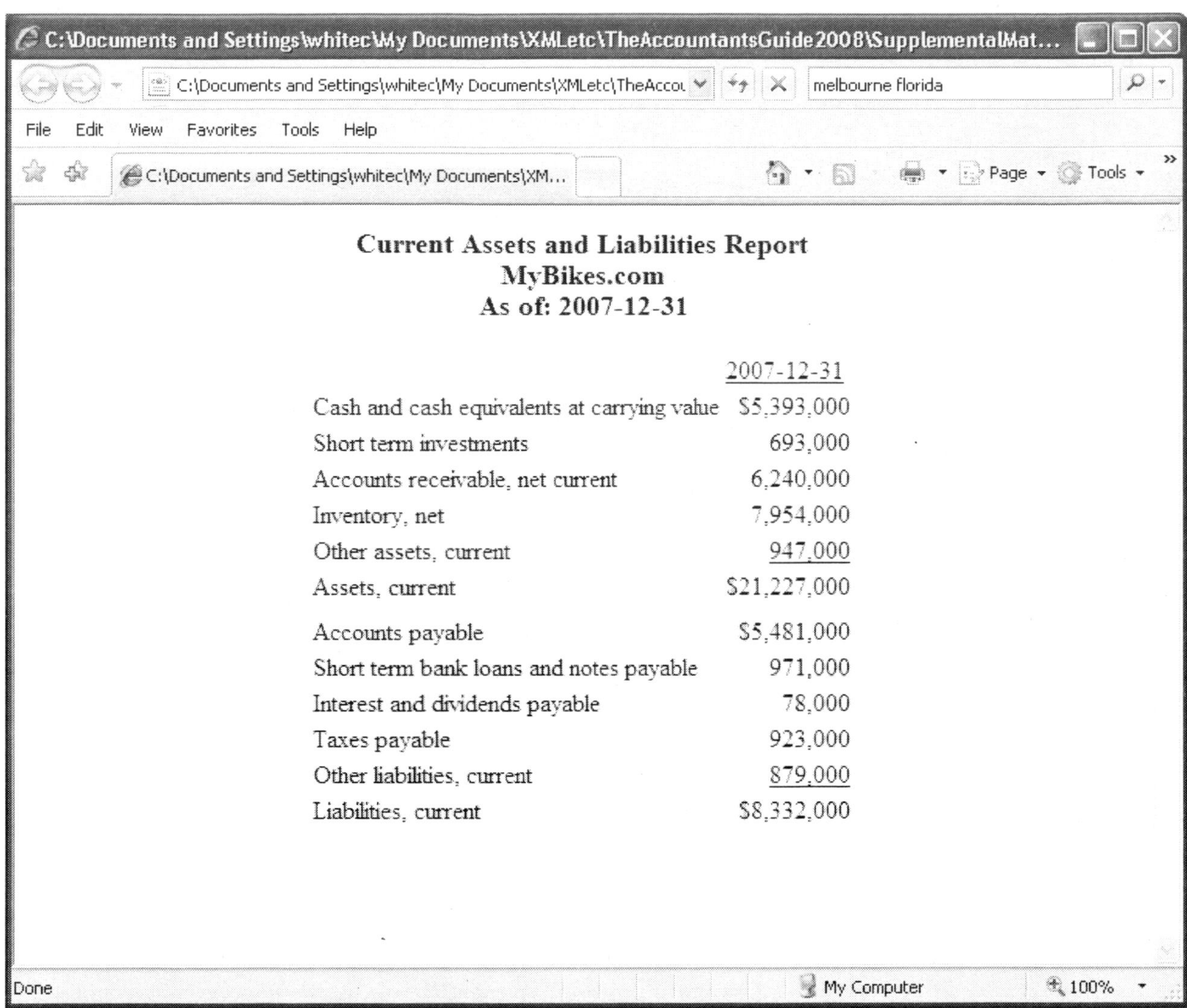

Current Assets and Liabilities Report
MyBikes.com
As of: 2007-12-31

	2007-12-31
Cash and cash equivalents at carrying value	$5,393,000
Short term investments	693,000
Accounts receivable, net current	6,240,000
Inventory, net	7,954,000
Other assets, current	947,000
Assets, current	$21,227,000
Accounts payable	$5,481,000
Short term bank loans and notes payable	971,000
Interest and dividends payable	78,000
Taxes payable	923,000
Other liabilities, current	879,000
Liabilities, current	$8,332,000

Hints: Below is a start for your *MyBikesCurrentAssetAndLiabilitiesReport.xsl* document:

```
<?xml version="1.0"?>
<!-- File name: MyBikesCurrentAssetsAndLiabilitiesReport.xsl – Author: add your
name    -->

<xsl:stylesheet xmlns:xsl="http://www.w3.org/1999/XSL/Transform"
xmlns:us-gaap="http://xbrl.us/us-gaap/2008-03-31" version="1.0">
        <xsl:template match = "/">
        <HTML>
        <CENTER>
        <H3>Current Assets and Liabilities Report<BR/>
        MyBikes.com<BR/>
        As of: <xsl:value-of select="//instant"/>
        </H3>
```

Open Notepad™ or your favorite text editor and start your **.xsl** document with this code. To access the value associated with a label attribute, use the following code: **<xsl:value-of select="//*prefix:element name*/@label"/>** . To format numbers, use the following patterns: For a $ sign use **'$#,##0'**; For no dollar sign use **'#,##0'**. To underline, use the HTML tag <U>. To get your numbers to align to the right, use the HTML tag <TD align="right">. When finished, first open your *MyBikesCurrentAssetsAnd LiabilitiesReport.xsl* file in IE to see if it is well-formed. Then open your *MyBikesCurrent AssetsAndLiabilities.xml* source document and see if the result looks similar to Figure 5-10.

__**Exercise 5-2**__: In this exercise you will write the XSLT instructions to create a Web page using the XBRL instance document created in Exercise 4-2 (I will refer to it as *MyBikesCurrentOperationsReport.xml*) as the __source__ document. When you created that XBRL instance document, you had to go to the **us-gaap v1.0** taxonomy to find the appropriate XBRL element name for each item. Each XBRL element in the **us-gaap** taxonomy also has a **standard label** in a label linkbase. Instead of writing complex XSLT instructions to access them, in this exercise we will modify the original XBRL instance document to include __a **label** attribute for each item__. For each item you will have to look up the Standard Label in the US GAAP taxonomy (i.e., for **CashAndCashEquivalents- AtCarryingValue** its standard label is "Cash and Cash Equivalents, at Carrying Value"). Open your *MyBikesCurrentOperationsReport.xml* file in Notepad™ or your favorite text editor and add the appropriate **label** to __each XBRL item__ in your instance document. This item should now be similar to the following: **<us-gaap:CashAndCash-EquivalentsAtCarryingValue contextRef="xxx" unitRef="USD" decimals="0" label="Cash and Cash Equivalents, at Carrying Value">**5393000**</us-gaap:Cash-AndCashEquivalentsAtCarryingValue >**.

Next add the **stylesheet** instruction **<?xml-stylesheet type="text/xsl" href="MyBikesCurrentOperationsReport.xsl"?>** to the prolog section of your *MyBikesCurrentOperationsReport.xml.*

Next open a new file in Notepad™ or your favorite text editor and create your XSLT file named *MyBikesCurrentOperationsReport.xsl* (see Hints below). Your goal is to write the XSLT instructions to create a current asset and liability report similar to Figure 5-11.

Figure 5-11: Current Operations Report for MyBikes.com

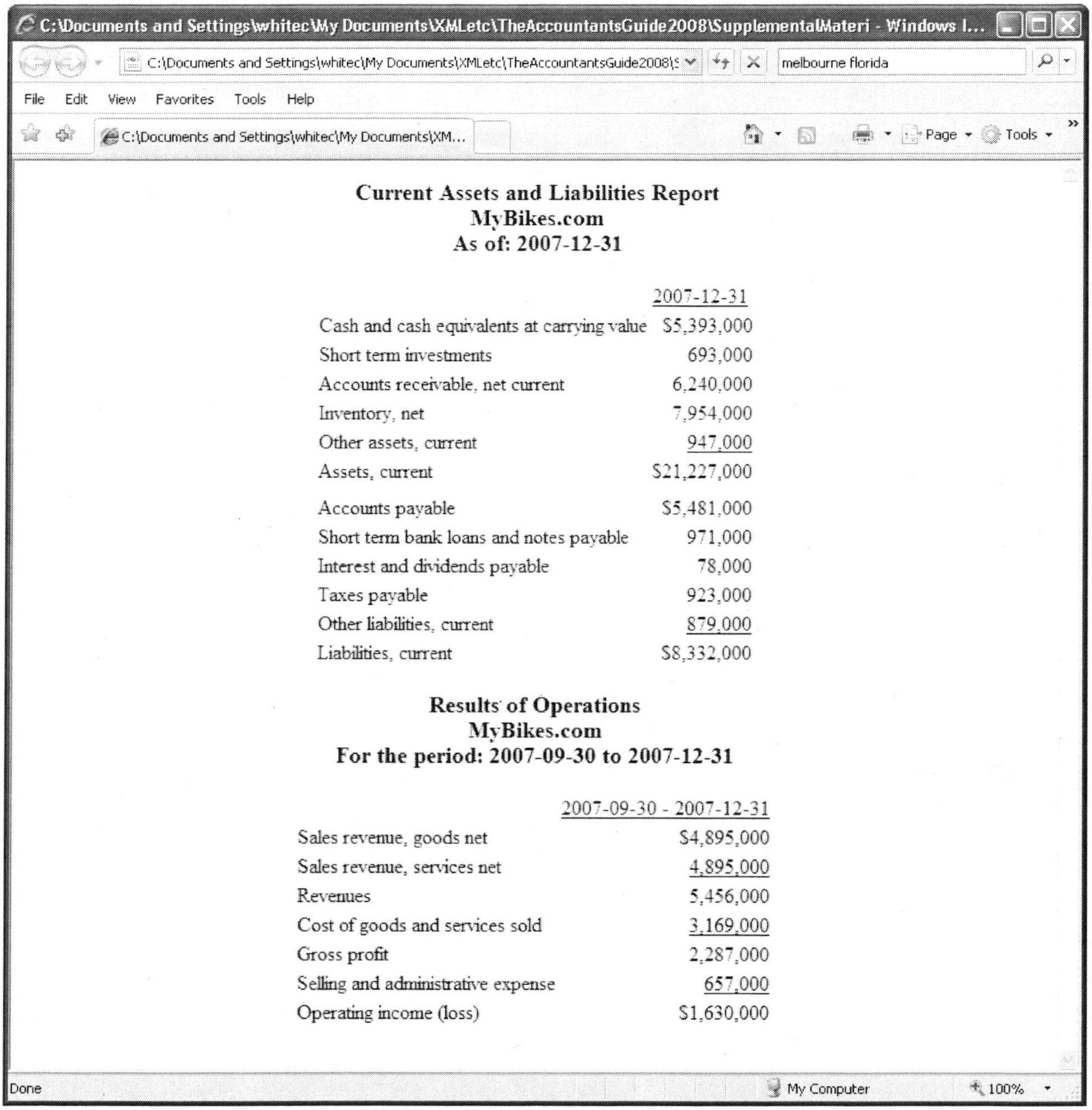

C:\Documents and Settings\whitec\My Documents\XMLetc\TheAccountantsGuide2008\SupplementalMateri - Windows I...

Current Assets and Liabilities Report
MyBikes.com
As of: 2007-12-31

	2007-12-31
Cash and cash equivalents at carrying value	$5,393,000
Short term investments	693,000
Accounts receivable, net current	6,240,000
Inventory, net	7,954,000
Other assets, current	947,000
Assets, current	$21,227,000
Accounts payable	$5,481,000
Short term bank loans and notes payable	971,000
Interest and dividends payable	78,000
Taxes payable	923,000
Other liabilities, current	879,000
Liabilities, current	$8,332,000

Results of Operations
MyBikes.com
For the period: 2007-09-30 to 2007-12-31

	2007-09-30 - 2007-12-31
Sales revenue, goods net	$4,895,000
Sales revenue, services net	4,895,000
Revenues	5,456,000
Cost of goods and services sold	3,169,000
Gross profit	2,287,000
Selling and administrative expense	657,000
Operating income (loss)	$1,630,000

Hints: Below is a start for your *MyBikesCurrentOperationsReport.xsl* document:
<?xml version="1.0"?>
<!-- File name: MyBikesCurrentOperationsReport.xsl – **Author:** *add your name* -->

<xsl:stylesheet xmlns:xsl="http://www.w3.org/1999/XSL/Transform" xmlns:us-gaap="http://xbrl.us/us-gaap/2008-03-31" version="1.0">

```
<xsl:template match = "/">
<HTML>
<CENTER>
<H3>Current Assets and Liabilities Report<BR/>
MyBikes.com<BR/>
As of: <xsl:value-of select="//instant"/>
</H3>
```

Open Notepad™ or your favorite text editor and start your **.xsl** document with this code. To access the value associated with a label attribute, use the following code: **<xsl:value-of select="//*prefix:element name*/@label"/>** . To format numbers, use the following patterns: For a $ sign use **'$#,##0'**; For no dollar sign use **'#,##0'**. To underline, use the HTML tag <U>. To get your numbers to align to the right, use the HTML tag <TD align="right">. When finished, first open your *MyBikesCurrentOperations Report.xsl* file in IE to see if it is well-formed. Then open your *MyBikesCurrent OperationsReport.xml* source document and see if the result looks similar to Figure 5-11.

<u>Exercise 5-3</u>: In this exercise you will write the XSLT instructions to create a Web page using the XBRL instance document created in Exercise 4-3 (I will refer to it as *MyBikesOperationsAndDisclosures.xml*) as the <u>source</u> document. When you created that XBRL instance document, you had to go to the **us-gaap v1.0** taxonomy to find the appropriate XBRL element name for each item. Each XBRL element in the **us-gaap** taxonomy also has a **standard label** in a label linkbase. Instead of writing complex XSLT instructions to access them, in this exercise we will modify the original XBRL instance document to include <u>a **label** attribute for each item</u>. For each item you will have to look up the Standard Label in the US GAAP taxonomy (i.e., for **CashAndCashEquivalents- AtCarryingValue** its standard label is "Cash and Cash Equivalents, at Carrying Value"). Open your *MyBikesOperationsAndDisclosures.xml* file in Notepad™ or your favorite text editor and add the appropriate **label** to <u>each XBRL item</u> in your instance document. This item should now be similar to the following: **<us-gaap:CashAndCash-EquivalentsAtCarryingValue contextRef="xxx" unitRef="USD" decimals="0" label="Cash and Cash Equivalents, at Carrying Value"**>5393000**</us-gaap:Cash-AndCashEquivalentsAtCarryingValue** >.

Next add the **stylesheet** instruction **<?xml-stylesheet type="text/xsl" href="MyBikesCurrentOperationsReport.xsl"?>** to the prolog section of your *MyBikesOperationsAndDisclosures.xml*.

Next open a new file in Notepad™ or your favorite text editor and create your XSLT file named *MyBikesOperationsAndDisclosuresReport.xsl* (see Hints below). Your goal is to write the XSLT instructions to create a current asset and liability report similar to Figure 5-12.

Figure 5-12: Current Assets, liabilities, Operations and Disclosures Report for MyBikes.com

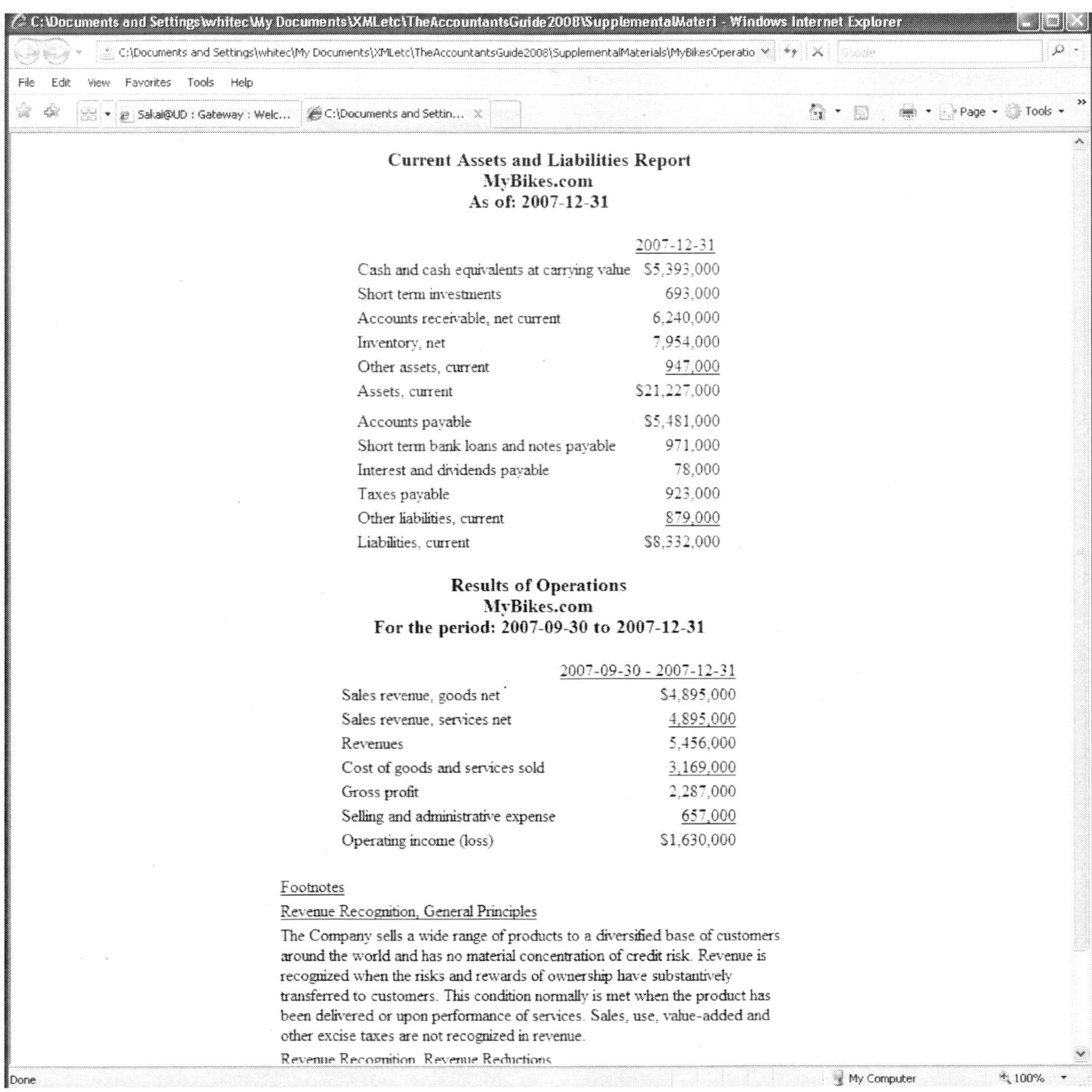

Current Assets and Liabilities Report
MyBikes.com
As of: 2007-12-31

	2007-12-31
Cash and cash equivalents at carrying value	$5,393,000
Short term investments	693,000
Accounts receivable, net current	6,240,000
Inventory, net	7,954,000
Other assets, current	947,000
Assets, current	$21,227,000
Accounts payable	$5,481,000
Short term bank loans and notes payable	971,000
Interest and dividends payable	78,000
Taxes payable	923,000
Other liabilities, current	879,000
Liabilities, current	$8,332,000

Results of Operations
MyBikes.com
For the period: 2007-09-30 to 2007-12-31

	2007-09-30 - 2007-12-31
Sales revenue, goods net	$4,895,000
Sales revenue, services net	4,895,000
Revenues	5,456,000
Cost of goods and services sold	3,169,000
Gross profit	2,287,000
Selling and administrative expense	657,000
Operating income (loss)	$1,630,000

Footnotes

Revenue Recognition, General Principles

The Company sells a wide range of products to a diversified base of customers around the world and has no material concentration of credit risk. Revenue is recognized when the risks and rewards of ownership have substantively transferred to customers. This condition normally is met when the product has been delivered or upon performance of services. Sales, use, value-added and other excise taxes are not recognized in revenue.

Revenue Recognition, Revenue Reductions

Hints: Below is a start for your *MyBikesOperationsAndDisclosuresReport.xsl* document:
<?xml version="1.0"?>
<!-- File name: MyBikesOperationsAndDisclosuresReport.xsl – **Author:** *add your name*
-->

<xsl:stylesheet xmlns:xsl="http://www.w3.org/1999/XSL/Transform" xmlns:us-gaap="http://xbrl.us/us-gaap/2008-03-31" version="1.0">

```
<xsl:template match = "/">
<HTML>
<CENTER>
<H3>Current Assets and Liabilities Report<BR/>
MyBikes.com<BR/>
As of: <xsl:value-of select="//instant"/>
</H3>
```

Open Notepad™ or your favorite text editor and start your **.xsl** document with this code. To access the value associated with a label attribute, use the following code: **<xsl:value-of select="//*prefix:element name*/@label"/>** . To format numbers, use the following patterns: For a $ sign use **'$#,##0'**; For no dollar sign use **'#,##0'**. To underline, use the HTML tag <U>. To get your numbers to align to the right, use the HTML tag <TD align="right">. When finished, first open your *MyBikesOperationsAndDisclosures Report.xsl* file in IE to see if it is well-formed. Then open your *MyBikesOperationsAnd Disclosures.xml* source document and see if the result looks similar to Figure 5-12.

Downloadable files:

Available from: www.SkipWhite.com/Guide2008/Chapter5/ *file name*:

- File name: UBLCatalogueWStylesheet (Figure 5-3 – Part 1)
  http://www.skipwhite.com/Guide2008/Chapter5/UBLCatalogueWStylesheet.xml
- File name: UBLCataloguePage.xsl (Figure 5-3 – Part 2)
  http://www.skipwhite.com/Guide2008/Chapter5/UBLCataloguePage.xsl
- File name: CreatePurchaseOrderPage (Figure 5-6)
  http://www.skipwhite.com/Guide2008/Chapter5/CreatePurchaseOrderPage.xml
- File name: PurchaseOrder (Figure 5-7)
  http://www.skipwhite.com/Guide2008/Chpter5/UBLPurchaseOrder.xml

References & more information:

HTML Help.com (www.htmlhelp.com)

HTML Tutorial, W3 Schools (http://www.w3schools.com/html/default.asp)

Kay, Michael, *XPath 2.0: Programmer's Reference*, Wrox Press (2004).

Kay, Michael, *XSLT 2.0: Programmer's Reference (3rd edition)*, Wrox Press (2000).

XSLT Tutorial, W3 Schools (http://www.w3schools.com/xsl/)

The Accountant's Guide to XBRL

Chapter 6: The Current State of XBRL

Overview

This chapter discusses the current state of XBRL in financial and business operations reporting around the world, some of the tools available for instance document creation and validation, and the future role of XBRL and related emerging technologies.

A number of major XBRL initiatives are in progress in the U.S. and around the world. In the U.S., the SEC and XBRL U.S. have teamed up to continue to fund and support the further development and implementation of XBRL as the reporting format for all publicly traded companies. Currently 13 U.S. taxonomies have achieved XBRL International's "Approved" status and one has achieved "Acknowledged" status. An "Acknowledged" taxonomy is one that has been tested for compliance with the XBRL 2.1 Specification. An "Approved" taxonomy is one that has been through an open review process after reaching "Acknowledged" status and has been used to create a number of instance documents to confirm that it adequately covers the data it purports to represent. Currently 18 international taxonomies have achieved "Acknowledged" status, including 16 country-specific taxonomies and two covering IFRS and global standards.

In addition, many tools are available for instance document and taxonomy creation and validation and for viewing, rendering, and analyzing XBRL financial statements. Companies creating SEC filings, for example, have a choice of using a spreadsheet-based tool, such as Rivet Dragon Tag, or a stand-alone software package, such as Fujitsu XWand. Companies can also contract for services with third party agents specializing in instance document creation and SEC filing, including EDGAR Online, Business Wire, and Merrill Corp. Financial analysts and other users have a choice of tools for viewing and analyzing XBRL instances, including Rivet Dragon View, IMetrix, and EDGARizer X.

To help you understand what is currently happening and what can be expected in the near future, we will discuss these activities and others affecting the world of XBRL financial reporting. This is emerging technology. It will evolve and will have a dramatic effect on accountants, clients, and the profession.

XBRL Around the World

The most significant aspect of XBRL financial reporting today results from regulatory and government agencies like the FDIC and SEC in the U.S., the Companies House and the HM Revenue & Customs in the U.K., and a number of stock exchanges requiring members to report in XBRL format. Oversight and regulatory agencies have long required members to report activities in a standard format – typically by filling in the blanks in a form designed for a specific purpose. Upon receipt of the form, the regulatory agency typically reviews and maps data from each individual member entity into a database or spreadsheet for further analysis – a very time consuming and error-prone task often requiring months of labor. Agency employees then face the unenviable tasks of trying to analyze massive amounts of data that are not always complete or comparable and then reconciling the not always reliable results. Such activities limit the agencies' ability to effectively regulate member entities.

FDIC

The U.S. FDIC, which regulates federally insured banks, is an interesting example of XBRL adoption. As a member of the Federal Financial Institutions Examination Council (FFIEC), the FDIC, along with the Federal Reserve Board (FRB]) and the Office of the Controller of the Currency (OCC), collects quarterly "Call Reports" from member banks. These Call Reports contain approximately 125 data items that indicate the financial health of the institutions. Some of these data items are defined in the XBRL Bank and Savings Institutions (BASI) taxonomy, while others represent items defined specifically for the FDIC Call Reports. Since a Call Report is designed for a specific reporting purpose and is not meant for general financial reporting, the FFIEC has developed its own stand-alone Call Report taxonomy.

Beginning with the third quarter of 2005, FDIC member institutions have been required to submit Call Reports as XBRL instance documents electronically to the FFIEC Central Data Repository (CDR). Member institutions have to create and validate their XBRL instance documents using the FFIEC's Call Report taxonomy prior to submission to the CDR. The requirement to validate prior to submission shifts the responsibility for validation to the preparer of the Call Report – a change that is having a major impact on the quality of the data submitted. Measurable benefits reported by the FFIEC include the following:

- Data accuracy has improved from 66% to 95%.
- Data inflow begins within 24 hours after closing dates as opposed to several weeks under the former system.
- An individual analyst can now analyze the data from 550 to 600 banks as opposed to 450 to 500 previously.
- Data can be published within one day of receipt as opposed to several days previously.
- Analysts' workload is completed within 41 days of the close of the quarter – a 15% improvement.

The results show immediate improvements in data quality, speed of analysis and data handling, and analysts' effectiveness. Member banks have also realized improvements in the form of more accurate data, more timely reporting, and dramatically fewer follow-up requests.

SEC

Since 1996, all domestic publicly traded companies have been required to submit all SEC filings in electronic form – first as electronic documents and later as documents in PDF and HTML format. The EDGAR (Electronic Data Gathering And Retrieval) database system, now almost 20 years old, has been the repository for all SEC filings with documents available for download; essentially a document repository. In February 2005, the SEC implemented a voluntary pilot program encouraging corporations to file financial statements in XBRL format as supplements to their regular annual filings (PDF and HTML documents). Early in 2006, the SEC implemented their "interactive data initiative" to encourage greater participation in the XBRL pilot program by including an incentive program consisting of expedited reviews of registration statements and annual reports. Later in 2006, they announced a commitment to overhaul the antiquated EDGAR system to support storage and access to XBRL filings – the data to support their interactive data initiative. They also committed funding to support XBRL US in their development of the US GAAP XBRL taxonomies and the creation of a new generation of interactive data software tools.

With funding from the SEC, XBRL US completed the development of version 1.0 of the US GAAP taxonomies in April, 2008; this is what we have been working with in this book. In partnership with the SEC, XBRL US plans to continuously review filings and issue a new version of the US GAAP taxonomy annually. As of this writing, they have released a new version for public comment and expect it to be released for use in February, 2009.

The SEC has now made available on its Web site a number of interactive data viewing and analysis tools (see Figure 6-1). If you have a computer with Internet access, go to: http://www.sec.gov/spotlight/xbrl/xbrlwebapp.shtml. These tools were developed by third-party software developers to demonstrate the potential uses and flexibility of financial information in XBRL format. If you click on Interactive Financial Reports, you will see the "Test Drive Interactive Data" that provides access to quarterly and annual financial statements filed with the SEC. From here, you can choose a company in the left-hand window and click the report you want to see and chart it or download it to Excel. If you click 3M Co/Annual Report (2007-12-31)/Consolidated Balance Sheet, and then click Export to Excel, this data will be loaded into your Excel spreadsheet (see Figure 6-2). Note that the data in Figure 1-1 are the current assets and liabilities from this statement.

Figure 6-1: SEC Interactive data viewers

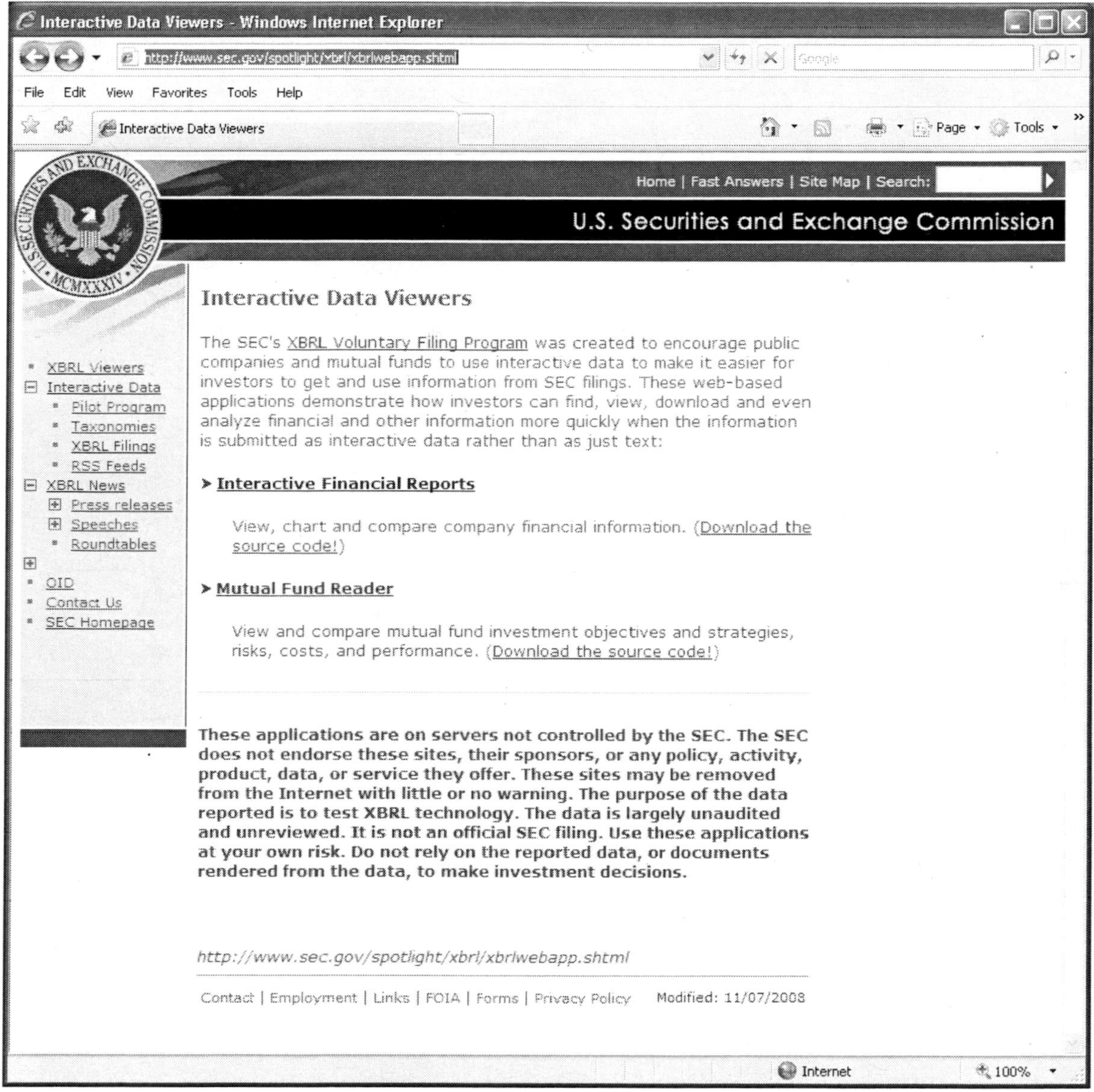

(http://www.sec.gov/spotlight/xbrl/xbrlwebapp.shtml)

Figure 6-2: 3M Company Consolidated Balance Sheet (12-31-2007)

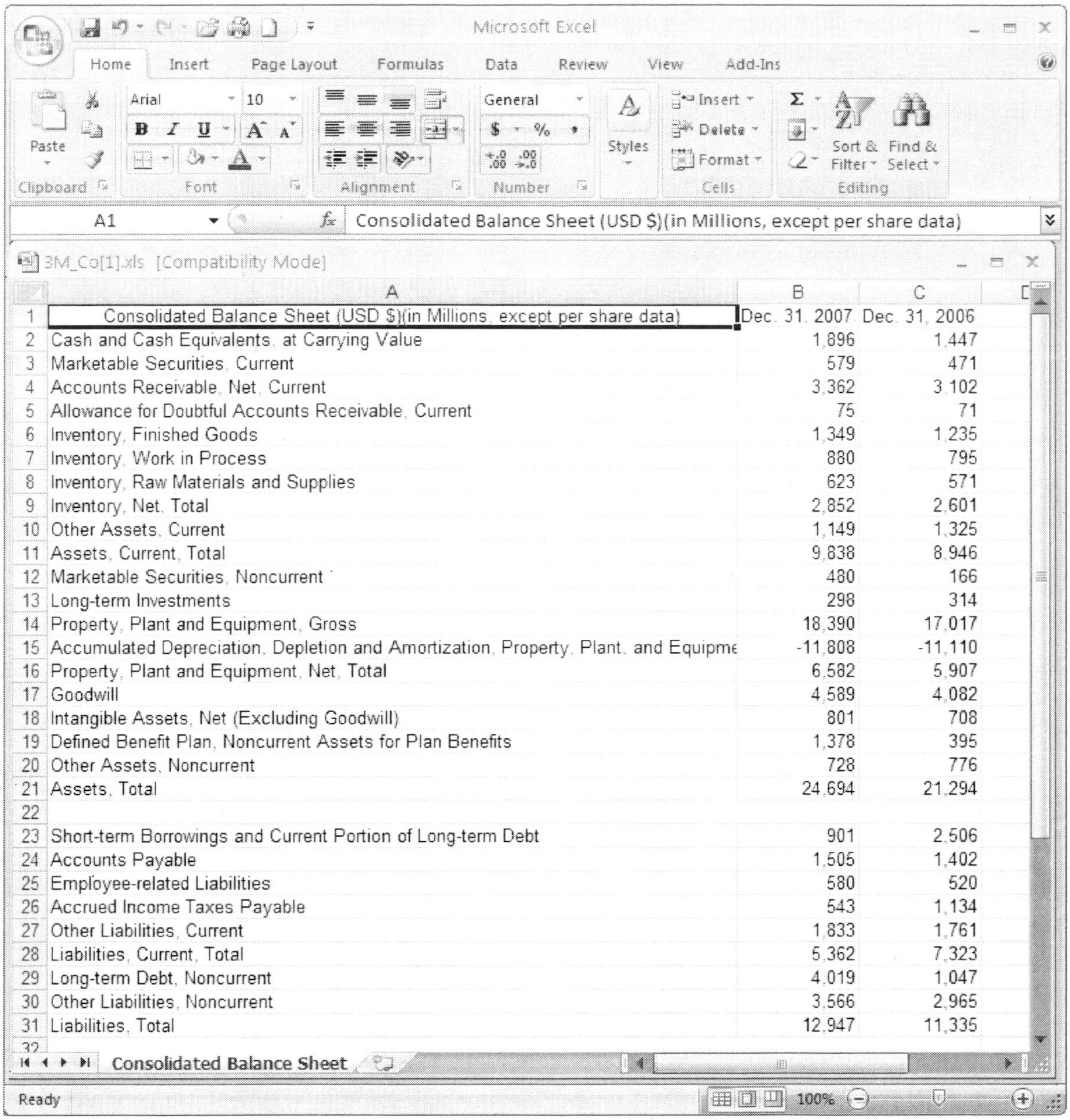

Microsoft Excel

A1 — Consolidated Balance Sheet (USD $)(in Millions, except per share data)

3M_Co[1].xls [Compatibility Mode]

	A	B	C
1	Consolidated Balance Sheet (USD $)(in Millions, except per share data)	Dec. 31, 2007	Dec. 31, 2006
2	Cash and Cash Equivalents, at Carrying Value	1,896	1,447
3	Marketable Securities, Current	579	471
4	Accounts Receivable, Net, Current	3,362	3,102
5	Allowance for Doubtful Accounts Receivable, Current	75	71
6	Inventory, Finished Goods	1,349	1,235
7	Inventory, Work in Process	880	795
8	Inventory, Raw Materials and Supplies	623	571
9	Inventory, Net, Total	2,852	2,601
10	Other Assets, Current	1,149	1,325
11	Assets, Current, Total	9,838	8,946
12	Marketable Securities, Noncurrent	480	166
13	Long-term Investments	298	314
14	Property, Plant and Equipment, Gross	18,390	17,017
15	Accumulated Depreciation, Depletion and Amortization, Property, Plant, and Equipme	-11,808	-11,110
16	Property, Plant and Equipment, Net, Total	6,582	5,907
17	Goodwill	4,589	4,082
18	Intangible Assets, Net (Excluding Goodwill)	801	708
19	Defined Benefit Plan, Noncurrent Assets for Plan Benefits	1,378	395
20	Other Assets, Noncurrent	728	776
21	Assets, Total	24,694	21,294
22			
23	Short-term Borrowings and Current Portion of Long-term Debt	901	2,506
24	Accounts Payable	1,505	1,402
25	Employee-related Liabilities	580	520
26	Accrued Income Taxes Payable	543	1,134
27	Other Liabilities, Current	1,833	1,761
28	Liabilities, Current, Total	5,362	7,323
29	Long-term Debt, Noncurrent	4,019	1,047
30	Other Liabilities, Noncurrent	3,566	2,965
31	Liabilities, Total	12,947	11,335

Consolidated Balance Sheet

While the Interactive Financial Reports viewer tool is useful for accessing, charting, and downloading financial statements to Excel, the Mutual Fund Reader tool is also useful to access risk and return information and to compare funds. Starting at the Interactive Data Viewers site (http://www.sec.gov/spotlight/xbrl/xbrlwebapp.shtml), if you click Mutual Fund Reader/Fidelity Contrafund/Fidelity Advisor New Insights Fund/Risk/Return

Summary (2008-03-10), you will see investment summary information provided by the Interactive Risk & Return Summary Report Viewer (see Figure 6-3).

Figure 6-3: Mutual Fund Risk & Return Viewer

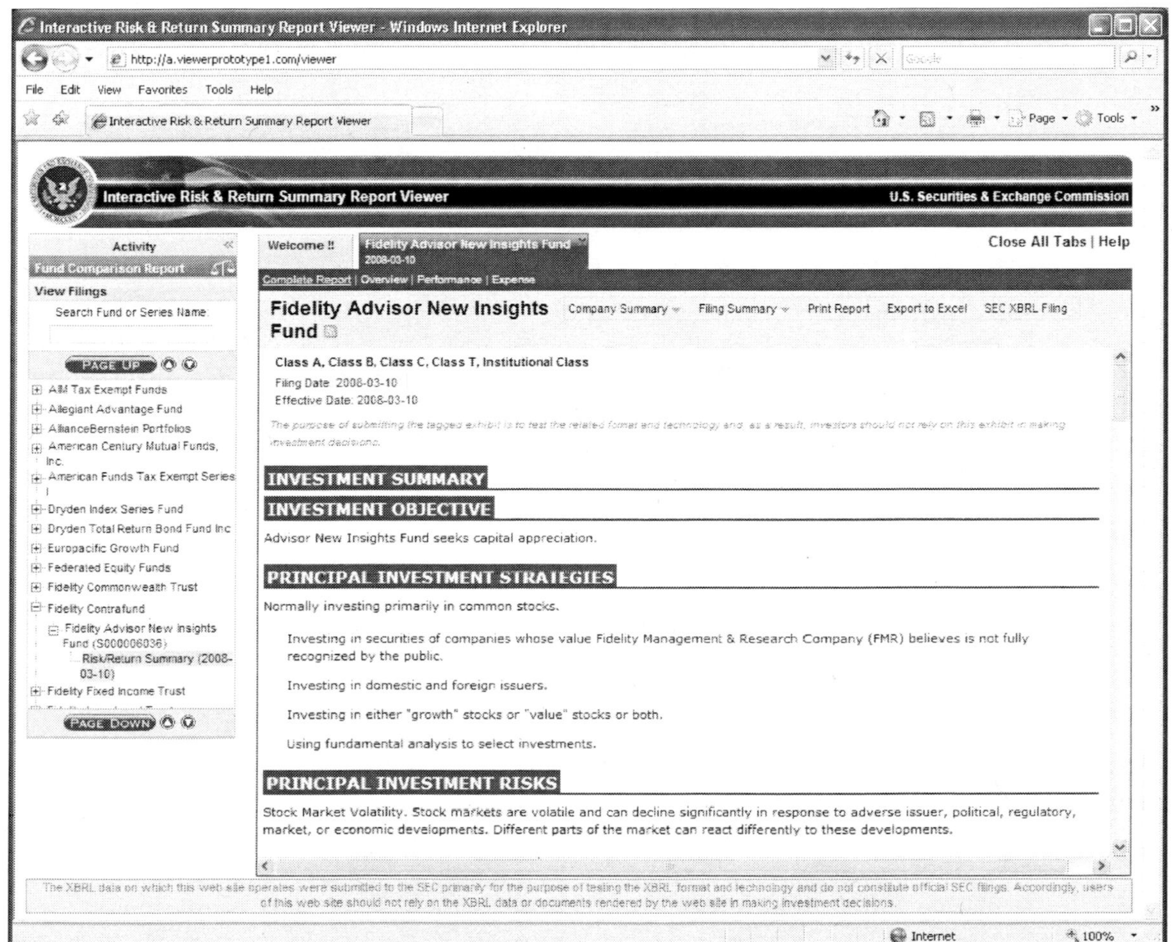

In May 2008, the SEC voted unanimously to propose mandating the use of XBRL for all public company filings to be phased in over three years. In Phase one, beginning in 2009, the 500 largest publicly traded companies will be required to "furnish" XBRL financial statements, in addition to their normal filings. The financial statements will be tagged using the US GAAP taxonomy and any necessary extension taxonomy including footnotes tagged as blocks of text (e.g. Footnote 1 might be tagged with the element name **SignificantAccountingPoliciesTextBlock**). In their second year of filing in XBRL format, companies will be required to tag footnote information in more detail and depth, as in the following example:

<SignificantAccountingPoliciesTextBlock contextRef= "xxx">
<ReceivablesPolicyTextBlock contextRef= "xxx">
<TradeAndOtherAccountsReceivablePolicy contextRef= "xxx">
Our trade accounts receivable policy is …
</TradeAndOtherAccountsReceivablePolicy>

In phase two, beginning in 2010, all other domestic and foreign accelerated filers will be required to begin filing in XBRL format. In phase three, beginning in 2011, all remaining companies will be required to follow suit. It is expected that the SEC will finalize its mandatory XBRL filing requirement in December, 2008. At this time, there is no requirement for assurance to be issued on XBRL filings.

In order to access all XBRL SEC filings go to http://www.sec.gov/index.htm and click Search for Company Filings and then XBRL Submissions.

PCAOB

In May 2005, the PCAOB (Public Company Accounting Oversight Board), established by the Sarbanes-Oxley legislation (2002), issued a set of guidelines for attestation engagements regarding XBRL financial information furnished under the SEC voluntary filing program (see http://www.pcaobus.org/Standards/Staff_Questions_and_Answers/2005/05-25%20.pdf). In summary, auditors with sufficient knowledge of the regulations, the company's financial statements, and XBRL taxonomies and instance documents may be engaged to attest and report on whether the XBRL-related documents accurately reflect the information in the corresponding EDGAR filings. Two major objectives of the examination procedures are to determine whether the XBRL data agree with official EDGAR filings and whether the XBRL instance documents are in conformity with applicable XBRL taxonomies and specifications. In 2008, the PCAOB prioritized the consideration of standards for auditing XBRL financial information. The expectation is that more detailed assurance guidelines will be forthcoming.

International Agencies

Canada: In January 2007, the Canadian Securities Administration launched an XBRL voluntary filing program. In May 2007, companies began furnishing financial statements to the SEDAR database. The SEDAR database system has been updated to support interactive data and The Taskforce to Modernize Securities Legislation in Canada (see http://www.tfmsl.ca/) recommends that the current paper-based disclosure model be abandoned in favor of an interactive, multimedia electronic system, with the expectation of providing users with more timely, comprehensive, and user-friendly access to corporate financial information.

Europe: Many government and regulatory agencies in Europe are implementing pilot programs and new projects involving XBRL reporting. The Irish Central Statistics Office (CSO), which is in charge of collecting economic data from companies, has conducted a pilot project in which all enterprises with more than 20 persons engaged in mining, manufacturing, and energy reported quarterly changes in stocks, acquisitions, and sales of capital assets in XBRL format. The special taxonomy for the CSO reporting project was implemented through an Excel ™ spreadsheet, developed by PricewaterhouseCoopers (PwC), which exported data as an XBRL instance document. The Spanish Stock Exchange Commission has begun accepting and disseminating member company data in XBRL format as part of its electronic administration program. The Committee of European Banking Supervisors is developing an XBRL taxonomy for EU bank reporting. In the UK, Customs House is now receiving audit-exempt accounts data in XBRL format. After 50,000 filings, Customs House reports it is experiencing less than a 1% filing rejection rate. Also in the UK, HM Revenue and Customs now receives corporate tax filings in XBRL format. They expect to have all companies submitting tax filings in XBRL format by 2010. The German Stock Exchange has conducted a pilot program in which it is collecting and redistributing quarterly reports in XBRL format.

Asia: The Japanese Securities and Exchange Commission and the Bank of Japan have adopted XBRL as a reporting standard and have launched an implementation project. The Korean GAAP Taxonomy was approved in 2004, and the Korean Stock Exchange is developing an XBRL-based public disclosure system for publicly traded companies. The Thailand Stock Exchange has created XBRL taxonomies as an initial step toward Thai companies filing financial data in XBRL format. The Accounting & Corporate

Regulatory Authority of Singapore now requires all financial statements to be filed in XBRL format.

Australia and New Zealand: The Australian Government Technical Interoperability Framework, a consortium including the Australian Accounting Standards Board, the Australian Stock Exchange, and industry and banking regulators, has recommended XBRL as a data content standard. Both Australia and New Zealand have adopted the Standard Business Reporting initiative, an XBRL-based program for companies filing information with government agencies.

XBRL is obviously gaining traction with governments, regulatory agencies, and stock exchanges around the world. Governments have many agencies that need to collect, analyze, and share massive amounts of financial information. Regulatory agencies must analyze large amounts of data in order to understand what their member entities are doing and fulfill their mandate. Likewise, stock exchanges must process massive amounts of data on a daily basis and regulate member activities. XBRL provides a standardized format with which to represent financial information. Entities reporting in XBRL format can validate their instance documents before transmitting them to the reporting authority. Once received by the reporting authority, the information should have a high degree of reliability, should be quickly reviewable, and should be directly processable by a database. From there it can be effectively and efficiently analyzed, processed, and reported using software applications. The result should be more accurate, timely, and transparent financial information.

XBRL Services and Tools

From consulting services to XBRL taxonomy creation and validation software, the supply of XBRL-related services and tools is growing rapidly. EDGAROnline, Inc. (www.edgar-online.com), Automated Filing Services, Inc. (http://www.sedaredgar.com/), Merrill Corporation (http://www.merrillcorp.com/cps/rde/xchg/merrillcorp/hs.xsl/565_989.htm), and BusinessWire (http://www.businesswire.com/portal/site/home/corefiling/), among others, provide XBRL consulting and implementation services. ClaritySystems' Clarity FSR (http://www.claritysystems.com/Product/FSR.aspx) is an ERP (Enterprise Resource Planning) software package that can automatically generate XBRL regulatory filings and GAAP to IFRS conversions. Rivet Software's DragonTag (http://www.rivetsoftware.com/dragontag), EDGAR Filings Ltd's EDGARizer X (http://www.edgarfilings.com/), Fujitsu Limited's Interstage XWand (http://www.fujitsu.com/global/services/software/interstage/xwand/cts/xbrlprocessor), and UBmatrix's UBmatrix Report Builder (http://www.ubmatrix.com/products/report_builder.htm), to name a few, are software tools to create, validate, and render XBRL instance documents. Though taxonomy creation is an advanced topic beyond the purpose of this book, most XBRL instance document tools also support extension taxonomy creation. For more information and references see the XBRL US tools and vendors Web site http://xbrl.us/Vendors/Pages/default-expand.aspx.

One tool that is free for educators and available at a discount for University computing labs and student purchase is Rivet Software, Inc.'s Dragon Tag™ ((http://www.rivetsoftware.com/dragontag). Dragon Tag™ is a Microsoft Office™ add-in package for Excel™ and Word™ that facilitates tagging financial information to create XBRL instance documents, reviewing the results, validating the documents, and rendering them as Web pages. Students can use it in the computer lab to gain experience with an XBRL tool and use it to create an extension taxonomy.

The starting point is an Excel™ spreadsheet enabled with Rivet Dragon Tag™ (notice the small tool bar over the A column in Figure 6-4). Notice that we will use the same spreadsheet containing 3M Company's current assets and liabilities (see Chapter 1, Figure 1-1). The Rivet DragonTag MS Office add-in software is available as a 30-day evaluation copy (www.rivetsoftware.com). Also, as mentioned earlier, it is free for faculty and available at reduced pricing for students and University computing labs.

Figure 6-4: 3M Company, Inc.'s current assets and liabilities

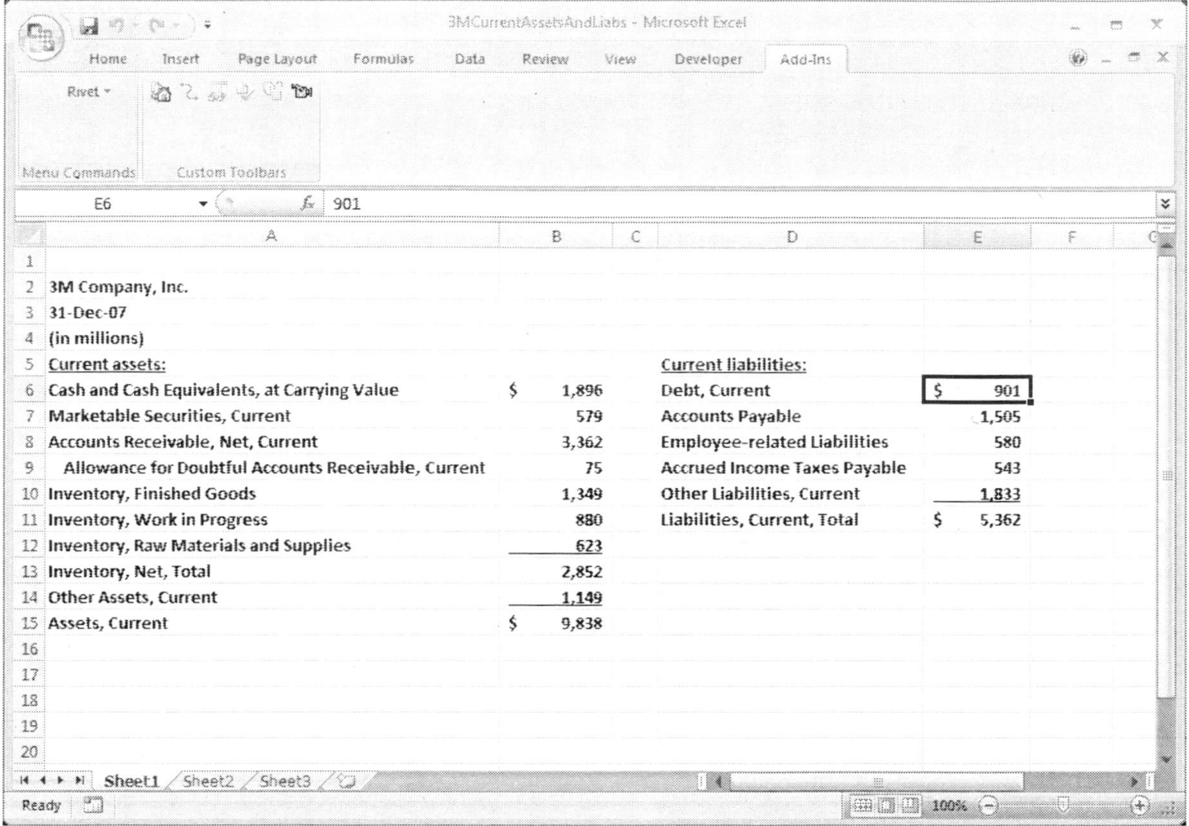

	A	B	C	D	E
1					
2	3M Company, Inc.				
3	31-Dec-07				
4	(in millions)				
5	Current assets:			Current liabilities:	
6	Cash and Cash Equivalents, at Carrying Value	$ 1,896		Debt, Current	$ 901
7	Marketable Securities, Current	579		Accounts Payable	1,505
8	Accounts Receivable, Net, Current	3,362		Employee-related Liabilities	580
9	Allowance for Doubtful Accounts Receivable, Current	75		Accrued Income Taxes Payable	543
10	Inventory, Finished Goods	1,349		Other Liabilities, Current	1,833
11	Inventory, Work in Progress	880		Liabilities, Current, Total	$ 5,362
12	Inventory, Raw Materials and Supplies	623			
13	Inventory, Net, Total	2,852			
14	Other Assets, Current	1,149			
15	Assets, Current	$ 9,838			
16					
17					
18					
19					
20					

The first step is to set up a profile for 3M Company indicating its name and identifying characteristics, including a unique identifier and indicating that it reports under U.S. GAAP for C&I. To set up a profile, click the first icon (the small house) on the add-in tool bar and fill in the blanks on the Entity Profile screen (see Figure 6-5). The only tricky part is the location of the Default Reporting Taxonomy. Since 3M Company reports under US GAAP for C&I companies, you must identify the location of the XBRL schema for this taxonomy. Since the taxonomy consists of a schema and its linkbases, the software looks for files in a specific file hierarchy. Copy the complete US GAAP taxonomy on to a flash drive. To do so, go to: http://xbrl.us/Pages/US-GAAP.aspx and click All Taxonomies (a zip file) in the left-hand panel. After unzipping and saving it, you will see a folder named "XBRLUSGAAP-Taxonomies-2008-03-31" with a rather strange file structure inside (do not change the file structure). To find the appropriate taxonomy schema, open the "ind" folder, then the "ci" folder, then click on the file named “us-gaap-ci-stm-dis-all-2008-03-31.xsd.” This is the complete US GAAP taxonomy including all statements and disclosures.

Figure 6-5: 3M Company’s profile

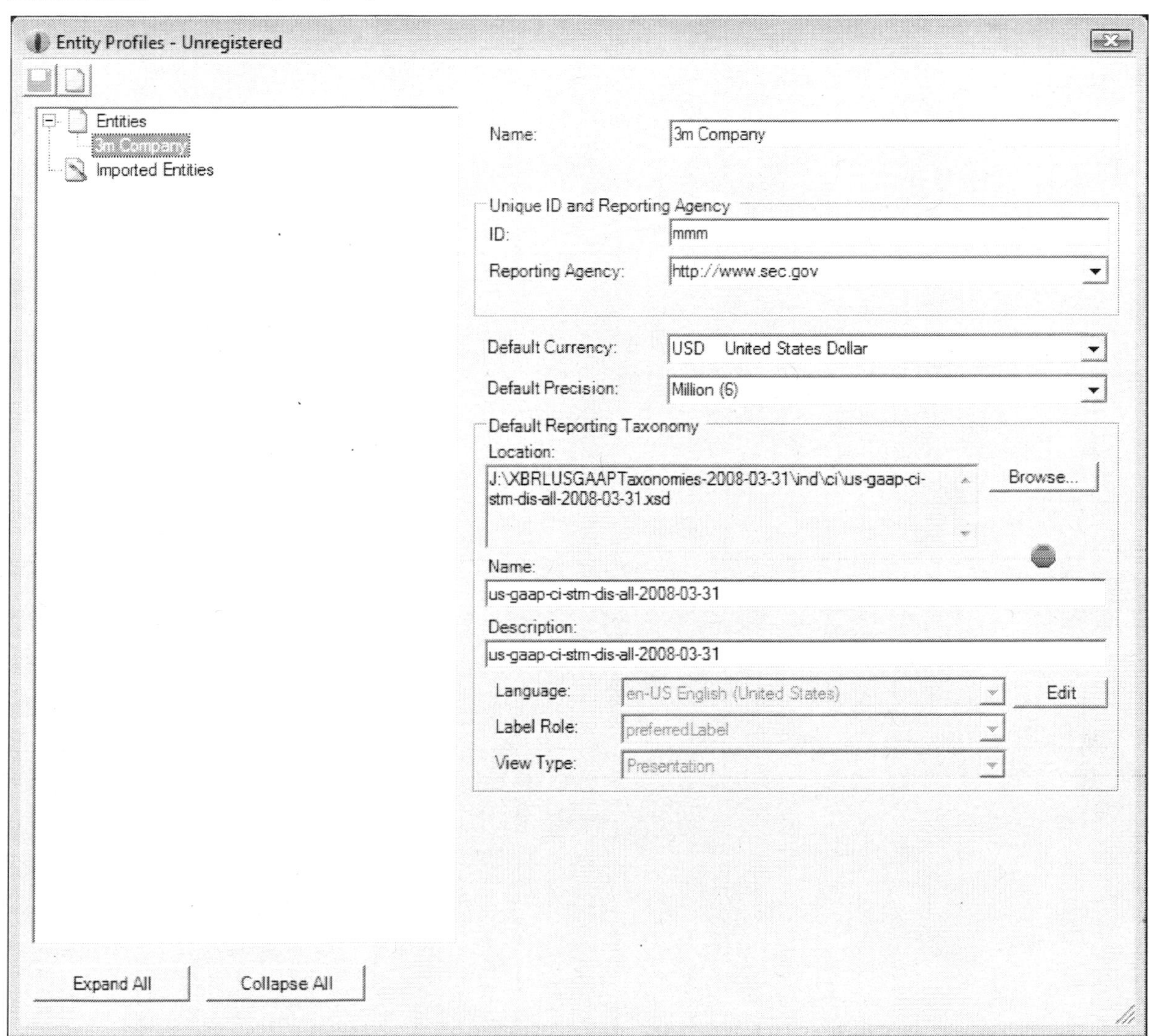

The next step is to open the default US GAAP taxonomy and start the markup process. First click the second icon on the add-on tool bar (the small arrow) and then double-click My taxonomies and then click the us-gaap taxonomy. Continue to click and open the Statement of financial position. You are now working with the Reporting Elements window and can begin “dragging and tagging” each individual item in the spreadsheet. As shown in Figure 6-6, you choose a reporting element from the US GAAP taxonomy and use it to tag a cell containing a balance in your spreadsheet. Notice that the cell changes to gray when it is tagged with an element name and the element name is marked with a star in the taxonomy indicating it has been used.

Figure 6-6: The Reporting Element Cash and Cash Equivalents

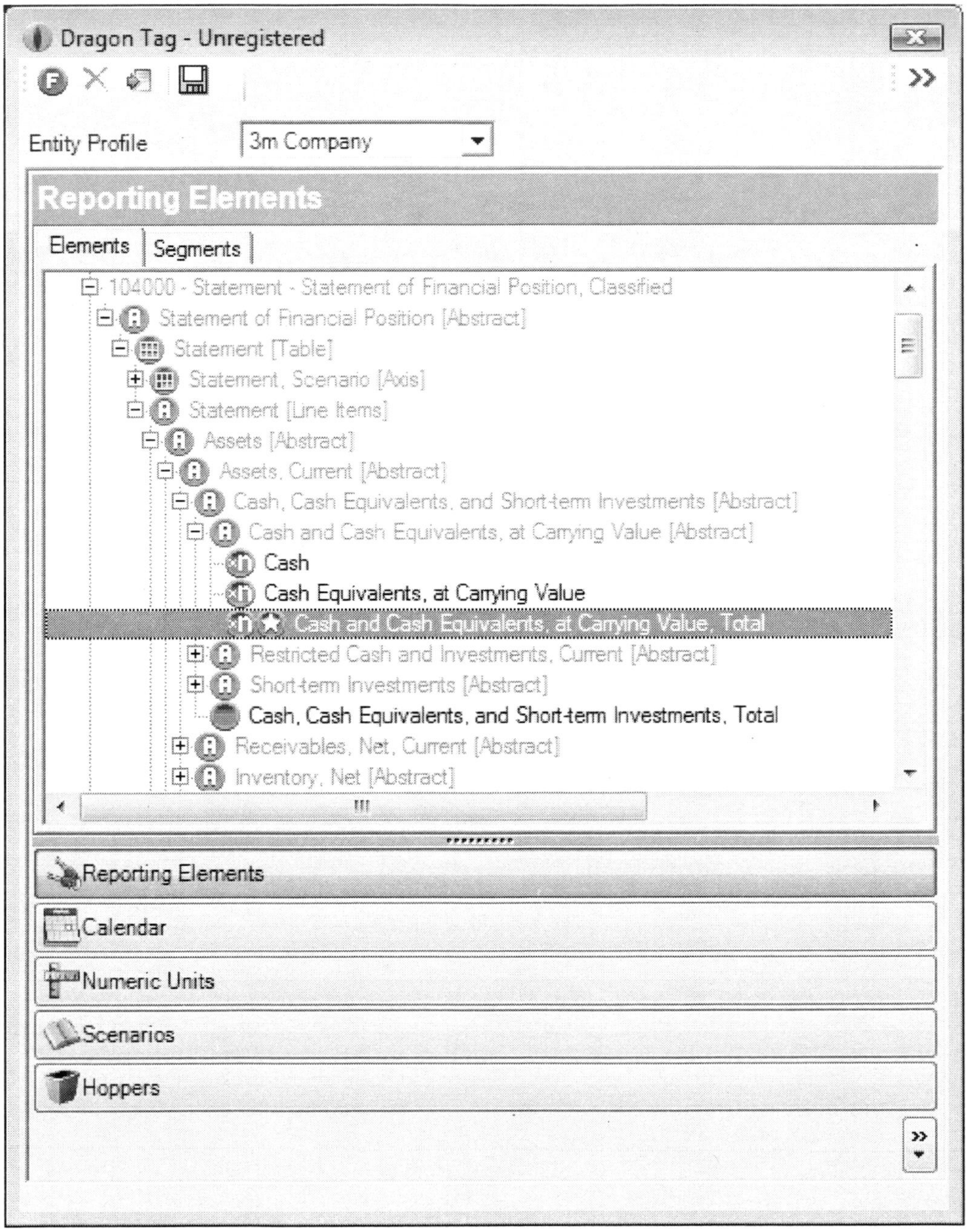

Each cell in your spreadsheet must be tagged with the appropriate element name. This is straightforward until you get to the "Inventory, Raw Materials and Supplies" item. When you look for this item in the Statement of Financial Position in the US GAAP taxonomy, you will find "Inventory, Raw Materials" and "Other Inventory, Supplies" but not the exact element name you are looking for. As mentioned previously, a rule for XBRL instance document creators is that if you don't find an element name where you expect to find it in a financial statement, look for it in the disclosures section. As shown in Figure 6-7, if you scroll down to Disclosure – Inventory and begin opening elements, you will find the element name you are looking for. The problem that you now face is that it is in the disclosure section and not in the financial statement where you need it to be. Moving the element is possible but doing so requires the creation of an extension taxonomy.

Creating an extension taxonomy is where an XBRL instance document tool like Dragon Tag shows its true value. You can use Dragon Tag to copy the element name in the disclosure and paste it in the financial statement and let the software take care of modifying the taxonomy schema and linkbases appropriately. To do so, first right-click the element name "Inventory, Raw Materials and Supplies" and select copy. Then right-click the element name "Inventory, Raw Materials" in the Statement of Financial Position (i.e., where you want to move it to) and select paste. You should now see the Modify Element Location screen as shown in Figure 6-8. With this wizard, you can do a variety of things such as "remove the element from its original location" (since I only want to "copy" it, I chose not to remove it, which also makes it available for use in a disclosure if needed) and I chose to place it after the "Inventory, Raw Materials" element in the financial statement hierarchy. Then I assigned a weight of 1, meaning it is a positive item for calculation purposes, and clicked OK. With these actions, you have created an extension taxonomy by building a modified version of the original US GAAP taxonomy (i.e., you did not change the original but created an extension) and this element is now available for use to tag the appropriate balance in the spreadsheet (see Figure 6-9).

Figure 6-7: The Inventory, Raw Materials and Supplies, Total element

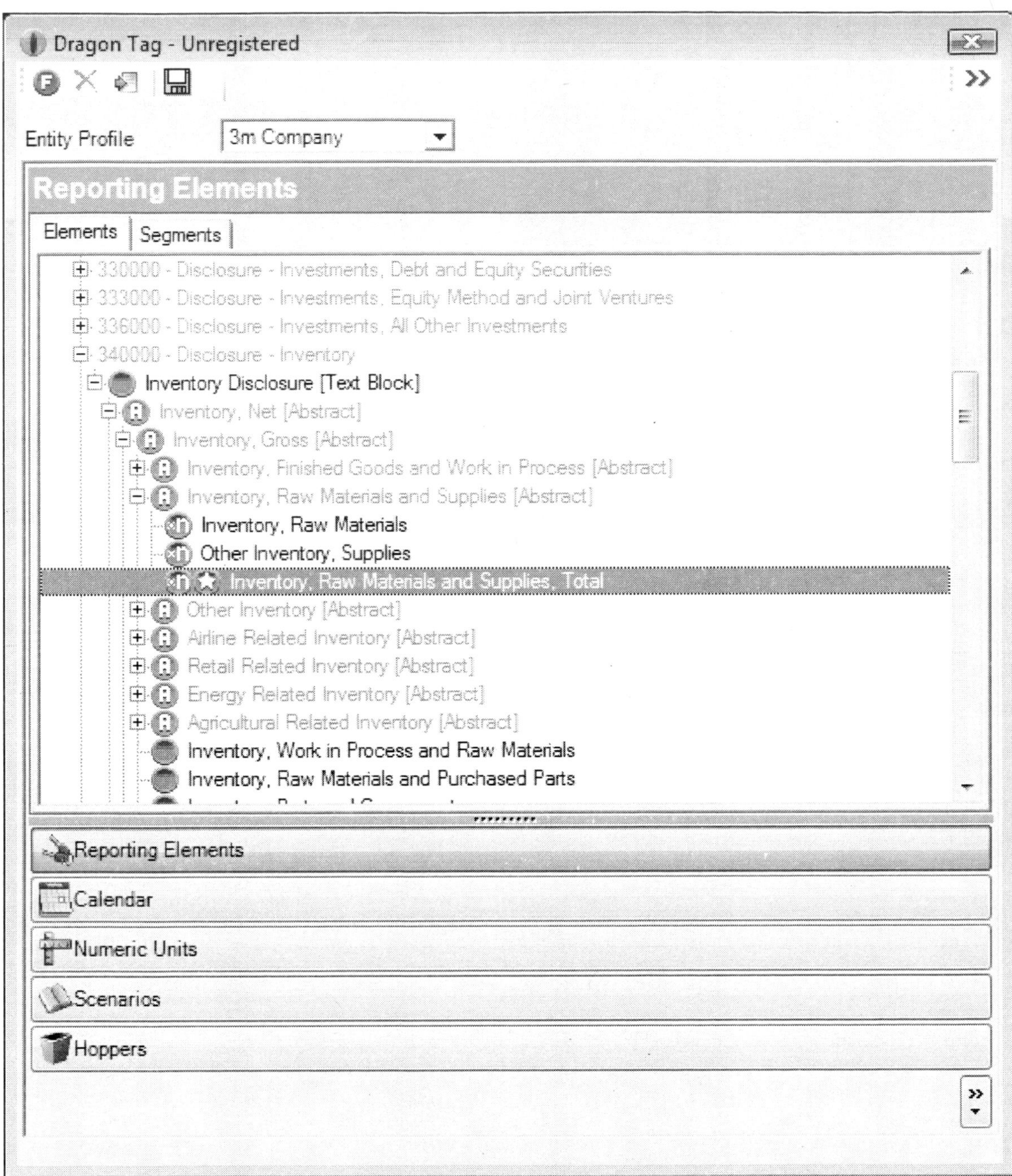

Figure 6-8: Dragon Tag's Modify Element Location (copy and paste function)

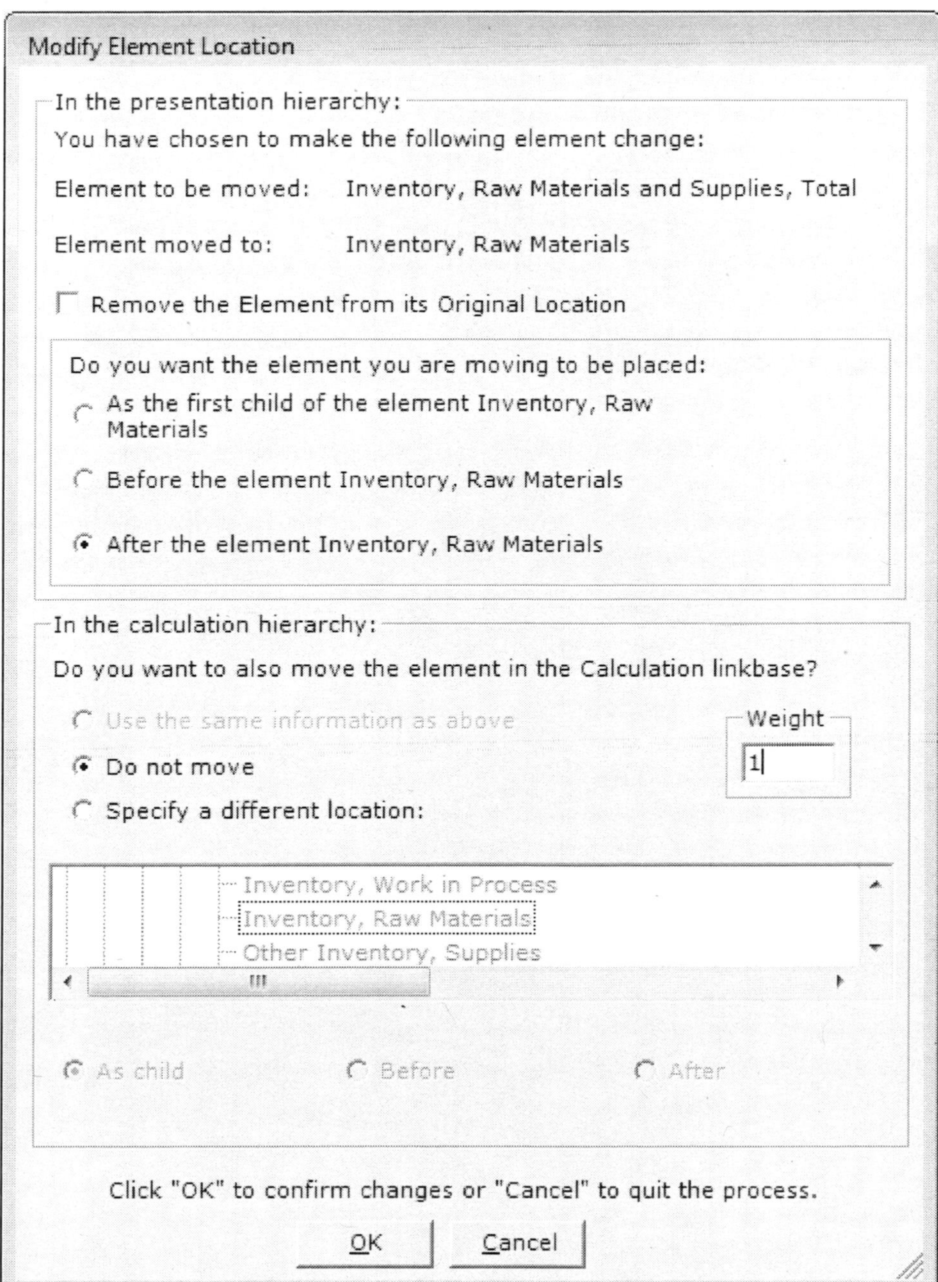

Figure 6-9: Inventory "extended" with the Inventory, Raw Materials and Supplies element

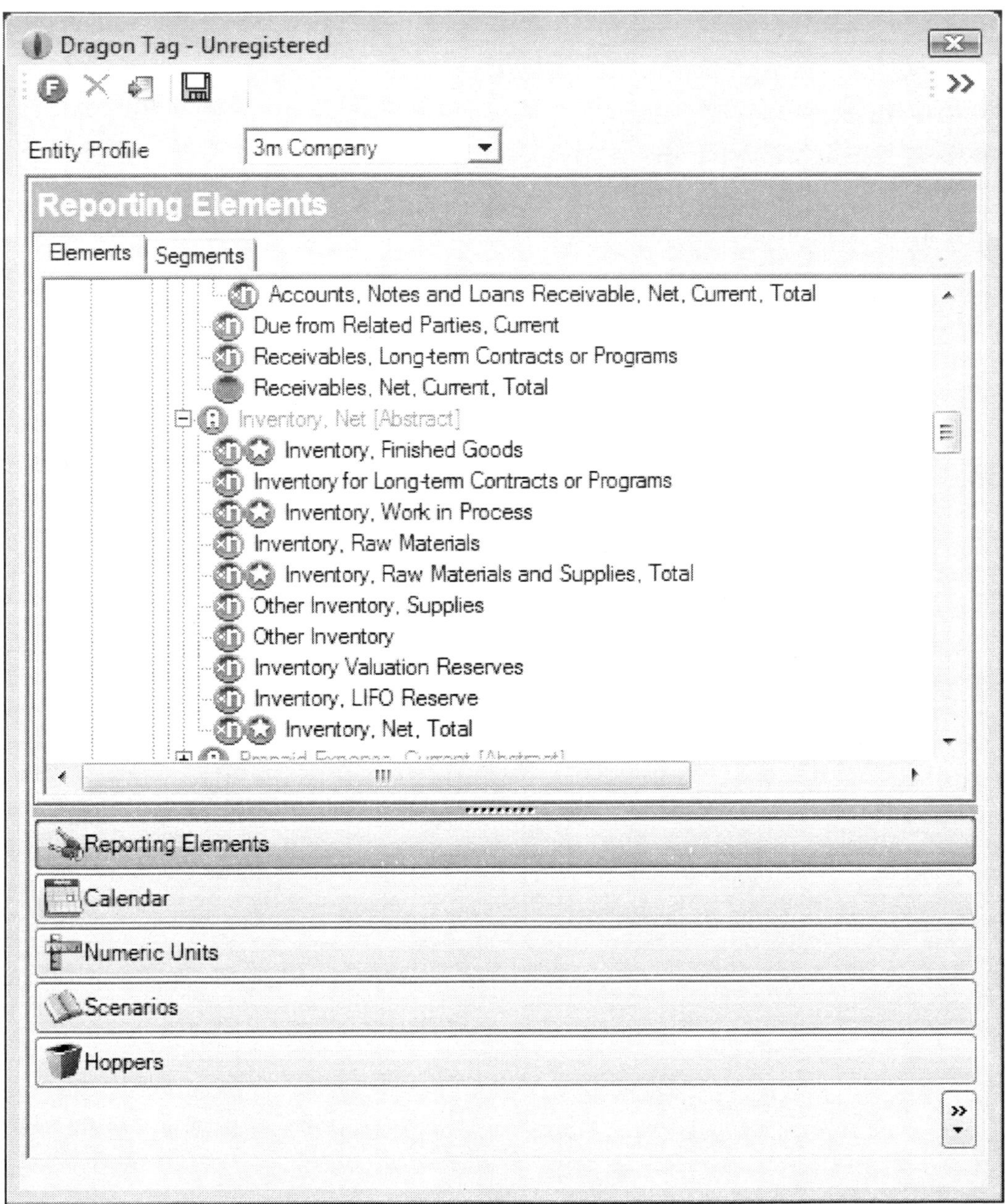

After tagging all balances in your spreadsheet with element names, you must also assign a calendar period to your items. To do this, click Calendar and then click My Calendar Periods/System Defaults/2007/TwelveMonthsEnded_31Dec2007 and drag and drop it on the asset column and the liabilities column in your spreadsheet (i.e., you can select an entire column by clicking the first item, holding down the Shift key, and clicking the last item in the column). The result should be the spreadsheet as shown in Figure 6-10. When items are completely tagged with a name and a calendar, they turn blue.

Figure 6-10: 3M Company's Current Assets and Liabilities completely tagged

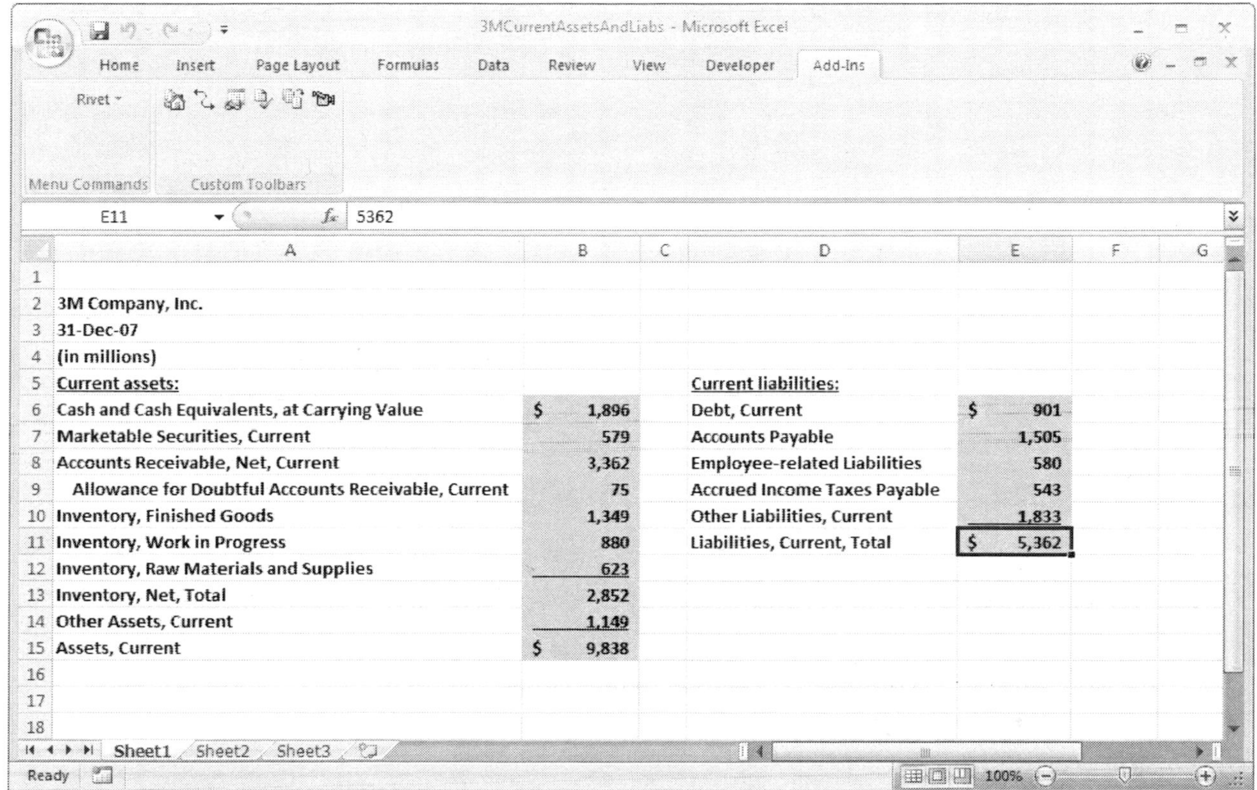

	A	B	C	D	E
1					
2	3M Company, Inc.				
3	31-Dec-07				
4	(in millions)				
5	Current assets:			Current liabilities:	
6	Cash and Cash Equivalents, at Carrying Value	$ 1,896		Debt, Current	$ 901
7	Marketable Securities, Current	579		Accounts Payable	1,505
8	Accounts Receivable, Net, Current	3,362		Employee-related Liabilities	580
9	Allowance for Doubtful Accounts Receivable, Current	75		Accrued Income Taxes Payable	543
10	Inventory, Finished Goods	1,349		Other Liabilities, Current	1,833
11	Inventory, Work in Progress	880		Liabilities, Current, Total	$ 5,362
12	Inventory, Raw Materials and Supplies	623			
13	Inventory, Net, Total	2,852			
14	Other Assets, Current	1,149			
15	Assets, Current	$ 9,838			

You can now use Dragon Tag to review your markup by clicking the third icon on the add-on tool bar (a spreadsheet with glasses). To validate your complete instance document, click the fourth icon (a spreadsheet with check mark); and to export your instance document as XBRL or a rendered Web page, click the fifth icon (the multiple spreadsheets). Always validate your instance document before exporting it. If you click the export icon and choose XBRL Preview, you should see the XBRL instance document as shown in Figure 6-11.

Figure 6-11: 3M Company's Current Assets and Liabilities XBRL instance document

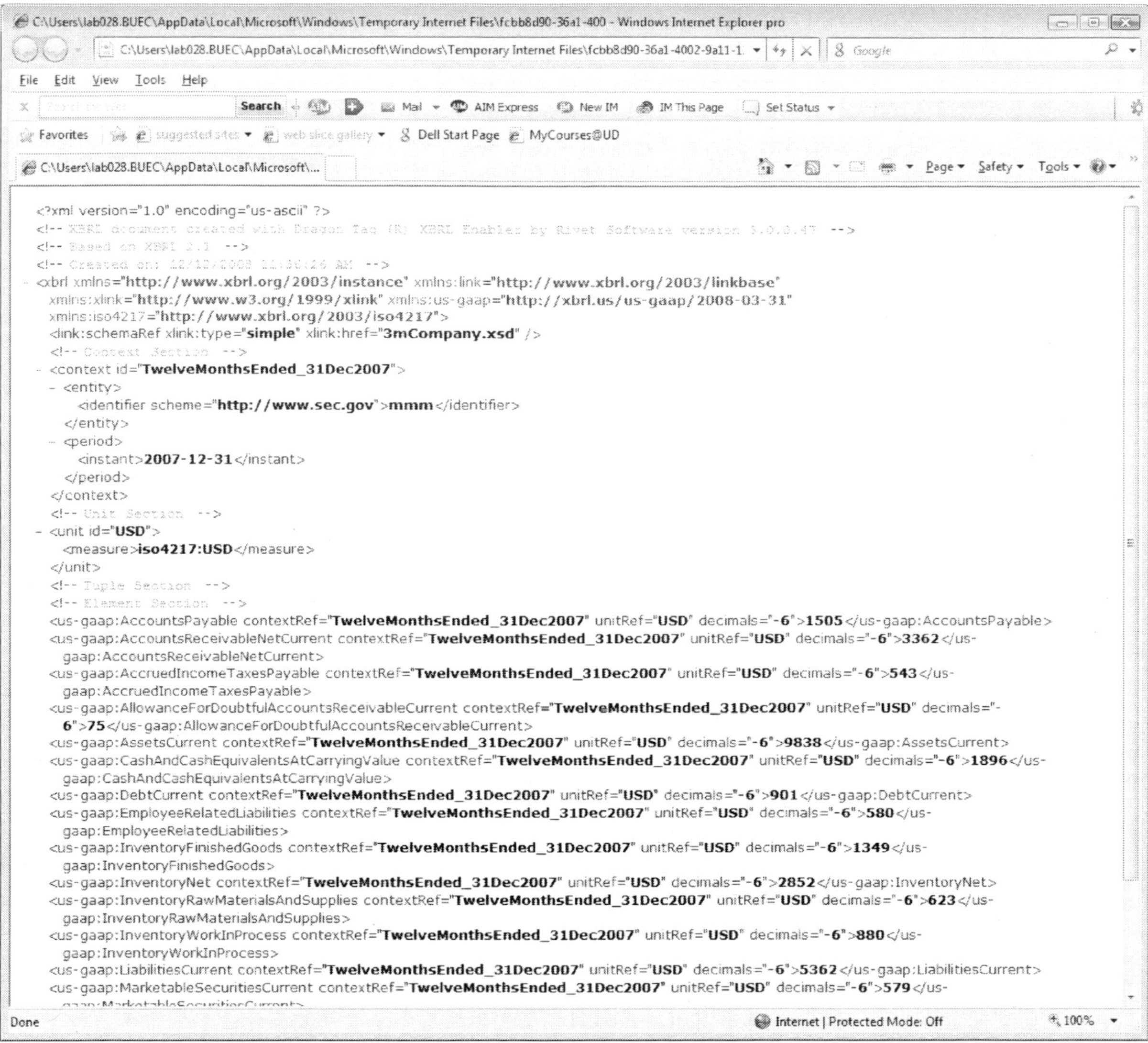

```
<?xml version="1.0" encoding="us-ascii" ?>
<!-- XBRL document created with Dragon Tag (R) XBRL Enabler by Rivet Software version 5.0.0.47 -->
<!-- Based on XBRL 2.1 -->
<!-- Created on: 12/10/2008 11:36:26 AM -->
- <xbrl xmlns="http://www.xbrl.org/2003/instance" xmlns:link="http://www.xbrl.org/2003/linkbase"
  xmlns:xlink="http://www.w3.org/1999/xlink" xmlns:us-gaap="http://xbrl.us/us-gaap/2008-03-31"
  xmlns:iso4217="http://www.xbrl.org/2003/iso4217">
  <link:schemaRef xlink:type="simple" xlink:href="3mCompany.xsd" />
  <!-- Context Section -->
- <context id="TwelveMonthsEnded_31Dec2007">
  - <entity>
      <identifier scheme="http://www.sec.gov">mmm</identifier>
    </entity>
  - <period>
      <instant>2007-12-31</instant>
    </period>
  </context>
  <!-- Unit Section -->
- <unit id="USD">
    <measure>iso4217:USD</measure>
  </unit>
  <!-- Tuple Section -->
  <!-- Element Section -->
  <us-gaap:AccountsPayable contextRef="TwelveMonthsEnded_31Dec2007" unitRef="USD" decimals="-6">1505</us-gaap:AccountsPayable>
  <us-gaap:AccountsReceivableNetCurrent contextRef="TwelveMonthsEnded_31Dec2007" unitRef="USD" decimals="-6">3362</us-
    gaap:AccountsReceivableNetCurrent>
  <us-gaap:AccruedIncomeTaxesPayable contextRef="TwelveMonthsEnded_31Dec2007" unitRef="USD" decimals="-6">543</us-
    gaap:AccruedIncomeTaxesPayable>
  <us-gaap:AllowanceForDoubtfulAccountsReceivableCurrent contextRef="TwelveMonthsEnded_31Dec2007" unitRef="USD" decimals="-
    6">75</us-gaap:AllowanceForDoubtfulAccountsReceivableCurrent>
  <us-gaap:AssetsCurrent contextRef="TwelveMonthsEnded_31Dec2007" unitRef="USD" decimals="-6">9838</us-gaap:AssetsCurrent>
  <us-gaap:CashAndCashEquivalentsAtCarryingValue contextRef="TwelveMonthsEnded_31Dec2007" unitRef="USD" decimals="-6">1896</us-
    gaap:CashAndCashEquivalentsAtCarryingValue>
  <us-gaap:DebtCurrent contextRef="TwelveMonthsEnded_31Dec2007" unitRef="USD" decimals="-6">901</us-gaap:DebtCurrent>
  <us-gaap:EmployeeRelatedLiabilities contextRef="TwelveMonthsEnded_31Dec2007" unitRef="USD" decimals="-6">580</us-
    gaap:EmployeeRelatedLiabilities>
  <us-gaap:InventoryFinishedGoods contextRef="TwelveMonthsEnded_31Dec2007" unitRef="USD" decimals="-6">1349</us-
    gaap:InventoryFinishedGoods>
  <us-gaap:InventoryNet contextRef="TwelveMonthsEnded_31Dec2007" unitRef="USD" decimals="-6">2852</us-gaap:InventoryNet>
  <us-gaap:InventoryRawMaterialsAndSupplies contextRef="TwelveMonthsEnded_31Dec2007" unitRef="USD" decimals="-6">623</us-
    gaap:InventoryRawMaterialsAndSupplies>
  <us-gaap:InventoryWorkInProcess contextRef="TwelveMonthsEnded_31Dec2007" unitRef="USD" decimals="-6">880</us-
    gaap:InventoryWorkInProcess>
  <us-gaap:LiabilitiesCurrent contextRef="TwelveMonthsEnded_31Dec2007" unitRef="USD" decimals="-6">5362</us-gaap:LiabilitiesCurrent>
  <us-gaap:MarketableSecuritiesCurrent contextRef="TwelveMonthsEnded_31Dec2007" unitRef="USD" decimals="-6">579</us-
```


This should look familiar to you. Notice that the Calendar period name, TwelveMonthEnded_31Dec2007, was used for the **context** element **id** and the corresponding **contextRef** attributes. To render the instance document as a Web page, click the export icon and choose Report Preview and you should see the Dragon Tag rendering as shown in Figure 6-12.

Figure 6-12: Dragon Tag rendered instance document

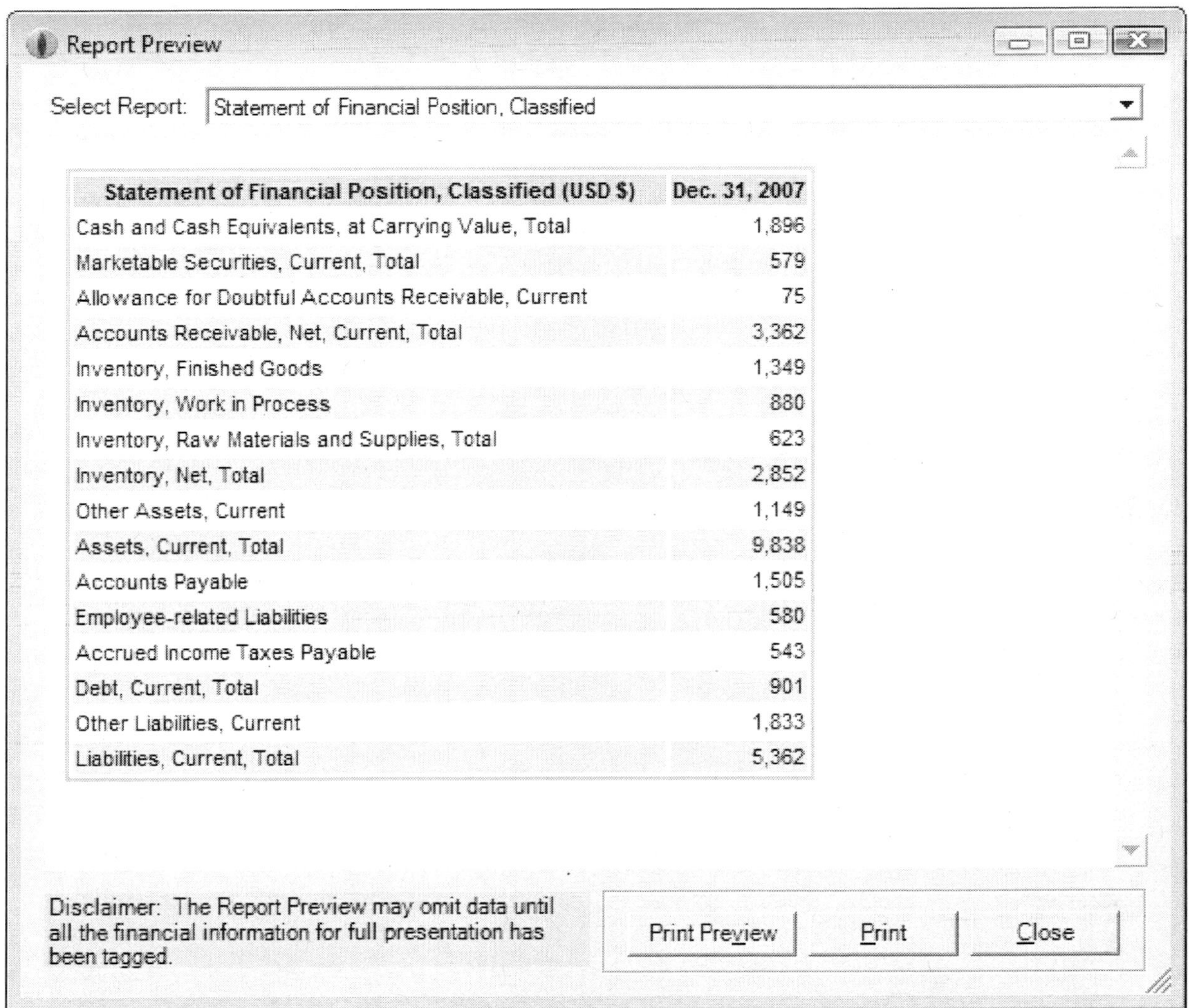

Statement of Financial Position, Classified (USD $)	Dec. 31, 2007
Cash and Cash Equivalents, at Carrying Value, Total	1,896
Marketable Securities, Current, Total	579
Allowance for Doubtful Accounts Receivable, Current	75
Accounts Receivable, Net, Current, Total	3,362
Inventory, Finished Goods	1,349
Inventory, Work in Process	880
Inventory, Raw Materials and Supplies, Total	623
Inventory, Net, Total	2,852
Other Assets, Current	1,149
Assets, Current, Total	9,838
Accounts Payable	1,505
Employee-related Liabilities	580
Accrued Income Taxes Payable	543
Debt, Current, Total	901
Other Liabilities, Current	1,833
Liabilities, Current, Total	5,362

Rivet Dragon Tag™ is a relatively simple tool to create instance documents, extend taxonomies, and validate XBRL instances. For anyone with a basic understanding of XBRL, it takes the tedious work out of instance document creation and provides easy- to-use tools for validation. Any entity reporting financial information in XBRL instance document format is concerned with validation. As you have seen in this book, the XBRL Specification 2.1 is quite complex, and coding even basic XBRL instance documents correctly requires specific knowledge of the rules and careful attention to detail. Validating that an XBRL instance document is coded correctly is important as it represents factual information about the reporting entity and needs to be precisely correct to be read and processed by computer applications. Validation of XBRL instance documents occurs on several levels, including the overall format for all XBRL instance documents, the appropriate elements and their syntactic use according to the taxonomy in which they are defined, and the appropriate relationships defined in linkbases. Validation is only possible with a software application like Rivet Dragon Tag™.

Other XBRL instance document and validation packages include the following:

- True North™, from DecisionSoft (http://www.decisionsoft.co.uk/index.html)
- Interstage XWand™, from Fujitsu (http://software.fujitsu.com/en/)
- Fujitsu also has an instance document creation and validation tool for academics, see: http://software.fujitsu.com/en/interstage-xwand/activity/xbrltools/index.html
- UBmatrix™ XBRL Taxonomy Designer, from UBmatrix (http://www.ubmatrix.com/products/products.asp)

As mentioned in Chapter 4, the XBRL taxonomies do not define every possible element and relationship used in every instance of financial reporting. Companies using XBRL frequently discover that they need to create "extension" taxonomies. Extension taxonomies follow the rules for all XBRL taxonomies as defined in the XBRL Specification 2.1 and are quite technical to create. One of the above mentioned tools is necessary to do it correctly. For more detailed information about creating extension taxonomies, see the *XBRL US GAAP Taxonomy Preparer's Guide* (http://xbrl.us/Documents/PreparersGuide.pdf).

The Future State of XBRL

Gordon Moore, co-founder of Intel, talking about computer chip technology in 1965, predicted that computing power would double every 18 months while costs remain constant or decline. Robert Metcalf, designer of the Ethernet local area networking protocol as a graduate student in the 1970's and founder of 3Com Corp. in 1981, observed that as you connect any number, "n," computers to a network their potential value is "n" squared (i.e., each has an exponential effect on the network). Moore's Law helps to explain why new information technologies are being introduced at an increasing rate, while Metcalf's Law applies to any network of users of a new technology and helps to explain why new technologies suddenly take off and begin to change the way things are done. In his book *Being Digital* (1995), Nicolas Negroponte states that these two laws are the driving force behind a world being transformed from one of atoms to one of bits (i.e., representing physical things composed of atoms in bits is rapidly transforming our world). XBRL is now on an exponential projection as predicted by Moore's and Metaclf's Laws.

XML and XBRL will become ubiquitous in accounting, operations, and financial reporting. The following projects in various stages of development will likely affect accountants, accounting, and financial and operations reporting:

- ICXML (Internal Control Markup Language) – a markup language to standardize the communication of risk assurance, internal control, and management certification information. ICXML is a working group of the OAGi (Open Applications Group for interoperability). It is focused on creating an XML vocabulary to describe the risk and control structure of an organization as defined in the COSO (Committee on Sponsoring Organizations) framework; store it as a "Risk and Control Library" containing information about business processes, risks, controls, testing procedures, etc.; and communicate it for purposes such as external audit and Sarbanes Oxley compliance. For an overview, see: http://www.idealliance.org/proceedings/xml04/papers/16/XML2004.html.
- SAML (Security Assertions Markup Language) – a markup language to standardize the communication of user authentication, entitlement, and attribute information. SAML 2.0 (10/29/2005) is the creation of the Security Services Technical Committee of OASIS (the Organization for the Advancement of Structured Information Standards), an international consortium for the development and adoption of e-business standards. SAML is an XML vocabulary to support e-business applications in which assertions need to be communicated about the identity, attributes, and entitlements of a human or computer application. For more information see: http://www.oasis-open.org/committees/tc_home.php?wg_abbrev=security.

- XACML (eXtensible Access Control Markup Language) – a markup language to standardize the expression of an entity's information systems security policy. XACML 2.0 (2/1/2005) is the creation of the Access Control Technical Committee of OASIS. XACML is an XML vocabulary for the creation, management, enforcement, and reporting of enterprise-wide information systems security policy. For more information see: http://www.oasis-open.org/committees/tc_home.php?wg_abbrev=xacml.
- A number of tax XML-based initiatives, including: TIGERS (Tax Information Group for EC Requirements Standardization) – a group which focuses on standards for electronic tax filings (see: http://www.taxadmin.org/fta/edi/1205ann.html) ; FSET (Federal/State Employment Tax) – an XML vocabulary for quarterly federal and state employment tax filings (see: http://www.irs.gov/taxpros/providers/article/0,,id=97766,00.html); OASIS Tax XML Technical Committee – an initiative to research and analyze personal and business tax reporting (see: http://www.oasis-open.org/committees/tc_home.php?wg_abbrev=tax#announcements).

In addition to these non-proprietary XML projects, several companies are working on their own proprietary initiatives. One is Approva™ Corporation (www.approva.net), a leader in the area of continuous controls monitoring and audit software. Approva™ is currently developing a controls definition language (XCDL) and a controls reporting language (XCRL). Another is Appian Corporation (www.appiancorp.com), a leader in Business Process Management software and solutions. Appian has developed an XML-based continuous controls monitoring and compliance suite known as the Sarbanes-Oxley Compliance Solution.

These and other emerging XML-based technologies will have a dramatic effect on accountants, our clients, and accounting as a profession. We are riding an exponential curve in which new information technology will continually change and reinvent our professional lives. XML, UBL, XBRL, and related emerging specifications will form the foundation for a brave new world of accounting, reporting, and analysis. Remember,

XBRL takes computer processing of accounting, financial, and business performance data to an entirely new level in which it can be precisely understood, reused, and processed with meaning. Consider *The Accountant's Guide to XBRL* as your introduction to an important information technology for the future of accounting and financial reporting.

Welcome aboard for the ride!

Glossary of new terms introduced in Chapter 6

Approved taxonomy: One that has been given approved status by XBRL International. It must comply with the guidelines in the Financial Reporting Taxonomy Architecture and have been through an open review process and been used to create a number of XBRL instance documents.

Exercise

Exercise 6-1: In this exercise you will access the U.S. SEC's EDGAR filing system and investigate and answer questions about a company currently reporting to the SEC in XBRL format. Since the SEC initiated its pilot program in 2005, momentum has been gathering and more and more companies have been including XBRL financials as supplemental materials with their required filings.

Instructions:

- Access the SEC EDGAR filing system: www.sec.gov /. Then click Search for Company Filings/XBRL Submissions
- Here you will find many companies filing SEC forms such as 8-Ks, 10-Qs, and 10-Ks in XBRL format
- Choose one of the following companies: Chevron (filing a 10-Q on 2008-11-06) or Adobe (filing a 10-Q on 2008-10-02). Then click on "html" in the left-hand column before their name, and then click on their XBRL instance document (it will likely be the first link with a **.xml** extension - if not, look to the right of the links for the words "instance document" or "ins")
- Questions to address:
    - What XBRL tagging tool did they use?
    - Why do they have so many context elements? Can you understand them?
    - What is Chevron's or Adobe's fiscal year? What is the context id for their balance sheet for their current quarter (for this 10-Q filing)? What is the context id for their income statement for their current quarter (for this 10-Q filing)?
    - What is the net income they are reporting for this quarter?
    - Which standard XBRL taxonomies are they using?
    - What is the MDA taxonomy used for?
    - What is the namespace prefix for their extension taxonomy? How large is their extension taxonomy? Why? Pick out one or two extension items and see if you can find a standard us-gaap element that they might have used

instead of their own extension element. How do you explain their use of the extension element?

- What is a segment? Where does it appear? Within a segment element, what does "explicitMember" and "dimension" mean?
- Are the financials in XBRL format understandable?

References:

Automated Filing Services, Inc., http://www.sedaredgar.com/.

BusinessWire, http://www.businesswire.com/portal/site/home/corefiling/.

Clarity FSR, ClaritySystems, http://www.claritysystems.com/Product/FSR.aspx.

Dragon Tag, Rivet Software, Inc., http://www. rivetsoftware.com/dragontag.

EDGARizer X, EDGAROnline, Inc., www.edgar-online.com.

Interstage XWand™, Fujitsu, Inc., http://software.fujitsu.com/en/.

Merrill Corporation, http://www.merrillcorp.com/cps/rde/xchg/merrillcorp/hs.xsl/565_989.htm.

Negroponte, Nicholas, *Being Digital,* Random House (NY) 1995.

Taskforce to Modernize Securities Legislation in Canada, http://www.tfmsl.ca/.

True North, DecisionSoft, Inc., http://www.decisionsoft.co.uk/index.html.

UBmatrix™ XBRL Taxonomy Designer, UBmatrix, Inc., http://www.ubmatrix.com/products/products.asp.

XBRL US GAAP Taxonomy Preparer's Guide, http://xbrl.us/Documents/PreparersGuide.pdf.

XBRL US tools and vendors, http://xbrl.us/Vendors/ Pages/default-expand.aspx.

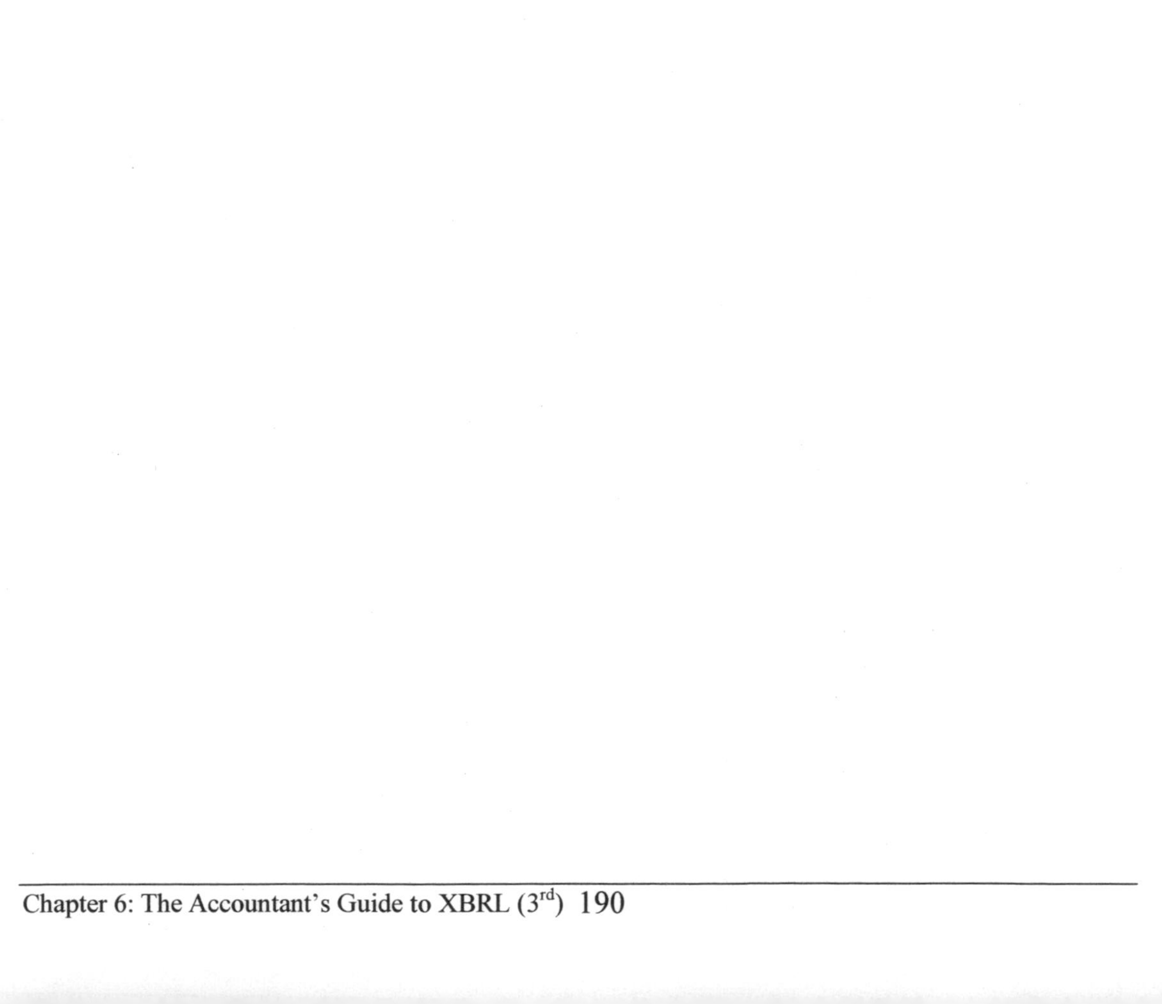

The Accountant's Guide to XBRL

Appendix: XBRL GL 2007

Overview

This appendix presents XBRL GL 2007, also known as "the journal taxonomy." The GL stands for "Global Ledger." The XBRL GL v1.1 specification (April 17, 2007) has reached recommendation status, which means it has been tested, has been used to create instance documents, and is now ready to be used for XBRL GL applications. The XBRL GL taxonomy is designed to enable the efficient handling of financial and business information contained within an organization. In contrast, the XBRL we have considered so far in this book has been for financial and business operations reporting.

Since all accounting systems are computerized, the XBRL GL taxonomy supports the representation of anything that is found in a chart of accounts, journal entries or historical transactions, financial and non-financial. XBRL GL is the taxonomy to use to tag the data behind the information in XBRL financial statements and operational reports. It is expected to have a big effect on businesses and their adoption of XBRL for internal processes and external reporting.

A Modular Set of Taxonomies

XBRL GL is a modular set of taxonomies to standardize the representation of data found in accounting and operational information systems. It consists of a core taxonomy that defines the overall structure of XBRL GL instance documents and core accounting concepts, such as accounting entry headers and entry details, and extension taxonomies for representing a variety of special and general journal information in operational information systems. Extension taxonomies "extend" the GL core to represent advanced business concepts useful for supplemental information surrounding transactions, multicurrency information, US/UK accounting, and tax and audit information. The namespace summary page for XBRL GL 2007 is: http://www.xbrl.org/int/gl/2007-04-17/GLFramework-REC-2007-04-17.htm, it will be referred to many times in this Appendix. If you go to this namespace and scroll down to the "Physical location of taxonomy files" section, you will see the XBRL GL "palette" of taxonomies (as shown in Figure A-1). These represent combinations of the various GL taxonomy schemas. They are presented as palettes because when combined the content of the container elements can vary depending on the combination of taxonomies used. We will work with the COR and BUS modules.

Figure A-1: XBRL GL taxonomy schema palettes

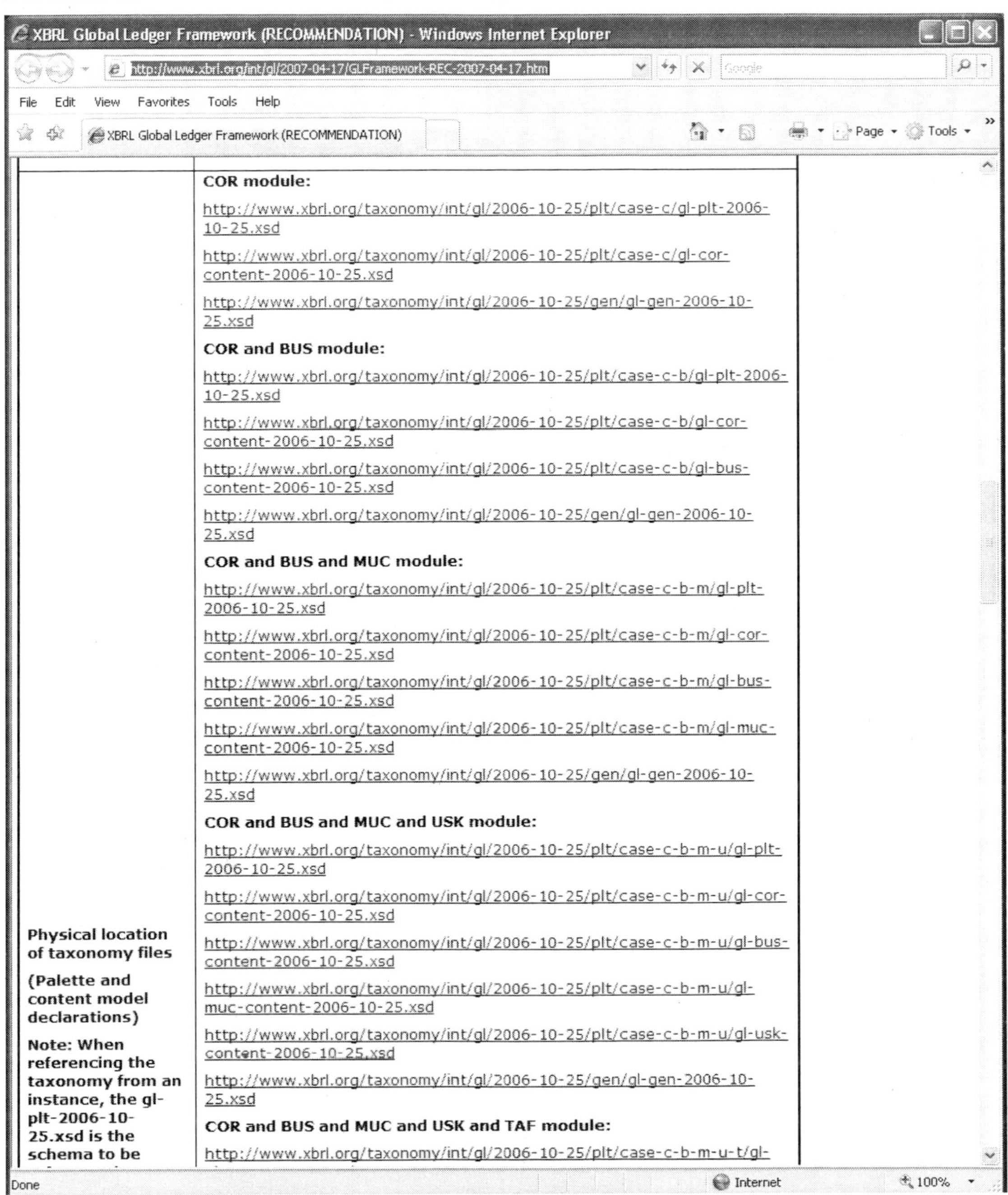

(http://www.xbrl.org/int/gl/2007-04-17/GLFramework-REC-2007-04-17.htm)

Notice that the first link within each module is to a schema with "plt" in its file name (as in gl-plt-2006-10-25.xsd). This is referred to as the "***palette taxonomy schema***" and is the one to use in a **schemaRef** element. Also notice that the next link within each module is to a schema with "content" in its file name (as in gl-cor-content-2006-10-25.xsd). This is referred to as the "***content taxonomy schema***" and in the COR and BUS module there are two of them – one for gl-cor-content and one for gl-bus-content. The content schemas are where you can look up the elements and their sequence in XBRL GL instance documents.

Unfortunately, as of this writing, there is not a handy human-friendly taxonomy viewer for the XBRL GL taxonomy. As a result, I will frequently make reference to finding things in GL schemas.

The XBRL GL core (gl-cor) taxonomy

The XBRL GL core taxonomy uses the preferred namespace prefix **gl-cor**. It defines a class of XBRL instance documents with the following overall structure:

```
<xbrl ... >
  <schemaRef ... >
    <gl-cor:accountingEntries>
      <gl-cor:documentInfo>
      <gl-cor:entityInformation>
      <gl-cor:entryHeader>
        <gl-cor:entryDetail>
```

It is important to realize that XBRL GL documents are also XBRL instance documents. As with all XBRL instance documents, the root element is **xbrl**, and its first child element is the **schemaRef** element. The XBRL GL portion of the instance document starts with the "container element" ***gl-cor:accountingEntries***. A container element is a complex element that contains a complete logical set of information. A single **gl-cor:accountingEntries** element provides the container in which a complete set of data representing an XBRL GL document is found. An XBRL instance document can contain more than one XBRL GL document, each within a **gl-cor: accountingEntries** structure. All of the elements within the **gl-cor:accounting**

Entries element are themselves container elements; the first of which is the ***gl-cor: documentInfo*** element. It can occur once and only once and contains information about the XBRL GL document itself. A particularly important element within the **gl-cor:documentInfo** element is the ***gl-cor:entriesType*** element. It is required to appear once and only once and is the first in the sequence of elements within the **gl-cor:documentInfo** element. The value contained within the **gl-cor:entriesType** element is one from an ***enumerated list*** defined in the **gl-cor** taxonomy that tells a software application the purpose of the XBRL GL document. The enumerated values and their meaning are as follows:

- **account** – information to fill in a chart of accounts.
- **balance** – a complete and validated list of entries for an account in a specific period.
- **entries** – a list of individual accounting entries.
- **journal** – a self-balancing (debit = credit) list of entries for a specific period, including beginning balance for that period.
- **ledger** – a complete list of entries for a specific account for a specific period.
- **assets** – a listing of open receivables, payables, inventory, fixed assets, or other information that can be extracted from but are not necessarily included as part of a journal entry.
- **trialBalance** – the self balancing (debit = credit) result of accumulation of a complete and validated list of entries for an entity in a complete list of accounts in a specific period.
- **other** – a catch-all value for other purposes.

These values tell a software application what to expect in the remainder of the GL instance document.

Interactive exercise A-1: In the following **gl-cor:documentInfo** element, which value from this enumerated list would you use for an XBRL GL instance document containing the details of an entity's open receivables accounts?

```
<gl-cor:documentInfo>
   <gl-cor:entriesType contextRef="xxx"> ____________</gl-cor:entriesType>
</gl-cor:documentInfo>
```

Notice that the **gl-cor:entriesType** element contains a **contextRef** attribute. This is because a GL instance document is also an XBRL instance document and therefore must follow its rules. As such, every element that contains a data value must have a **contextRef** attribute, and when an element has a numeric value it must also have a **unitRef** attribute and a **decimals** attribute.

In addition to the required **gl-cor:entriesType** element, the **gl-cor:documentInfo** element can contain the following selected optional elements in sequence:

- **gl-cor:uniqueID**
- **gl-cor:language**
- **gl-cor:creationDate**
- **gl-bus:creator**
- **gl-cor:periodCoveredStart**
- **gl-cor:periodCoveredEnd**
- **gl-bus:sourceApplication**
- **gl-bus:targetApplication**

These elements are optional. For a complete list go to the second link under the **COR and BUS module** (the gl-cor-content taxonomy schema) and scroll down to **documentInfoComplexType**.

The next element in the **gl-cor:accountingEntries** element is the ***gl-cor: entityInformation*** container element. It contains information about the entity to which the GL information pertains, such as entity name, e-mail addresses, phone and fax numbers, and Web site URIs. Most of the elements within the **gl-cor:entityInformation** element are defined in an extension taxonomy known as the "advanced business concepts" taxonomy.

The XBRL GL advanced business concepts (gl-bus) taxonomy

The XBRL GL advanced business concepts taxonomy uses the preferred namespace prefix **gl-bus**. It defines a number of elements which can be used to augment the XBRL GL core elements with a wide variety of information about the entity, including inventory measurements, information sources, customers, vendors, employees, and other pertinent information for tracking resources, events, and agents involved in business transactions. Elements from the **gl-bus** taxonomy appear throughout the **gl-cor:accountingEntries** structure. The following selected optional elements can appear, in sequence, within the **gl-cor:entityInformation** element in an XBRL GL instance document:

- **gl-bus:entityPhoneNumber**
    - **gl-bus:phoneNumberDescription**
    - **gl-bus:phoneNumber**
- **gl-bus:entityFaxNumberStructure**
    - **gl-bus:entityFaxNumberUsage**
    - **gl-bus:entityFaxNumber**
- **gl-bus:entityEmailAddressStructure**
- **gl-bus:organizationIdentifiers**
- **gl-bus:entityWebSite**
- **gl-bus:contactInformation**
- **gl-bus:businessDescription**
- **gl-bus:fiscalYearStart**
- **gl-bus:fiscalYearEnd**
- **gl-bus:organizationAccountingMethodStructure**
    - **gl-bus:organizationAccountingMethod**
    - **gl-bus:organizationAccountingMethodPurpose**
    - **gl-bus:organizationAccountingMethodStartDate**
    - **gl-bus:organizationAccountingMethodEndDate**

- **gl-bus:accountantInformation**
- **gl-bus:reportingCalendar**

These elements are used when needed in the **gl-cor:entityInformation** container element and always appear in sequence. Many of these elements have elements nested within them (e.g. the **gl-bus:entityPhoneNumber** and **gl-bus:entityFaxNumberStructure** elements). Also, many of these have an enumerated list of values that must be used. The **gl-bus:phoneNumberDescription** element, for example, has the following enumerated list of values to choose from: **bookkeeper, controller, direct, fax, investor-relations, main, switchboard,** and **other**. Likewise, the **gl-bus:organizationAccountingMethod** element has the following enumerated list of values to choose from: **accrual, cash, modified cash, modified accrual, encumbrance, special methods, hybrid methods,** and **other methods**. As discussed above, you can find a complete list by going to the appropriate context taxonomy schema.

Interactive exercise A-2: In the following **gl-cor:entityInformation** element shell, fill in the blanks with the appropriate information:

Controller's office: phone number 302-831-2990

Fiscal year: July 1, 2007 to June 31, 2008

Method of accounting: encumbrance

```
<gl-cor:entityInformation >
  <gl-bus:entityPhoneNumber>
    <gl-bus:phoneNumberDescription contextRef=“xxx”>___________</gl-bus:
       phoneNumberDescription>
    <gl-bus:phoneNumber contextRef=“xxx”>____________________</gl-bus:
       phoneNumber>
  </gl-bus:entityPhoneNumber>
  <gl-bus:fiscalYearStart>_______________</gl-bus:fiscalYearStart>
  <gl-bus:fiscalYearEnd>_______________</gl-bus:fiscalYearEnd>
  <gl-bus:organizationAccountingMethodStructure>
    <gl-bus:organizationAccountingMethod contextRef=“xxx”>__________</gl-
       bus:organizationAccountingMethod>
  </gl-bus:organizationAccountingMethodStructure>
  </gl-cor:entityInformation>
```

Always remember that sequence is enforced in all containers in XBRL GL instance documents.

The gl-cor:entryHeader element

The next element in the **gl-cor:accountingEntries** element is the ***gl-cor:entryHeader*** container element. It contains information about a set of entry detail items and the specific entry details themselves. The entry header can be used as a container to group entry details for different purposes; such as a group of invoices for audit purposes or a group of journal entries from a particular journal. The **gl-cor:entryHeader** element contains a variety of optional elements from the **gl-cor** and **gl-bus** taxonomies including the following:

- **gl-cor:postedDate** – the date the detailed items within this header were posted to the original journal; may be helpful for audit purposes.
- **gl-cor:enteredBy** – the name of the person who entered this information in the original system; may be helpful for audit purposes.
- **gl-cor:enteredDate** – the date the detailed items within this header were actually entered into the original system; may be helpful for audit purposes.
- **gl-cor:sourceJournalID** – a code from an enumerated list to identify the source journal; such as "**sj**" for sales journal or "**gj**" for general journal or "**pj**" for accounts payable journal.
- **gl-bus:sourceJournalDescription** – a term or phrase to describe the source journal.
- **gl-cor:entryType** – a standard word from an enumerated list to differentiate between types of entries, such as "**standard**" for actual accounting entries as opposed to "**adjusting**" or "**budget**" or "**eliminating**" or "**tax**".
- **gl-bus:entryOrigin** – indicates whether the detailed items within this header were "**imported**" from an automated system or "**entered**" manually.

A complete list can be found in the **gl-cor** content taxonomy schema (http://www.xbrl.org/taxonomy/int/gl/2006-10-25/plt/case-c-b/gl-cor-content-2006-10-25.xsd). Also, you can have multiple **gl-cor:entryHeader** elements within a single XBRL GL instance document. An example is an XBRL GL instance document to report the information on invoices as posted to a Sales Journal, where each invoice is represented by its own **gl-cor:entryHeader** container element. Another example is invoices from vendors (vouchers) posted to a Purchases Journal, where each voucher is represented by its own **gl-cor:entryHeader** container element.

Interactive exercise A-3: In the following **gl-cor:entryHeader** element shell, fill in the blanks to represent the following information:

A Sales journal with standard entries manually entered by a human

Posted on December 12, 2008

Entered on December 10, 2008

<gl-cor:entryHeader>
<gl-cor:postedDate contextRef="xxx">________________</gl-cor:postedDate>
<gl-cor:enteredDate contextRef="xxx">________________</gl-cor:enteredDate>
<gl-cor:sourceJournalID contextRef="xxx">___</gl-cor:sourceJournalID>
<gl-bus:sourceJournalDescription contextRef="xxx">______________</gl-bus: sourceJournalDescription >
<gl-cor:entryType contextRef="xxx">________________</gl-cor:entryType >
<gl-bus:entryOrigin contextRef="xxx">________________</gl-bus:entryOrigin>
</gl-cor:entryHeader>

To help you get a feel for the proper use of XBRL GL, there are two locations where you can find annotated example instance documents. The first set of annotated instance documents is provided by the XBRL GL Working Group (http://www.xbrl.org/GlobalLedgerWGNotes/). If you go to this location and scroll down to "Best Practices Annotated Instances – Published 2007-08-01" and click "Annotated instances – HTML version" and scroll down, you will see a page with links to a number of sample XBRL GL instance documents for different purposes (see Figure A-2). The second set of annotated instance documents is provided by IPHIX (http://iphix.net/index.htm), an XBRL GL consulting firm (http://gl.iphix.net/) (see Figure A-3).

Figure A-2: Sample XBRL GL documents

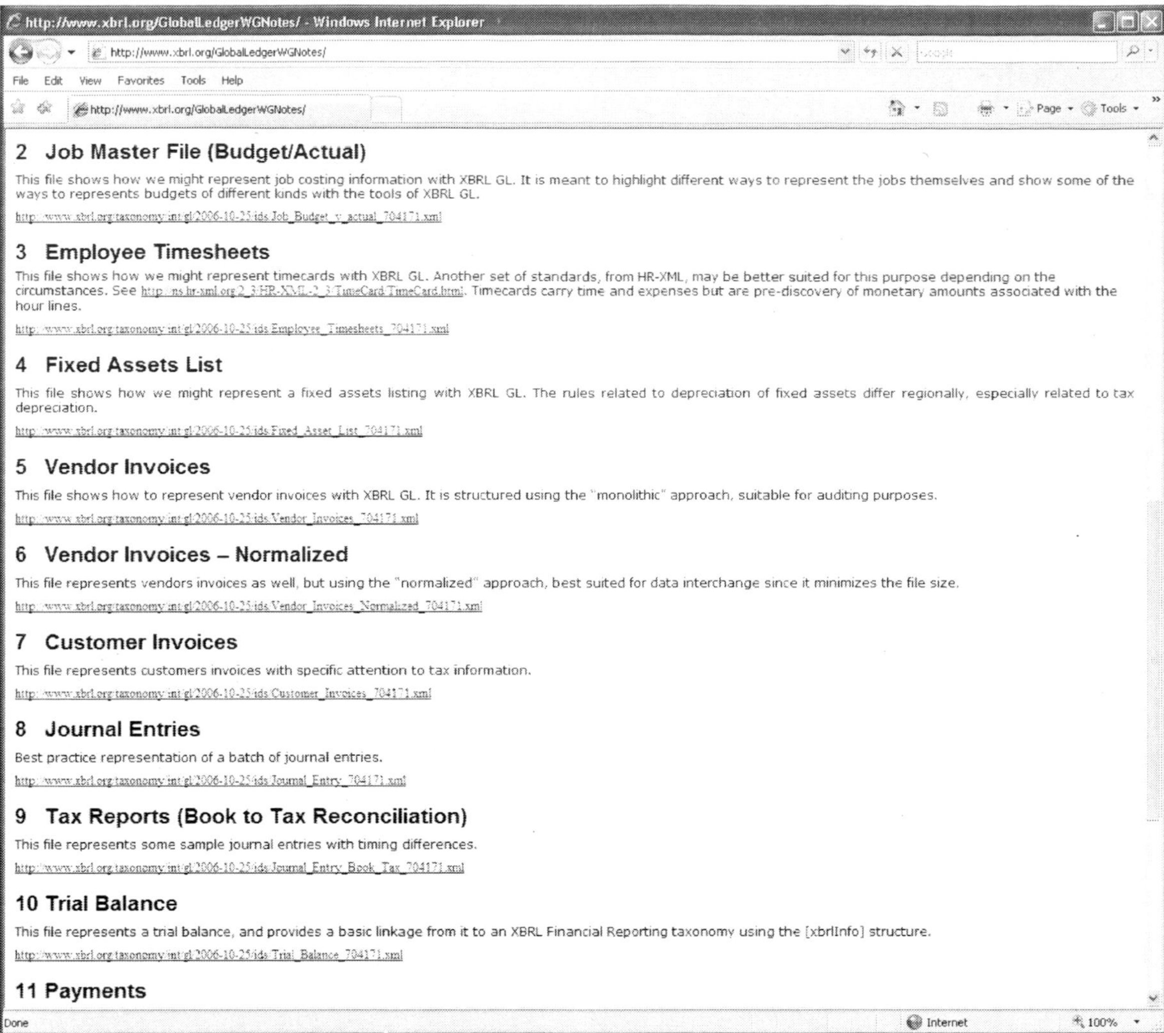

(http://www.xbrl.org/Global LedgerWGNotes/)/Annotated instances – HTML version

Figure A-3: IPHIX annotated XBRL GL instance documents

(http://gl.iphix.net/)

At each of these locations, you will find sample annotated XBRL GL instance documents for a variety of purposes. Notice that the overall structure of each type of instance document is the same (i.e., each follows the overall structure for all GL instances starting with **gl-cor:accountingEntries**) but each uses different parts and elements of the XBRL GL specification as appropriate for its own purpose.

The gl-cor:entryDetail element

The ***gl-cor:entryDetail*** element(s) are found within a **gl-cor:entryHeader** element and contain the transaction or event details being reported in an XBRL GL instance document. Though **gl-cor:entryDetail** elements will differ depending on the purpose of the GL instance document and the information being reported, the following is a basic structure including only **gl-cor** and **gl-bus** elements – all are optional:

- **gl-cor:lineNumber** – a unique number for each **entryDetail** item.
- **gl-cor:account** – a container element to identify account information if needed.
- **gl-cor:amount** – the amount being reported.
- **gl-cor:debitCreditCode** – a code from an enumerated list, such as "**D**" or "**debit**" or "**C**" or "**credit**".
- **gl-cor:postingDate** – the accounting significance date.
- **gl-cor:identifierReference** – a container element to identify document sources:
    - **gl-cor:identifierDescription** – a word of phrase such as the name of a vendor.
    - **gl-cor:identifierType** – a required item within **identifierReference** using a code from an enumerated list to identify the source, such as "**C**" or "**customer**" or "**V**" or "**vendor**".

- **gl-cor:documentType** – a term from an enumerated list to identify the type of document the entry came from, such as "**voucher**" for an invoice from a vendor or "**check**" or "**receipt**".
- **gl-cor:documentReference** – to specifically identify the source document the entry came from, such as "Voucher number 123456".
- **gl-cor:documentDate** – to record the date of the source document.
- **gl-cor:xbrlInfo** – a container element to identify other XBRL information:
    - **gl-cor:summaryReportingElement** – to identify which XBRL reporting element this item amount rolls up to.
- **gl-bus:measurable** – a container element to identify measurable information about an entry, such as information from a line item on a voucher including an item's description, how many, and a unit cost.

XBRL GL 2007 is designed to be flexible so as to support the reporting of a wide variety of detailed accounting transaction and business event information. And the **gl-cor: entryHeader** and **gl-cor:entryDetail** container elements reflect this flexibility – a GL instance document reporting the contents of a sales journal would use different elements than one reporting the contents of a voucher from a vendor. In all cases, the XBRL GL document designer would choose the appropriate elements as needed from the appropriate GL content taxonomy schemas and use them to contain the values to be reported.

Interactive exercise A-4: In this exercise, you will locate a sample XBRL GL instance document and use it as a guide to enter the following information in the following **gl-cor:entryDetail** element.

First, point your browser to http://gl.iphix.net/ and click *Accounts Payable/Vendor Management* then *Invoices* and you should see an annotated GL instance listing vendor invoices. Then scroll down to the first **gl-cor:entryDetail** element (see Figure A-4) and use it as your guide to enter the following information in the shell provided.

An invoice from: Joe's Place dated December 13, 2008

One item for $53.55 and another for $24.99 (in U.S. dollars)

The voucher was dated November 27, 2008 and was posted on December 1, 2008 and is unpaid at this time.

```
<gl-cor:entryDetail>
  <gl-cor:lineNumber contextRef="xxx">___</gl-cor:lineNumber>
  <gl-cor:amount contextRef="xxx" unitRef="USD" decimals="2">______</gl-
        cor:amount>
  <gl-cor:postingDate contextRef="xxx">___________</gl-cor:postingDate>
  <gl-cor:identifierReference>
        <gl-cor:identifierDescription>___________</gl-cor:identifierDescription>
        <gl-cor:identifierType contextRef="xxx">___</gl-cor:identifierType>
        </gl-cor:identifierReference>
  <gl-cor:documentType contextRef="xxx">_________</gl-cor:documentType>
  <gl-cor:documentDate contextRef="xxx">__________</gl-cor:documentDate>
  <gl-cor:xbrlInfo>
        <gl-cor:summaryReportingElement contextRef="xxx">_______________
          </gl-cor:summaryReportingElement>
  </gl-cor:xbrlInfo>
```

```
    </gl-cor:entryDetail>

<gl-cor:entryDetail>
  <gl-cor:lineNumber contextRef="xxx">____</gl-cor:lineNumber>
  <gl-cor:amount contextRef="xxx" unitRef="USD" decimals="2">________</gl-
       cor:amount>
  <gl-cor:postingDate contextRef="xxx">___________</gl-cor:postingDate>
   <gl-cor:identifierReference>
       <gl-cor:identifierDescription>______________</gl-cor:identifierDescription>
       <gl-cor:identifierType contextRef="xxx">___</gl-cor:identifierType>
       </gl-cor:identifierReference>
  <gl-cor:documentType contextRef="xxx">_________</gl-cor:documentType>
  <gl-cor:documentDate contextRef="xxx">__________</gl-cor:documentDate>
  <gl-cor:xbrlInfo>
       <gl-cor:summaryReportingElement contextRef="xxx">_______________
         </gl-cor:summaryReportingElement>
       </gl-cor:xbrlInfo>
    </gl-cor:entryDetail>
```

Remember, each **gl-cor:entryDetail** element contains the details of a single accounting transaction or business event (e.g. a line item on a voucher) and each must have a unique gl-cor:lineNumber (e.g. 01 and so on sequentially).

Other XBRL GL taxonomies: gl-muc, gl-usk, and gl-taf

In the examples presented so far, we have only used elements from the **gl-cor** and **gl-bus** taxonomies. There are, however, three other special purpose XBRL GL taxonomies. The multicurrency taxonomy, with the preferred namespace prefix ***gl-muc***, defines elements to be used to describe entries and transactions involving multiple currencies that appear in a **gl-cor: entryDetail** element. Such elements as: **gl-muc:amountCurrency, gl-muc:amount OriginalExchangeRateDate, gl-muc:amountOriginalAmount,** and **gl-muc:amount OriginalCurrency**, could be used directly following a **gl-cor:amount** element to fully describe a multicurrency transaction. A complete list can be found in the **gl-cor** content taxonomy schema within the COR and BUS and MUC module: http://www.xbrl.org/ taxonomy/int/gl/2006-10-25/plt/case-c-b-m/gl-cor-content-2006-10-25.xsd (see Figure A-1). The advanced US-UK accounting taxonomy, with the preferred namespace prefix ***gl-usk***, defines elements to be used for more sophisticated US-UK accounting entries and transactions. Many of these appear in the **gl-cor:entryHeader** element and include reversing and recurring entries. The tax and tax audit taxonomy, with the preferred namespace prefix ***gl-taf*** defines elements to be used by international tax agencies for tax audit purposes. These can appear in the **gl-cor:entryDetail** element. A complete list of both the **gl-usk** and **gl-taf** elements can be found in the content taxonomy schemas at the XBRL GL namespace: http://www.xbrl.org/int/gl/2006-10-25/gl-2006-10-25.htm (see Figure A-1).

To learn more about how to use XBRL GL 2007 to create instance documents, see the annotated sample instance documents referenced earlier.

Summary

XBRL GL 2007 is designed to make possible the efficient handling of financial and operations information by providing a standard way to represent journal entries, general and special ledger information, and detailed operations information. It uses a number of container elements and a number of enumerated lists for values for specific types of elements (see http://www.xbrl.org/taxonomy/int/gl/2006-10-25/gen/gl-gen-2006-10-25.xsd). XBRL GL 2007 is a very complex specification that is independent of any specific chart-of-accounts, reporting methodology, or information system. At the same time, it compliments XBRL financial reporting by providing the details behind the items being reported on financial statements, including all of the specific information needed for detailed reporting, budget planning, and audit work papers. It is an emerging specification that is growing in use and is expected to have a major impact on the future of accounting, accounting information systems, and XBRL reporting.

XBRL GL will become the foundation technology for tagging accounting transactions and events, moving them between information systems, and then reporting them. XBRL is a data-level technology. Tagging accounting transactions and business events and recording them in databases using the XBRL GL standard will make them more readily understandable and usable as the foundation for financial and operations reports. XBRL GL will provide the detailed data behind the financial and operations reports and will be the information key to transparency in reporting. Like all emerging technologies, XBRL GL will evolve and become more useful and user-friendly over time.

Glossary of new terms introduced in this Appendix

Container element: An element whose purpose it is to "contain" other elements. It is a complex element that contains a complete logical set of other elements. XBRL GL contains a number of container elements that make up its overall structure; as follows:

<gl-cor:accountingEntries>
  <gl-cor:documentInfo>
  <gl-cor:entityInformation>
  <gl-cor:entryHeader>
    <gl-cor:entryDetail>

Content taxonomy schema: A GL taxonomy schema describing the sequence and available elements for a specific palette of GL taxonomies. For example, in the GL COR and GL BUS module, the GL COR content taxonomy schema and the GL BUS content taxonomy schema together define the sequence and available elements for this combination of taxonomies to be used in GL instance documents.

Enumerated list: A list of predefined values. It is a computer term indicating that the value found in an element must be one found in a predefined list, such as in one of the XBRL GL taxonomies.

gl-bus: A module taxonomy of XBRL GL for reporting advanced business concepts. This taxonomy defines elements to help track business details surrounding resources, events, and agents involved in transactions. It includes elements representing inventory measurements, business events metrics, and internal and external agents.

gl-cor: A module taxonomy of XBRL GL for reporting core accounting transaction concepts. This taxonomy defines elements used in representing the core structure of XBRL GL instance documents, including journal entry details.

gl-cor:accountingEntries: The overall container element for the XBRL GL instance document. It identifies the start of a GL instance document and contains all other GL elements within it.

gl-cor:amount: Contains a value for an **gl-cor:entryDetail** element. There can be one and only one **gl-cor:amount** element in each **gl-cor:entryDetail** element. It is a simple element containing a value representing an accounting item such as a journal entry amount or a line item amount on an invoice.

gl-cor:documentInfo: The first container element within the **gl-cor:accountingEntries** element. It is a container element that can appear once and only once in a GL instance document and contains information about the GL instance document itself, including document identifiers and descriptive information.

gl-cor:entityInformation: The second container element within the **gl-cor:accounting Entries** element. It is a container element that can appear once and only once in a GL instance document and contains additional information about the entity about which the GL information pertains, including name and Web site and e-mail information. The majority of these elements are defined in the **gl-bus** taxonomy.

gl-cor:entriesType: The first element within the **gl-cor:documentInfo** element. It is required, and it contains a value from an enumerated list of codes designed to describe the purpose of the XBRL GL instance document. These codes are used by a software application reading the document to identify its purpose.

gl-cor:entryDetail: A container element containing line-item amounts. It that can appear multiple times within the **gl-cor:entryHeader** element. Each **gl-cor:entryDetail** element has a **gl-cor:lineNumber** element and a **gl-cor:amount** element. It can also contain information about accounts, posting date (the accounting significance date), account memo, identifiers, and measurements.

gl-cor:entryHeader: The third container element within the **gl-cor:accountingEntries** element. It is a container element that can appear multiple times within a GL instance document and contains information such as the date the entries were posted to a computerized system, who entered them, etc. It also contains all of the GL document's **gl-cor:entryDetail** elements

gl-muc: A module taxonomy of XBRL GL for reporting multicurrency concepts. This taxonomy defines elements necessary for identifying currencies and including details of transactions.

gl-taf: A module taxonomy of XBRL GL for reporting taxation concepts. This taxonomy defines elements useful for identifying tax and tax audit details. It should also be useful for international tax authorities.

gl-usk: A module taxonomy of XBRL GL for reporting advanced US/UK accounting concepts. This taxonomy defines elements necessary for more sophisticated Saxonic accounting, including US, UK, Canada, Australia, and others.

palette taxonomy schema: A combination of taxonomy schemas to support an XBRL GL instance document. These have been compiled by XBRL International to support the GL COR taxonomy and the various GL extension taxonomies – gl-bus, gl-muc, gl-usk, and gl-taf.

XBRL GL: The new XBRL taxonomy for accounting transactions and business events, also know as the "journal" taxonomy. This taxonomy is designed to represent data in accounting journals and accounting systems. It is currently undergoing testing and revision before reaching the "recommendation" status.

Exercise

Exercise A-1: Using the data below, create an XBRL GL instance document for the outstanding invoices received from vendors (vouchers) for MyComputers.com, Inc. The company reports under US GAAP in US Dollars.

Company data:

MyComputers.com, Inc. (www.nasdaq.com: MYCC)

Outstanding invoices received from vendors (Vouchers)

For the week of: September 24, 2008 to September 30, 2008

First voucher:

Invoice - Number 452643

Office Depot, Inc (MYCC: ID 54689)

Date: 2008-09-22

Terms: 2% 10 Net 30

Items:

Description	Quantity	Price	Amount	Code
Printer cartridges	10	22.50	225.00	prncrt
Paper	1 box	19.95	19.95	paper
Envelopes	5 boxes	5.95	29.75	envp

Date received: 2006-04-11
Date entered & posted: 2006-04-12
Entered by: Your name
Location: Main invoice file
Identifier: MYCC Voucher# 34567

Second voucher:

Invoice - Number 29905

Dell, Inc (MYCC: ID 499823)

Date: 2006-04-11

Terms: 2% 10 Net 30

Items:

Description	Quantity	Price	Amount	Code
Laptop: XPS M1710	5	1990.00	9950.00	LPXpsm1710
Laptop: XPS M140	12	550.00	6600.00	LPXpsm140
Desktop: XPS 600	4	1395.00	5580.00	DTxps600

Date received: 2006-04-12
Date posted & posted: 2006-04-13
Entered by: Your name
Location: Main invoice file
Identifier: MYCC Voucher# 34568

Exercise A-2: Write the XSLT code to create the following "outstanding vouchers report:"

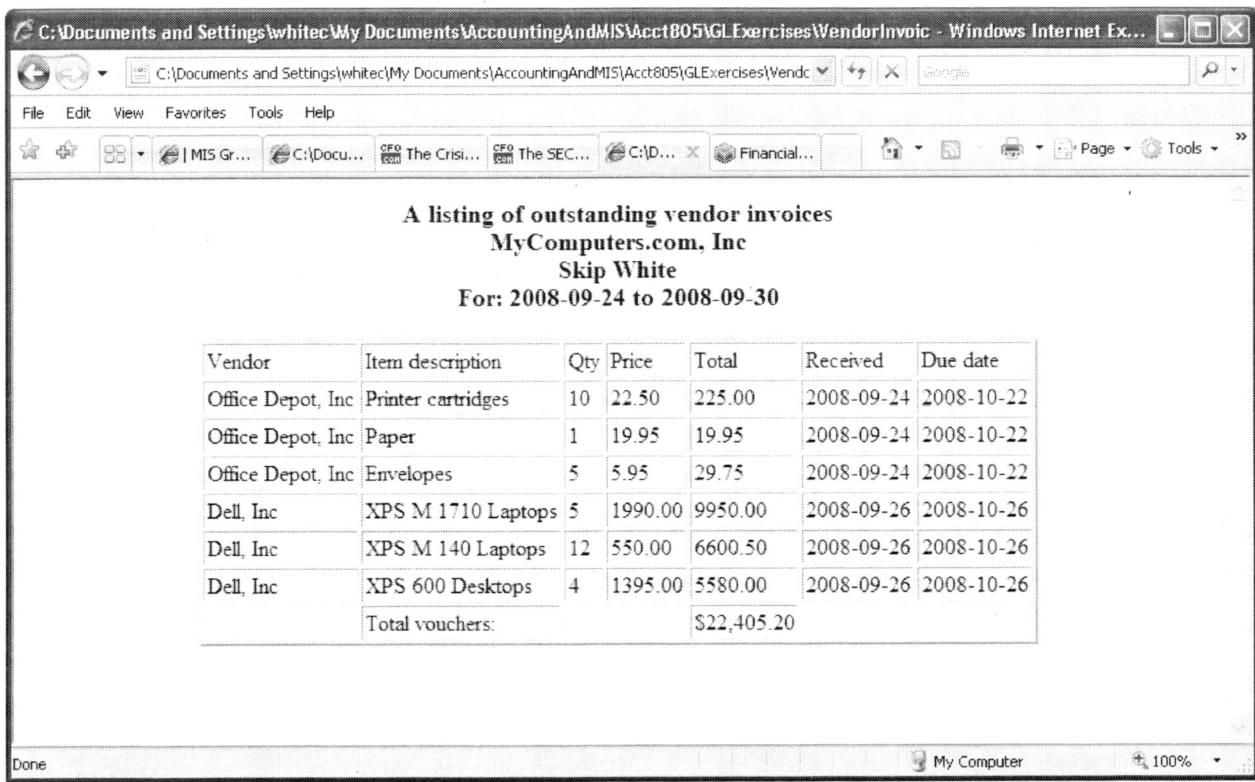

A listing of outstanding vendor invoices
MyComputers.com, Inc
Skip White
For: 2008-09-24 to 2008-09-30

Vendor	Item description	Qty	Price	Total	Received	Due date
Office Depot, Inc	Printer cartridges	10	22.50	225.00	2008-09-24	2008-10-22
Office Depot, Inc	Paper	1	19.95	19.95	2008-09-24	2008-10-22
Office Depot, Inc	Envelopes	5	5.95	29.75	2008-09-24	2008-10-22
Dell, Inc	XPS M 1710 Laptops	5	1990.00	9950.00	2008-09-26	2008-10-26
Dell, Inc	XPS M 140 Laptops	12	550.00	6600.50	2008-09-26	2008-10-26
Dell, Inc	XPS 600 Desktops	4	1395.00	5580.00	2008-09-26	2008-10-26
	Total vouchers:			$22,405.20		

Hint: You should use a **<for-each select= "//gl-cor:entryDetail>** loop to select the data values with which to populate the main table.

References & More Information

IPHIX, Annotated GL instance documents, http://gl.iphix.net/.

XBRL GL 2007, http://www.xbrl.org/int/gl/2006-10-25/gl-2006-10-25.htm.

XBRL gl-cor & gl-bus taxonomy, http://www.xbrl.org/taxonomy/int/gl/2006-10-25/plt/case-c-b/gl-cor-content-2006-10-25.xsd.

XBRL GL Working Group, http://www.xbrl.org/Global LedgerWGNotes/.

Answers:

Interactive exercise A-1: In the following **gl-cor:documentInfo** element, which value from this enumerated list would you use for an XBRL GL instance document containing the details of an entity's open receivables accounts?

<gl-cor:documentInfo>
<gl-cor:entriesType contextRef="xxx"> _assets_ **</gl-cor:entriesType>**
</gl-cor:documentInfo>

Interactive exercise A-2: In the following **gl-cor:entityInformation** element shell, fill in the blanks with the appropriate information:

Controller's office: phone number 302-831-2990

Fiscal year: July 1, 2007 to June 31, 2008

Method of accounting: encumbrance

<gl-cor:entityInformation >
<gl-bus:entityPhoneNumber>
<gl-bus:phoneNumberDescription contextRef="xxx">_controller_**</gl-bus: phoneNumberDescription>**
<gl-bus:phoneNumber contextRef="xxx">_302-831-2990_**</gl-bus: phoneNumber>**
</gl-bus:entityPhoneNumber>
<gl-bus:fiscalYearStart>_2007-07-01_**</gl-bus:fiscalYearStart>**
<gl-bus:fiscalYearEnd>_2008-06-30_**</gl-bus:fiscalYearEnd>**
<gl-bus:organizationAccountingMethodStructure>
<gl-bus:organizationAccountingMethod contextRef="xxx">_encumbrance_**</gl-bus:organizationAccountingMethod>**
</gl-bus:organizationAccountingMethodStructure>
</gl-cor:entityInformation>

Interactive exercise A-3: In the following **gl-cor:entryHeader** element shell, fill in the blanks to represent the following information:

A Sales journal with standard entries manually entered by a human

Posted on December 12, 2008

Entered on December 10, 2008

```
<gl-cor:entryHeader>
  <gl-cor:postedDate contextRef="xxx">_2008-12-12_</gl-cor:postedDate>
  <gl-cor:enteredDate contextRef="xxx">_2008-10-2008_</gl-cor:enteredDate>
  <gl-cor:sourceJournalID contextRef="xxx">_sj_</gl-cor:sourceJournalID>
  <gl-bus:sourceJournalDescription contextRef="xxx">_sales journal_</gl-bus:
      sourceJournalDescription >
  <gl-cor:entryType contextRef="xxx">_standard_</gl-cor:entryType >
  <gl-bus:entryOrigin contextRef="xxx">_entered_</gl-bus:entryOrigin>
  </gl-cor:entryHeader>
```

Interactive exercise A-4: In this exercise, you will locate a sample XBRL GL instance document and use it as a guide to enter the following information in the following **gl-cor:entryDetail** element.

First, point your browser to http://gl.iphix.net/ and click *Accounts Payable/Vendor Management* then *Invoices* and you should see an annotated GL instance listing vendor invoices. Then scroll down to the first **gl-cor:entryDetail** element (see Figure A-4) and use it as your guide to enter the following information in the shell provided.

An invoice from: Joe's Place dated December 13, 2008

One item for $53.55 and another for $24.99 (in U.S. dollars)

The voucher was dated November 27, 2008 and was posted on December 1, 2008 and is unpaid at this time.

```
<gl-cor:entryDetail>
  <gl-cor:lineNumber contextRef="xxx">_01_</gl-cor:lineNumber>
  <gl-cor:amount contextRef="xxx" unitRef="USD" decimals="2">_53.55_</gl-
      cor:amount>
  <gl-cor:postingDate contextRef="xxx">_2008-12-01_</gl-cor:postingDate>
  <gl-cor:identifierReference>
      <gl-cor:identifierDescription>_Joe's Place_</gl-cor:identifierDescription>
      <gl-cor:identifierType contextRef="xxx">_vendor_</gl-cor:identifierType>
      </gl-cor:identifierReference>
  <gl-cor:documentType contextRef="xxx">_voucher_</gl-cor:documentType>
  <gl-cor:documentDate contextRef="xxx">_2008-11-27_</gl-cor:documentDate>
```

```
<gl-cor:xbrlInfo>
      <gl-cor:summaryReportingElement contextRef="xxx">_us-gaap:
      AccountsPayable</gl-cor:summaryReportingElement>
 </gl-cor:xbrlInfo>
   </gl-cor:entryDetail>

<gl-cor:entryDetail>
  <gl-cor:lineNumber contextRef="xxx">_02_</gl-cor:lineNumber>
  <gl-cor:amount contextRef="xxx" unitRef="USD" decimals="2">_24.99_</gl-
      cor:amount>
  <gl-cor:postingDate contextRef="xxx">_2008-12-01_</gl-cor:postingDate>
  <gl-cor:identifierReference>
      <gl-cor:identifierDescription>_Joe's Place_</gl-cor:identifierDescription>
      <gl-cor:identifierType contextRef="xxx">_vendor_</gl-cor:identifierType>
      </gl-cor:identifierReference>
  <gl-cor:documentType contextRef="xxx">_voucher_</gl-cor:documentType>
  <gl-cor:documentDate contextRef="xxx">_2008-11-27_</gl-cor:documentDate>
  <gl-cor:xbrlInfo>
      <gl-cor:summaryReportingElement contextRef="xxx">_us-gaap:
      AccountsPayable</gl-cor:summaryReportingElement>
   </gl-cor:xbrlInfo>
     </gl-cor:entryDetail>
```

About the Author

Clinton E. White, Jr. (Skip) is a Professor of Accounting & MIS and the Area Head of MIS in the Department of Accounting & MIS at the University of Delaware; where he has been on the faculty since 1987. He has a DBA from Indiana University (1981) in Accounting, MIS, and Numerical Methods, an MBA from the University of Louisville (1975) in Finance and Economics, and a BA from Western Kentucky University (1969) in History and Government. His first academic position was on the faculty of the Department of Accounting & MIS at the Penn State University from 1981 to 1987. He has published numerous articles in a variety of academic and practitioner journals including MIS Quarterly, the Journal of MIS, Information & Management, Computers & Security, and the Journal of Accountancy. For a summary of his recent academic work see: http://www.lerner.udel.edu/personnel/acctmis/list/white.HTML.

Professor White is probably most widely known for his seminars, lectures, and workshops to academics and practitioners on emerging information technologies. His academic career has been devoted to the study of emerging information technologies and their application in business and accounting and MIS education. He has been conducting seminars and workshops since the mid-1980's on the emerging technologies of the time; including, DOS, Hypertext, multimedia, HTML, The Web, Java Script, XML, XBRL, and Web Services. Most recently he has been devoting research, writing, and lecturing efforts to emerging XML-based vocabularies such as XBRL.